DEMOCRATIC ACCOUNTABILITY

Leif Lewin

Democratic Accountability

Why Choice in Politics Is Both
Possible and Necessary

HARVARD UNIVERSITY PRESS

Cambridge, Massachusetts, and London, England   2007

Copyright © 2007 by the President and Fellows of Harvard College
All rights reserved
Printed in the United States of America

ISBN-13: 978-0-674-02475-5
ISBN-10: 0-674-02475-3

The Cataloging-in-Publication Data is available from the Library of Congress.

Contents

DEMOCRATIC ACCOUNTABILITY

CHAPTER **1**

Introduction:
The Politics of Blame Avoidance

Accountability as a Democratic Value

Politicians are blamed for almost all of the bad things that happen in the world: economic setbacks, miserable public service, crises, wars, terrorism. Their reply is, not unexpectedly, that others, not they, are responsible for such problems.[1] "It is beyond my control!" they exclaim with John Malkovich's Vicomte de Valmont in *Dangerous Liasons,* a movie set in eighteenth-century France before the revolution. It was with these words, viewers of the film will recall, that the Vicomte sought to steel himself against all moral inhibition, the better to seduce and destroy the innocent Madame Tourvel, in the lovable person of Michelle Pfeiffer.

More precisely, politicians tend to rely on arguments formulated by political theorists to explain why they have no control. We will deal with seven of these arguments in this book, each of them in a separate chapter following this one:

1. Politicians have no control because history pushes onward independently of human interaction and intent (Fukuyama, Chapter 2).
2. Politicians have no control because force and violence decide the course of events (the *Ventotene Manifesto,* Chapter 3).
3. Politicians have no control because the world market is the superior force (Martin and Schumann, Chapter 4).
4. Politicians have no control because they must cooperate with others (Lijphart, Chapter 5).
5. Politicians have no control because the bureaucracy rules (Niskanen, Chapter 6).

1

6. Politicians have no control because something different than intended often occurs (Merton, Chapter 7).
7. Not even the Leader has control, for in the end he is just the instrument of Fate (Hitler, Chapter 8).

Thus, in large part, the research question in this book is empirical: is it true that politicians, in specific situations, have no control over events? The answer depends of course partly on what we mean by this formulation and how politicians themselves understand their role. The thesis that politicians have no freedom of action at all is far too broad. Rather, politicians feel that they have *constraints* over their action. An important task for the present study is therefore to analyze the way politicians reason when they launch their various plans and policies. How do they try to break with conventional thinking to get rid of the constraints and find a freedom to choose?

But the issue of control has a normative component as well. John Plamenatz has reiterated that ideological conceptions, such as the theory of blame avoidance, are empirical only in a superficial sense. At first sight they appear, certainly, to contain scientific statements: "We must note, first of all, that ideology is overtly descriptive and explanatory. Sets of beliefs or theories that are ideological purport to tell us how things are or were, and how they come or came to be so."

In a deeper sense, however, ideological conceptions involve moral values that give guidance to conduct. In Plamenatz's words, an ideology is "primarily persuasive" but "secondary prescriptive." An ideology, he says, resembles a fable by Aesop or La Fontaine: "it is, on the face of it, a tale though a tale that points to a moral. If there were only the moral and not the tale, there would be no ideology." The converse is also true: without the tale there would be no ideology, either. Political ideologies consist, in other words, both of values and of statements about reality. Plamenatz describes the interaction between these two elements:

> Many sets of beliefs or theories that are ideological are also overtly prescriptive; they include injunctions and advice to men as to how they should behave, and they make value judgements. But the injunctions and advice, and the value judgements, are supported by assertions that purport to describe and explain relevant facts. Unless this were so, the set of beliefs would not be ideological. So, too, it would not be ideological if, in addition to its descriptive and prescriptive elements, it merely expressed the feelings of its propagators. To be ideological, it must be a set of beliefs to which a

community or social group ordinarily resort in situations of a certain kind. They may, of course, resort to it (or to some part of it) to express or relieve their feelings, but it is their resorting to it that makes it ideological.[2]

The traditional belief to which democratic theorists have "resorted" is that politicians do have control and consequently are responsible. Responsibility is the bridge that combines the theory of blame avoidance with democratic theory. In the last chapter (Chapter 9), we analyze the argument that events are out of politicians' control in a broader context and discuss the reformulation of democratic theory, which now, in the shadow of the blame avoidance discussion, seems to be under way in political science.

In this more general discussion, it seems useful to distinguish between two central arguments. The first argument is, as mentioned, that politicians are not adrift, carried by currents they cannot resist. Rather, if they just use their imagination, they will find that they have a wide latitude for real choice. According to the second argument, these choices can be understood and evaluated by the citizens. That voters have alternatives is a core element of democratic theory. They do not have to develop these alternatives themselves ("participatory democracy"); rather, politicians present the voters with alternatives, which the voters then judge ("trustee democracy"). In other words, in democracies, citizens' choice is not only possible but also necessary.

If politicians have no control, they are not responsible, either. According to the view that guides this study, politicians are the agents and the citizens the principals. In place of the term *responsibility,* we will use the more narrow and precise term *accountability:* this word refers to the duty of an agent to account for his actions to his principal, who in turn can punish him if he fails to perform according to expectation. This is expressed in such statements as "according to the constitution, the government is accountable to Parliament"; or "should the police be more accountable to the public?" Responsibility, by contrast, is the broader concept: one is morally responsible for a given action or activity. "Now that you're thirteen, you should have more sense of responsibility"; or "the head of a large company has many responsibilities."[3]

Accountability means, then, that a person must follow the rules stipulated and achieve the goals prescribed; otherwise, he will be punished. We want to hold people accountable for their actions and omissions. To do so, we need standards for judging conduct, testing performance, and determining who will be exempt or excused. Holding people accountable works best when we can identify minimal conditions of good conduct and performance, as when someone breaks the law or fails a test. For this reason, accountability should be considered an important but rudimentary form of responsibility.

In a richer meaning, however, responsibility reaches beyond accountability. The question is not what will put you in prison, cost you money, or cause you to lose a job or a professional license; it is whether and to what extent you care about your duties and act accordingly. An ethic of responsibility calls for understanding as well as conformity; it looks to ideals as well as obligations. Even when responsibility is appropriate in its demands, we expect it to be based on an inner sense of rightness.[4]

For it to be possible, then, to say that a politician is responsible for a given action, it must be the case that said politician has a purpose behind what he is doing, that he enjoys a certain autonomy, and that he is able to work out strategies and distinguish alternatives. In the words of Robert Dahl,

> Adult human beings are metaphysically free, or possess free will, in that in some sense they are capable of choosing how they shall act, and possess the capacity to reason. Consequently they are responsible for their actions. Taking responsibility involves determining what one ought to do, which requires gaining knowledge, reflecting on motives, predicting outcomes, criticizing principles, and so forth. Since a responsible person arrives at moral decisions that he expresses to himself in the form of imperatives, we may say that he gives laws to himself, or is self-legislating (or self-determining). In short, he is autonomous.[5]

After that the voters can have their say. Becoming a politician means taking the step from a "responsible man" to an "accountable agent," who must answer on election day to the citizens for the policies he has pursued.

Of course, the many meanings of these concepts are not exhausted by this distinction. Legal, social, and economic philosophers often use these words in a highly specialized way.[6] For our purpose, however, the distinction is sufficient. Our point of departure is *accountability as a democratic value:* in a democracy, the politicians should be accountable to the citizens. Our understanding of democracy is that it is a system where the citizens have the power to dismiss the government; democracy includes the right of the people "to kick the rascals out."[7] In our time, these fundamental constitutional questions have been brought to a critical stage in the discussion of the so-called democratic deficit of the European Union. In seven separate analyses (including one chapter on the EU), we will scrutinize arguments that claim that politicians could *not* be held accountable. In the concluding chapter, we will see how these deliberations fit into the present discussion on democracy.

Politics as Rational Action

If we return to the first argument (that politicians do have a choice), another point of departure for this study is the idea of *politics as rational action.* It is certainly not my purpose here to give an overview of the rich literature on rational choice theory. But a few points and distinctions might be useful, so that the reader will know what kind of study to expect.

I have not set out to write a technical book on rational choice theory. Rather, I make the philosophical assumption that politicians know what they want and, when they cannot get everything they want, work out strategies to get as much of what they want as possible. It is better, in their view, to get something than nothing at all. This does not mean that everything is negotiable. There is a moral limit to how much one can compromise. Rational politics, in my view, takes shape in the span between deontology (which forbids any deviation from one's convictions) and consequentialism (which permits any deviation so long as the results are better than they would otherwise have been). As we shall see below, in connection with the various concrete cases, it is the charge of the politician to decide where this boundary exists, where compromise is no longer permitted. The outcome is not decided beforehand. There are no given victors. What happens depends on how different actors attempt, given the limits on the room for maneuver, to realize as many of their preferences as possible.[8]

Second, the focus is on individual actors and their way of reasoning. William Riker and Peter Ordeshook have, in my mind, presented the idea of intentional explanations beautifully, when they imagine themselves looking down on a man from a balcony. The man is walking along a street in a certain direction—a northerly one, let us say. There is no more reason to believe that, one minute later, this man will still be walking toward the north than that he will be walking toward the east, south, or west. But as soon as we find out what purpose the man has in going out for a walk—to drop by the kiosk to pick up an evening paper, for example—we can both predict and explain the rest of his walk with great confidence. The man has a goal for his actions, and a will to attain it. He conducts a purposeful action.[9] The assumption of politics as rational action implies, then, that the explanation lies in the intentions of actors.[10]

Third, scholars distinguish between so-called thin and broad rationality. The former involves a simple means-ends model. Broad rationality, on the other hand, obtains when preferences are rational in a more substantive sense. That is, preferences ought to have a content of a certain kind, and there should be some kind of evidence for the desirability of the objective sought.[11] It is rationality in this more advanced sense that is at issue when we speak of democratic accountability.

From the assumption of rationality follows, in other words, an effort to find explanations for human behavior by studying what is going on in the heads of the various actors. It involves studying and reconstructing their purposes, calculations, preferences, and intentions. Thus, we repudiate the determinist view of society, which takes an interest only in such external factors of importance for political action as occupation, income, education, religion, region, or ethnic affiliation. In the analytical current I represent, such characteristics are regarded as important background variables, but not as decisive for the outcome—which is always affected by individual decision makers. In its search for patterns and correlations, the determinist view of society resembles the explanatory models of natural science. The distinguishing feature of a study of politics as rational action, by contrast, is that it focuses on individuals who at times are both willing and able to *break* with such patterns—whether for good or for ill.

Critical Cases as Counterexamples

The empirical study in this book takes the form of an examination of *critical cases*. The purpose of a case study is to elucidate a theory through a detailed analysis of a particular concrete question. Are the correlations observed the ones presumed in the theory? Do the conditions give rise to the expected outcome? Or does the case indicate that the theory should be reconsidered?

The cases counter the prognoses that could be deduced from the seven arguments about politicians having no control. (The chapter on the seventh argument—that not even the Leader has control—has a somewhat different design.) In other words, we will discuss cases when history did not push onward in a certain direction independently of what the politicians did, when force and violence actually were controlled, when the world market was resisted, when the bureaucracy was disciplined, when consequences did occur as planned, and so on.

Ever since the days of John Stuart Mill, social scientists have been engaged in a detailed methodological discussion about how to choose cases for elucidating a theory. Mill himself distinguished between the "method of agreement" and the "indirect method of difference." According to the former, the cases chosen should exhibit what the theory describes. If, for example, the theory concerns the powerlessness of politicians in the face of growing bureaucracies, then the countries studied should have growing bureaucracies. The objection to this method is that it allows no variation in the dependent variable. This inspired Mill to launch the second method, whereby not only countries with growing bureaucracies are chosen, but also, for the sake of comparison, countries in which the bureaucracy has not grown.[12] The style of analysis I use in this study is closer to Mill's first method, in that I follow what is called the "most likely principle": I choose such cases that afford the theory the greatest possible chance of being confirmed. The phenomena under study are accordingly the ones set out in the theory. If the theory is not even confirmed in such a maximally favorable case, then there is probably something wrong with it. Choosing a "most likely" approach means subjecting one's criticism of the theory to the strongest possible test.

Even if we today have moved from the mechanistic and deterministic world to the stochastic world of probabilities and uncertainties, then, crudely speaking, a single counterexample is enough to falsify a deterministic theory: if but a single apple had soared up to the sky rather than falling to the ground, Newton's law of gravitation would have been disproved. It is true that, as they are formulated, many of the theories criticized in this book could be considered deterministic: "history is predetermined," "nation-states must go to war," "globalization wipes out the freedom to choose," "the bureaucrats, not the politicians, control politics," and so on. But such a reading would make things too easy for ourselves. These theories should not be regarded, underneath the surface, as postulating natural laws, but as making empirical generalizations. With such an interpretation, the reader will understand, the selection of cases becomes strategic. The researcher must take measures to ensure that when he calls the rule into question, he is not studying the exception. The case should be typical for the theory. If the theory does not hold true even there, it is not likely to be tenable. It is for this reason that, in quantitative analysis, one uses frequencies, probabilities, representativity, and the like for the cases under study. In qualitative analysis, by contrast, one must ensure the relevance of the cases through another design.[13]

Seymour Martin Lipset and his colleagues are the methodological fore-runners in the search for such a design. When, in their pathbreaking study of union democracy, they identified "deviating behavior," they demonstrated the methodological power of the critical case study, with the new and often surprising insights that such a method affords. One begins by describing the theory and the most likely outcome. The next step is to study a case where the theory is not confirmed and, finally, to return to the theory and look for ways in which it can be revised in order to improve its predictive power.[14] As Karl Popper has argued, refuting theories with the help of empirical testing is what science is all about.[15]

The term *critical case*, then, should be understood in two different ways. On the one hand, the case must be significant for the theory. On the other, the case can be used to call the theory into question.

In an oft-quoted essay, Alexander George states that it is possible to work with only a few cases if the cases are selected carefully by a "structured, focused comparison."[16] Another scholar points out that the fewer the cases, the more powerful the theory required.[17] The idea is that a carefully selected case contains, in fact, many observations. Or, as King, Keohane, and Verba say in *Designing Social Inquiry*, the qualitative selection could be a way to "increase the number of observations": "[I]t may be possible within even a single conventionally labelled 'case study' to observe many separate implications of our theory. Indeed, a single case often involves multiple measures of the key variables; hence, by our definition, it contains multiple observations."[18]

Our study shifts the level of analysis from the macro to the micro level. It is the deliberations of individual actors that are reconstructed. In the empirical study of politics as rational action, "[the] emphasis is on rational and strategic individuals who make choices within constraints to obtain their desired ends, whose decisions rest on their assessment of the probable actions of others, and whose personal outcomes depend on what others do. The approach is methodologically individualist, yet its focus is not on individual choice but on the aggregation of individual choices. Rational choice is . . . a model that offers the microfoundations of macroprocesses and events."[19]

"Analytical narratives" combine historical analysis with the systematic study of rational choice. Thus, "the explicit and testable predictions" made by various theories "not only explain some action, they also serve to highlight deviations."[20] My approach, in other words, is historical and empirical. "Process-tracing" is the term usually used to refer to the careful reconstruction of politicians' calculations and their beliefs about their room for maneuver. In an anthology on analytical narratives, Bates et al. describe this research process as follows: "We identify agents; some are individuals, but others are collective actors, such as elites, nations, electorates, or legislatures. By reading documents, laboring through archives, interviewing, and surveying the secondary literature, we seek to understand the actors' preferences, their perceptions, their evaluation of alternatives, the information they possess, the expectations they form, the strategies they adopt, and the constraints that limit their actions."[21]

This approach leads to in-depth analyses for each and every case. As said, this is necessary if one wishes to go beyond the cliché of determinism and reconstruct politicians' assessments of what concrete options they had in a given situation.

The blame-avoidance arguments criticized in this book are logically related to each other in a chain (see Figure 1.1). This chain in turn constitutes a model for how one may conceive of the political process. It starts with the deliberation already made in this chapter: that it is meaningful not only to speak of history as a collective concept but also to disaggregate it into the interests of individual actors.

I begin each chapter with an analysis of the argument. I then proceed to an examination of a counterexample. Finally, in the third section of each chapter, I analyze further the nature of the specific constraint removed.

My first thesis, then, is that history is not predetermined. I reject the view that the course of development is fixed in advance, such that politicians have no choice and that they consequently cannot be held accountable for what takes place. This Hegelian philosophy has reappeared, following the fall of the Berlin Wall and the end of the Cold War, in the form of the idea that liberal democracy is the final goal of history. The good is said to no longer have any enemy. According to determinism, history is a locomotive propelled by its own power. The opposite notion is what I would call the Machiavellian interest theory: that the outcome depends on how skillfully different actors maneuver to promote their interests. In the second part of

Chapters:

1. Introduction: The politics of
blame avoidance

2. History is not
predetermined

3. Nation-states need not
go to war

4. Globalization has not wiped
out the freedom to choose

5. Power-sharing does not
exclude accountability

6. Implementation may
well be immaculate

7. Consequences may well
be as intended

8. Action can be meaningful
even if irrational

9. Conclusion: The necessity
for choice

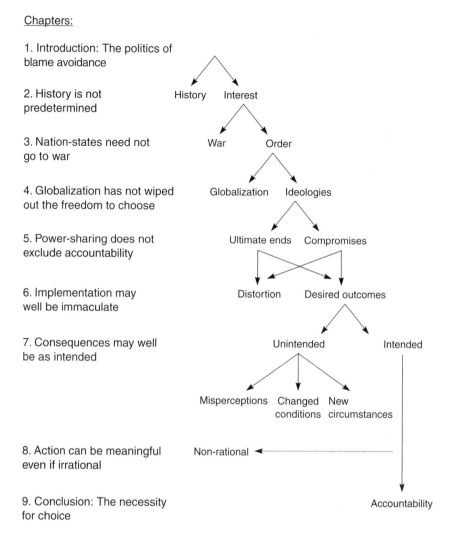

Figure 1.1. Disposition of the book.

Chapter 2, I take my counterexample from the intervention undertaken in
Europe after World War II by the American secretary of state, George Marshall. The continent lay in ruins, the Red Army was victorious, and many
believed Communism would sweep all the way to the Atlantic. Marxist doctrine predicted the victory of socialism. Yet, that is not what happened. Why
did not all of Europe become Communist after 1945? How did, in this case,

Machiavelli defeat Hegel? The third part of Chapter 2 looks more closely at the nature of counterfactual analysis. How does it happen that some actors discern alternatives to what is apparently taking place, and impart to history another course than the one expected?

Yet, some scholars claim, although history is not advancing by any motor of its own but rather is driven by individual interests, lawlike regularities that are beyond the control of politicians can nonetheless arise. For example, there are those who consider war inevitable. My argument in Chapter 3, accordingly, is that nation-states need not go to war. I thus criticize the view—championed by such theorists as Hobbes and Lenin—that a policy of peace and order stands no chance. Law is said to reside in the barrel of a gun. The counterexample I take up is the emergence of the European Union. "The first argument" in this context indicates that it is in fact possible to counter just such a vicious circle of violence. "The second argument" implies that this intervention has been continuously evaluated by the citizens, not always in a positive way but rather in a delicate interplay between a pushing elite and a more Euro-skeptical public who sometimes has found the union too remote from ordinary citizens and the leaders no longer accountable to them.

Pointing to the world market is the most classic way of evading responsibility. The social order in our time has become international. Politicians are said to be incapable of asserting their will against the world market; accordingly, they cannot be held accountable. I argue, however, that globalization has not wiped out the freedom to choose. In Chapter 4, I take my counterexample from the environmental work of the United Nations—which is by no means an unqualified success, but which cannot be totally ignored either. What responsibility do politicians bear in a market economy? Is the market, as is sometimes claimed, an insurmountable obstacle for political action? Is the market superior to politics and are politicians consequently not accountable?

It is in fact possible, I would argue, to stand up for certain values, for an ideology, also in an internationalized world. But to set one's stamp on society's development, one must enjoy the support of others—in a democracy, a majority. Cooperation is necessary in politics, yet it makes the lines of accountability unclear. "It is not my fault, but rather that of my collaborators," says the politician. But power-sharing does not exclude accountability. A faithfulness to ultimate ends is not, to be sure, all that is required in politics. To get anything done, one must also stitch together a majority—and that means compromise. Yet this does not release politicians from responsibility. In an analysis of the political crisis in Italy in the early 1990s, I inquire into the question of the moral implication of a politics of compromise. Whom should the citizens hold accountable when everyone cooperates?

Once political decisions are made, of course, they must also be implemented. Bureaucrats are thus the next scapegoat in the theory of blame avoidance. It is the bureaucrats who are actually to blame, say the politicians. It is on account of the bureaucrats that, when political decisions are to be implemented, the result is distortion rather than the outcome desired. My counterargument, therefore, is that: implementation may well be immaculate. Are politicians really putty in the hands of bureaucrats, as they claim? Following a discussion of Margaret Thatcher's success in taking command of British public administration, I explore whether bureaucracy should be regarded as a constraint, not as an instrument for policy realization, and analyze two models for the relationship between politicians and bureaucrats in a representative democracy.

"This is not how I wanted it to be," the politician pleads, in yet another attempt to evade responsibility. In social life, after all, unforeseen consequences arise all the time. Yet the consequences may well be as intended. It is a standard view in the social sciences nowadays that the consequences often prove different than intended. Showing how misperceptions, changed conditions, and new circumstances lead to policy failure has become routine. Against this background, it seems to me, a certain revision in our perspective is called for. With an eye to furnishing the needed corrective, I take a look at the strategy followed by the Swedish Social Democrats in order to maximize their electoral vote. I argue that this is a prime example of how politicians are sometimes able, with the help of a careful analysis of consequences, to successfully reach their goal. However, access to specialists is often needed for this. Yet what is the appropriate role of experts in a democracy? What is their responsibility—and what is the responsibility of politicians? What is the risk of delegating too much power to the experts, so that they become an unnecessary constraint on the politicians' freedom of action?

In order to deepen our analysis, finally, it may be fruitful to consider situations in which the idea of politics as rational and accountable action is not confirmed. The extreme counterexample is that of Adolf Hitler and National Socialism. Hitler's decision to remain in Berlin to the end was not "rational"—not, at any rate, in the utilitarian sense in which we tend to use that word. Yet action can be meaningful even if irrational. That is, on a metaphysical level, Hitler felt responsibility other than the one enjoined by democracy. Instead of being "accountable to the voters," Hitler sought to be "responsible to History." Fate is the ultimate constraint for freedom of action.

In the final chapter, I summarize my results and discuss the emergence of the new doctrine of democracy, which some people call "republicanism." What distinguishes popular rule from other forms of government, in my estimation, is precisely that the people are able—without spilling blood or resorting to civil war—to get rid of a government that has lost their favor. Whereas democracy is a method for the peaceful change of power, the coup d'état is the rule of succession in a dictatorship.

Thus, we may say that accountability is the topic, the assumption of politics as rational action the theory, and case studies the method for the book hereby introduced.

History Is Not Predetermined

The End of History

Like a voice from the other side of the grave—that is how many viewed Francis Fukuyama's declaration that the fall of Communism meant the end of history.[1] The furious uproar[2] provoked by this claim may above all have been due to the fact that, although Fukuyama's joy over democracy's victory over Communism certainly expressed what many people felt, "he used a tone and a set of concepts that many found unsettling and in some ways offensive."[3] Had not this very way of thinking been condemned, after all, by Karl Popper almost half a century before? Was it not the sheerest superstition to believe that history had a goal, that the course of development was predetermined? Simply put, had not historicism shown itself to be untenable?

Popper's critique of historicism[4] proceeded from the notion that man has a fundamental drive to liberate himself from his original social milieu (the "closed society"), the prototype of which was the tribe. The closed society, he explained, was static: its norms were considered unalterable. The open society, by contrast, is marked by individualism, equality, reason, and science. It also, however, deprives man of the security he felt in the tribe, by placing on him the burden of personal responsibility. Man is now free to choose, but he thereby becomes accountable for his actions. For this reason, the open society has enemies. There is a temptation to try to flee from one's responsibility. Unable to endure the unpredictability of civilization or the duties of moral responsibility, these enemies spin theories about history's fated return to the womblike security and irresponsibility of the closed society.

Popper himself defined "historicism" as follows: "I mean by 'historicism' an approach to the social sciences which assumes that historical prediction is their principal aim, and which assumes that this aim is attainable by discovering the 'rhythms' or the 'patterns', the 'laws' or the 'trends' that underlie the evolution of history." And he added: "I am convinced that such historicist doctrines of method are at bottom responsible for the unsatisfactory state of the theoretical social sciences."[5]

It was in the mid-nineteenth century—in the course of the famous *Methodenstreit* in the German social sciences[6]—that the word "historicism" entered usage. The theories then prevalent within the social sciences were accused of fastening too firmly to transitory phenomena. It was during the crisis of culture following World War I that the concept made its breakthrough. Traditions from the past were reassessed. A series of scholars—Troeltsch, Mannheim, Meinecke, Croce—argued that everything must be understood in its historical context. The static and universalist view of the world inherited from medieval times was being replaced by a new view—the keynote of which was change, and the consequence of which was a relativizing of all values and ideals.

The approach to method is considered the most important aspect of this viewpoint. With historicism, a new methodology was introduced. Its tendency was "to link evaluation with genetic explanation . . . [such] that each event is to be understood by viewing it in terms of a larger process of which it was a phase, or in which it played a part; and [such] that only through understanding the nature of this process can one fully understand or evaluate concrete events. It is partly because of this emphasis upon relating each event to some larger developmental process that historicism has come to be identified with holism and a belief in historical prediction."[7] But historicism means more than just the recognition that all human relations and ideals are subject to change. What makes the approach so controversial are the implications for the scholarly method that it involves.[8] A characteristic feature of the historicist outlook is the notion that "the analysis of an underlying historical trend can provide an illuminating context for the interpretation of contemporary issues."[9]

Of course, Popper's critique did not go unanswered. Ronald Levinson, for example, furnished an erudite and committed defense of Plato.[10] It is undeniably difficult, moreover, to reconcile a doctrine of eternal and unchanging truths with a theory of development. Indeed, to the extent that the ancient Greeks had any notion of change, it was change for the worse, not the better—that is, away from a golden past, rather than toward any enticing future final goal. When Platonism was wedded to Christianity, however, historicism became an incontestable fact. According to Saint Augustine, who formulated the official church view of history, there is an ongoing implacable struggle between good and evil throughout history. The victory of the one, however, is fated from the start; the triumph of the Kingdom of God is predestined.[11] Such was the doctrine to which people gave allegiance for over a thousand years.

The Renaissance saw the great voyages of discovery, the invention of the printing press, and the writing of encyclopedias. As a result of these and associated developments, an awareness of scientific progress spread, and the self-confidence of man increased. The idea was born that man could be master of his own fate—a dangerous notion that ultimately undermined the belief in absolute monarchy. Democracy began to sprout—only to end in a blood bath. The lesson of the French Revolution, according to Burke, was that this is what happens when politics is fitted more to man's arguments than to his nature. The old idea returned that history has a goal over and above the hopes and strivings of man. The modern form of historicism was born. It was impossible, clearly, to contravene the laws of history. Unless the meaning of history were ascertained, and policies adjusted to suit, nothing but failure was to be expected.

Hegel next became the philosopher of the hour. He had originally embraced the ideas of the French Revolution and seen Napoleon as the incarnation of the world spirit; subsequently, however, his views became increasingly conservative. On the abstract level, Hegel averred, history was the realization of reason: a process bringing about the liberation of man. The reality of freedom was achieved through the state—not just in the negative sense, in that lawless and arbitrary treatment of citizens ceased, but also and above all in the positive sense, in that subjects of the state first attained their full development upon being incorporated into the state. Yet, private desires were merely a moment—and a one-sided moment at that—of the objectively rational will of the state. A ceaseless struggle took place in history between master and slave. This "contradiction"—a favorite word in Hegelian philosophy—could be overcome only by political means: through the ideal state, wherein "freedom is realized" and the various classes and estates are subordinated to the state in a harmonious competition.

Following the catastrophic defeat of the various German states, Hegel became seized with the idea of German nationalism. The ascending kingdom of Prussia became, for him, the seat of world reason and the final goal of history. In the decades after Napoleon's fall, he dwelt in that country as an honored citizen—and an energetic champion of its monarchy, its church, its civil-service aristocracy, its feudal property relations, and its ever greater military power. His grand historical narrative thus ended in a rather flat defense of prevailing conditions in his homeland. Oppositionally inclined students of Hegel, however, asked whether we ought not instead—by the very premises of the Hegelian philosophy—to expect progress to continue, and the synthesis constituted by Prussia to be superseded in a new dialectical leap.

Of these students, Karl Marx would become the most renowned. It is in Hegel's view of history, namely, that both totalitarian ideologies of the twentieth century have their philosophical roots. Marx replaced his mentor's idealist view of history with his own materialist one. Few would wish today to deny the historicist character of Marx's thought, notwithstanding the many telling points made by Maurice Cornforth in his indignant reply to Popper.[12] In Marxism, quite plainly, the classless society looms in the distance as the final goal of history.

Hegel's philosophy also inspired National Socialism. At the end of the nineteenth century, an aggressive type of conservatism made its appearance, for which liberalism and democracy were the main enemy. The state, in this view, was not an "atomistic structure" composed of separate individuals, but a collective organism with a will of its own—and a pronounced need to assert itself vis-à-vis other states. Policy could not be established by consulting the inhabitants at occasional intervals; rather, the will of the state had to be divined by the sovereign. These ideas cascaded into the Nazi cult of the leader. Frustration at the defeat of Germany in World War I, together with rampant inflation and soaring unemployment, put wind in the sails of this movement, which grew by leaps and bounds in the ecstatic expectation of the final victory of the thousand-year Reich.

For Fukuyama, too (to return to the main character in our tale), the clear authority is Hegel—or, more strictly, the interpretation of Hegel made by Alexander Kojève, a Russian emigrant and philosopher who became a cult figure at a famous seminar in Paris in the 1930s. The names of Hegel and Kojève are cited constantly in Fukuyama's work, as are bits and pieces of the older tradition adumbrated above. In view of the debate over historicism during the last half-century, and considering the perspective I have set out here—which is now common among historians of political ideas—the most striking thing about Fukuyama's famous piece is that it contains no discussion of the critique of historicism. "What I suggested had come to an end," he heedlessly says, "was not the occurrence of events, even large and grave events, but History: that is, history understood as a single, coherent, evolutionary process." Fukuyama regards this process as predetermined, as moving toward a particular goal. It is a question of "directional history," as the recurrent phrase has it.

Fukuyama's point of departure is that the fall of Fascism, of subsequent right-wing dictatorships, and later of Communism as well, means something unique in the history of humanity. The good has no enemy anymore. Liberal democracy has triumphed for good—something we have undeniably heard before, one critic notes acidly, citing President Wilson's optimism following World War I.[13] Another critic expresses surprise that a writer in our time should need reminding that it has been said many times before that political struggle is over and that everyone has joined in a common ideology ("We are all socialists now," said King Edward VII in 1895).[14] Fukuyama's argument that such a claim is accurate—this time, at least—is founded on the basic Hegelian concept of "contradictions": these, he avers, no longer exist in postmodern society. One may therefore make so bold as to write a "universal history" of humanity, that is an account of history not as "a blind concatenation of events, but [as] a meaningful whole" moving toward a predetermined goal. The methodological objections to such an enterprise are well-known, as we have seen. "Here there is a lot to disagree with," writes one reviewer. "He seems to ascribe to [history] a direction independent of human intent and interest. More to the point, he ignores what is the main motor of human history, in this and previous centuries: namely, collective political action, action by groups, be these classes, nations, states."[15] In the estimation of another commentator, the idea that human progress is the result of direction by "the Idea, the Force, God, or some other demi-urge" means that "the role of human interaction and debate, the piecemeal building of notions through the accretion of thousands of insights, the practical, democratic building of ideas by everyone, is denied. Indeed the most undemocratic of methodologies is used to conclude the achievement of democratic perfection."[16] Fukuyama's entire framework is paradoxical: he uses the Marxist concept of directional history to prove that Marxism is wrong and dead and that Liberalism has won. Or, as one critic points out, "Marxist ideology is alive and well in Fukuyama's arguments to refute it."[17]

The drive that imparts direction to history, according to Fukuyama, is

"the Mechanism of Desire." More precisely, natural science is the best expression of this desire: "We have selected modern natural science as a possible underlying 'mechanism' of directional historical change, because it is
the only large-scale social activity that is by consensus cumulative and
therefore directional." Natural science differs from painting, poetry, art, or
architecture in that it improves better over time. It is not a given, after all,
that modern artists are superior to their counterparts of a previous age. The
natural sciences, by contrast, achieve progress: scientists of a later generation know more than their predecessors did. Our increased knowledge in
the areas of natural science and technology enables us to master the world
more fully than we formerly could. Is it conceivable that history will at
some point change direction, such that this store of knowledge is lost?
Fukuyama finds this improbable. There certainly have been and still are
contrary tendencies—from Rousseau to Khomeini. In earlier ages, moreover, entire civilizations disappeared without a trace. With the scientific
skills we have acquired, however, such a thing will not happen now. In scientific research, the fundamental mechanism of desire has attained its most
complete expression. This mechanism will continue to mark the progress of
humanity and to impart to history its direction.

Setbacks can, of course, occur. A new Hitler or Pol Pot is not unthinkable.
Such deviations, however, are temporary—they are exceptions—while the
universal progress of humanity is the rule.

On the one hand, then, development pushes onward independently of
human interaction and intent. On the other hand, the human desire for
knowledge is presented as the motor. Fukuyama employs, in other words,
"a willy argument that moves back and forth between a voluntarist and a
determinist pole . . . This 'end of history' relies on everyone believing the
end of history has come, on knowing what 'liberal democracy' means, and
on events not contradicting the belief unmanageably. This neither proves
anything, nor is much on which to hang hopes of global unity."[18]

Does scientific progress necessarily lead, then, to democracy? It is characteristic of Fukuyama, with his voracious intellectual appetite, that he takes
delight in complicating his historical account: the matter, he explains, is not
really that simple. The desire to understand the world and thus master it is
not enough to explain the movement of universal human history toward
liberal democracy. There is another necessary factor: the "Struggle for
Recognition." Here again Fukuyama cites Hegel, insisting that "it is solely by
risking life that freedom is obtained." Hegel's "first man" sought more than

just material things—a piece of meat to eat, an animal skin to wear, a cave in which to dwell. Above all else, he desired the recognition of other people. The section on man's struggle for recognition takes up a large portion of Fukuyama's book and issues in an imaginative reinterpretation of man's historical progress. *Thymos* is the concept Fukuyama takes from ancient philosophy to describe how the need for recognition develops into a striving for honor and self-respect. *Thymos* has far-reaching consequences for both master and slave (the opposition between who imparts to history its tension and who drives it forward, in the well-known fashion). The master shows he is free by putting his life at risk; his tragedy, however, is that he risks his life to be recognized by a slave, who is unworthy of recognizing him. The slave, too, is dissatisfied. Having subordinated himself to another, he has lost his humanity. Yet this total lack of recognition leads the slave to demand change—and thus to drive history forward. The slave regains his humanity—which he had lost due to his fear of a violent death—through labor. Over time, however, this labor changes its character. Instead of being done out of a fear of punishment, it is increasingly performed out of a sense of duty and discipline.

One might find it prudent at this point to set the book aside for a moment and to ask why we should accept Fukuyama's claim that the struggle for recognition is more fundamental than, say, the drive for security that Fukuyama so despises—a drive that furnished the foundation for Hobbes's equally grandiose theory of human development and the emergence of the state. Why should we conclude that the struggle for recognition is more distinctive of man than is his fear of being slain in the war of all against all? It is a highly speculative genre into which Fukuyama has ventured. Indeed, his account is all the more bewildering because he begins by saying that man is rational, thirsty for knowledge, and possessed of a strong interest in natural science and technology and then proceeds to describe him as an emotional, prestige-seeking "beast with red cheeks." "Here Fukuyama is most unconvincing," one critic points out. "Liberal democracy is his solution to the riddle of history not because it really solves the question of *thymos*. To the contrary, Fukuyama supplies numerous arguments to suggest it may well fall very short. Ultimately this solution 'succeeds' only because Fukuyama substitutes the static Platonian anthropology of a tripartite soul dominated by reason for the original one he had found on the key category of recognition translated as *thymos*."[19]

There are also many threats to Fukuyama's idyllic world. Critics have pointed out how far from reality it finds itself. As one understatement reads, "All is not altogether well in former Yugoslavia, the former Soviet Union, vast tracts of the Third World and many American cities . . . well, actually there's a little bit of history still to run here."[20] As is clear in retrospect, there were a good many problems during the 1990s: "The triumph of the liberal program does not mean 'the end of History' because modern liberalism is itself a heterogeneous, contested, and deeply unfinished business."[21]

This is also the main burden of Samuel Huntington's critique. "It is erroneous . . . to jump from the decline of Communism to the global triumph of liberalism and the disappearance of ideology as a force in world affairs." An ideology can always come back, for one thing. "Revivals are possible"—just look at economic liberalism, which many believed was dead during the decades of Keynesianism but staged a comeback in the late 1970s. For another, bloody schisms can arise within an ideology—as between Protestants and Catholics, for example, notwithstanding the ideological consensus on Christianity that had emerged in Europe around 1500. The fact that war is not likely to break out between liberal democracies such as France and Germany is a valid but irrelevant point. A hundred years ago one could have said that Pennsylvania and Virginia would not fight again. That did not prevent the United States from engaging in world wars. One trend in history is the amalgamation of smaller units into larger ones. And between these great blocs war is actually likely—with the consequent threat to liberal democracy. China is probably the best example. In the course of their industrialization, Britain, France, Germany, Japan, the United States, and the Soviet Union all became expansionist and imperialist states. China finds itself in the midst of such industrialization now. Perhaps that country will be more peaceful than other great powers have been. It is more likely, however, that it will end up following the familiar pattern. "A billion Chinese engaged in imperial expansion are likely to impose a lot of history on the rest of the world." A belief in the definitive victory of liberalism is dangerous: "To hope for the benign end of history is human. To expect it to happen is unrealistic. To plan on it happening is disastrous."[22]

How does Fukuyama explain, then, that the struggle for recognition leads humanity to liberal democracy? His vivid description of the fight for prestige would seem to indicate that Hobbes was right—that the trend of development is toward civil war and that one possible solution to this problem would be set up a dictatorship: Leviathan. Once again, the concept of contradiction proves critical to the argument. For Hegel, the French Revolution was the event that made the vision of liberty and equality real. The former slaves put their lives at risk, just as their masters had done before them, and thereby showed that they had overcome the fear of death, which had made them into slaves. The contradictions in history had come to an end. Democracy is achieved not for economic reasons, but as a result of man's struggle for recognition.

However, when we have come thus far in Fukuyama's reconstruction of human history, he surprises us yet again. He asks whether we should not perhaps agree with Nietzsche that this state of affairs "is not a cause for celebration, but an unparalleled disaster." If democracy is a victory for the slaves, is it not also a victory for slave morality? Are we not rendered flat and shallow by democracy? Do we not become bored by prosperity and peace? Are not the denizens of democracy people without pride, "men without chests"? The revolutionaries who battled Ceausescu's security police in Romania, the brave Chinese students who stood up to the tanks in Tiananmen Square, the Lithuanians who fought Moscow for their national independence, the Russians who defended their parliament and president—these "were the most free and therefore the most human of beings. They were former slaves who proved themselves willing to risk their lives in a bloody battle to free themselves. But when they finally succeed, as they eventually must, they will create for themselves a stable democratic society in which struggle and work in the old sense are made unnecessary, and in which the possibility of their ever again being as free and as human as in their revolutionary struggle has been abolished." This is certainly a strange way to greet those whom Fukuyama hopes will join him in rejoicing over the irrevocable victory of democracy. Or as Stephen Holmes puts the point: "Becoming free is everything, being free is nothing. How can Fukuyama preach such a message to the millions of men and women still groaning under the bitter legacy of decades of totalitarian rule? Welcome, he tells them, you have just been released from Communist unhappiness into democratic meaninglessness. Welcome to the vacuum at the heart of liberal society, where life is no longer worth living."[23]

At this point, however, Fukuyama's resolution fails him, and he considers the matter anew. He confesses his doubts about the scenario he has developed so vividly—giving vent, so to speak, to an objection to his objection. First he says, "It is difficult for those of us who believe in liberal democracy to follow Nietzsche very far down the road that he takes." But this concession to political correctness, it seems, lasts no more than a brief sober moment, for Fukuyama soon returns to his argument that the former slaves will find no satisfaction in democracy. "No regime—no 'socio-economic system'—is able to satisfy all men in all places . . . Rather, the dissatisfaction arises precisely where democracy has triumphed most completely: it is a dissatisfaction *with* liberty and equality." When Fukuyama speaks with forked tongue in this manner, he undermines his own thesis. The import of the idea he takes from Nietzsche is that, when all is said and done, history may not have come to an end. It can always begin again, due to the dissatisfaction mentioned: "Thus those who remain dissatisfied will always have the potential to restart history."

In his concluding metaphor, Fukuyama says that human history is like a wagon train strung out along a road. Some wagons will soon be pulling into town sharply and crisply, while others will be bivouacked back in the desert or else stuck in ruts in the final pass over the mountains. Several wagons will come under attack by Indians, with the result that some, stunned by the battle, will end up losing their direction. One or two wagons will tire of the journey and decide to set up camp permanently along the road. Others, finally, will find alternative routes to the main road. "But the great majority of the wagons will be making the slow journey into town, and most will eventually arrive there . . . [A]ny reasonable person looking at the situation would be forced to agree that there had been only one journey and one destination." This is undeniably an apposite picture for those wishing to claim that history is predetermined. But then, in a confusing final twist, the war within the author comes to the surface again. He suggests that people may end up being bored with democracy and that history may therefore start anew. The very last sentence in the book reads: "Nor can we in the final analysis know, provided a majority of the wagons eventually reach the same town, whether their occupants, having looked around a bit in their new surroundings, will not find them inadequate and set their eyes on a new and more distant journey."

Reading Fukuyama is a great intellectual experience. He gives evidence that he is no less brilliant than his most illustrious forebears among philosophers of history. But his unwillingness to discuss Popper's critique of historicism puts his entire presentation in a peculiar light. Such an ignorant—some would say arrogant—attitude toward opponents indisputably amounts to a startling break with the rules of academic debate. Those who venture out on an old theme without bothering to address the well-known objections to it expose themselves to the full force of the established critique.

Fukuyama is no exception in this regard. Oblivious of Hegel's mistake in portraying Prussia as the final destination of history, or of President Wilson's overoptimism regarding the prospects for peace, Fukuyama rashly generalizes from his own time, converting contingent institutions into something definitive and permanent, uninhibitedly translating his own time into something definitive and permanent. Unaffected by all those other attempts to ascertain the ultimate motive power within human nature, he abandons himself to an unchecked subjectivism—as when he blends scientific commonplaces ("the natural sciences are cumulative") with the most imponderable comparisons ("for man, recognition is more important than security"). Supremely uninterested in any effort to support his claims or even to argue for them, he arbitrarily distinguishes between the "direction" of history and its various "dead ends." The reader is tempted to cry out: Why not precisely the opposite? Why not regard oppression, rather than liberation, as the recurring pattern? Why not view the Holocaust and the atomic bomb, rather than liberal democracy, as the ultimate expression of the human desire to master nature? Why not—in a world of gaping fissures between rich and poor countries—see war and conflicts of interest among states, instead of eternal peace, as the normal condition?

Fukuyama one-sidedly emphasizes consistency as the scientific ideal, but he is unconcerned that truth—operationalized as the empirical testing of hypotheses—is a competing scientific ideal. With his concept of contradiction, the author gives himself a free hand to interpret the course of development according to a previously laid-out schema. Fukuyama reserves for himself the prerogative of deciding which phenomena qualify as "contradictions," and which of them are "overcome"; nor are these empirical interpretations preceded either by definitions or by hypotheses. When, finally, it remains unclear whether a "consistency" is attained within liberal democracy—that is, whether the former slaves end up being "altogether satisfied"—the reader is left in the dark on the main question: does the author really stand behind his thesis that history has come to an end? Or do his reservations get the better of his thesis, so that the conclusion of the entire extravagant presentation ends up being merely banal—that history will likely keep chugging along, because new groups who want to express their discontent will appear? Fukuyama's book, in other words, both inspires and provokes. But it does not convince. This latest attempt at showing that history is predetermined does not bear up under scrutiny any more than its predecessors did. We cannot claim that history has ended just because Communism fell.

The Politics of Containment

When political scientists seek to evaluate a general theory (such as that history is predetermined and has now come to an end), they try—as I explained in the introductory chapter—to find critical cases for testing the theory. I will look for a counterexample to illustrate the opposite thesis (that actors could formulate alternatives). In this spirit, we now continue our discussion by traveling back in time a bit more than a half-century and asking the following question: Why did not the whole of Europe become Communist after World War II? The continent, after all, lay in ruins. The vitality of the European democracies appeared to have ebbed out. The victorious Red Army incorporated one after another of the countries of Eastern and Central Europe into the Soviet empire. To be sure, Stalin had changed the socialist vision from that of world revolution to "socialism in one country." But now his ambitions once more exceeded the boundaries of the Soviet Union, and a third type of foreign-policy doctrine was staked out, appositely termed "socialism in one zone."[24] In Western Europe, too, moreover, Communists had strengthened their position. In April 1944, for example, the French Communists were given two posts in the provisional Résistance government of General de Gaulle. This event set a precedent for many other Communist parties. Stalin contentedly declared that "a new type of government," and thus a new instrument for Marxism-Leninism, had been acquired. The goal was not just to win a war between states but also to further revolution.[25]

In the United States, the foreign-policy establishment watched the European situation with growing alarm. One might liken these troubled experts to doctors who ascertain that a given illness will develop along certain lines and thereupon decide to intervene—in order to induce the illness to develop along different and more desirable lines. Their intervention was the Marshall Plan.[26]

How did the State Department decision makers reason when they came up with the Marshall Plan? What was their view of history and the choices available to them?

When the victorious powers had divided the continent into separate spheres of influence, the major responsibility for Greece had fallen to Great

Britain. The British then appointed a government for the country, against which the Greek Communists revolted, with the support of Communist governments in Albania, Yugoslavia, and Bulgaria. It seemed at first that, with the aid of the British military, the sitting government would be able to survive. In February 1947, however, Britain declared that its assistance to Greece and Turkey would shortly cease. The British did not have the wherewithal to continue the aid in spite of the fact that Greece was hard-pressed by the Communist guerrillas. The start of the policy process leading to the Marshall Plan was this unpleasant surprise that the British government gave to the U.S. government.

The sensational solution presented by the American president to address this quandary has become known as the Truman Doctrine. On 12 March 1947, President Truman proclaimed in a speech before Congress that U.S. foreign policy had to be changed, in order to meet the threat that totalitarian regimes continued to pose—and not just to Greece: "It must be the policy of the United States to support free peoples who are resisting attempted subjugation by armed minorities or by outside pressures."[27]

This was merely a declaration of principle and had to be complemented by a program of economic measures. This was the conclusion of the secretary of state, George Marshall, after a trip to Moscow. In March and April of that same year, he took part in extended meetings in the Soviet capital. His private conversations with Stalin on the future of Europe convinced him that the Russians were deliberately seeking to delay the economic recovery of Europe, probably in order to prepare the way for Communism. Marshall therefore instructed his colleague George Kennan to undertake a broad study of American aid policy. The object was to ensure that not only the enemies from the war—Nazis and Fascists—but also Communists would exercise no influence in a rebuilt liberal Europe free of narrow nationalism.

American key actors had been confronted with the enemy's long-range vision and now met this challenge with a purposeful intention to countercheck this development.

The next step was to give the policy a more concrete formulation. In a speech at Harvard University on 5 June 1947, Marshall launched what was thereafter known as the Marshall Plan, with the express purpose of injecting vitality into the tottering democracies of Europe. The speech at Harvard was as famous as it was lacking in detail. Marshall spoke of European economic dislocations, of the "breakdown of the business structure of Europe," and of the inability of European states to pay for food and other necessities. The remedy lay in "breaking the vicious circle and restoring the confidence of the European people in the economic future of their own countries and of Europe as a whole." The aid must be designed to "provide a cure rather than a mere palliative." He concluded, however, by stressing that the initiative had to come from Europe. The United States should not develop a unilateral program for getting Europe on its feet again: "This is the business of the Europeans."[28]

In the course of the Marshall Plan's implementation, a range of different interests came to coincide. At the same time as a series of practical problems for the occupation forces in Europe craved a solution, the State Department was working intensively to give substance to the new foreign policy sketched out in the speeches by Truman and Marshall. (The two addresses had been, after all, not just noteworthy but also imprecise.) The practical problems, in time, would be solved step by step. As for the new doctrine, it was given the finishing touches in committees and working groups, in memoranda and speeches, among congressmen and State Department officials. The process was characterized both by conflict and by compromise. When at last the Marshall Plan was approved by Congress, it marked a definitive break with the isolationism that had characterized American foreign policy between the wars. The Cold War had begun.

In Germany, a supranational organ was established to control the important Ruhr area. A United Nations committee had decided to appoint an economic commission for Europe, and there was strong support for such international initiatives among younger officials in the U.S. administration. They were worried about a future division of Europe into blocs, and they wished to support a system of economic and political integration through the organizations of the United Nations. (Europe divided into blocs all the same, of course; yet integration did eventually take place—in the West—and on a scale exceeding the most optimistic expectations.) Among these officials was John Foster Dulles, who had been appointed to the State Department because the president needed Republican support in Congress for the Marshall Plan.[29]

European reactions to Marshall's speech were immediate and positive. The French foreign minister, Georges Bidault, invited his British counterpart, Ernest Bevin, to Paris for consultations. It was more questionable, of course, whether the Soviet foreign minister, Vyacheslav Molotov, ought to be invited as well; yet, they decided to do so. Molotov, unsurprisingly, launched an immediate attack on the Marshall Plan, which he claimed vio-

lated the sovereignty of recipient countries and facilitated American infil-
tration. The Soviet delegation thereupon left Paris. The international division into blocs was becoming clearer and clearer. Stalin's reply was to mo-
bilize the various Communist parties—through the organization
Kominform—in an offensive against the governments that supported the
Marshall Plan. These parties described the Marshall Plan as "an instrument
of preparation for war" and as "a means for the economic and political en-
slavement of Europe."[30]

In the United States, too, the Marshall Plan was hotly debated. President
Truman came under criticism by both the Left and the Right, as well as by a
majority of voters—thirsty for peace and fearful of a new war. What were
the aims of the president and his secretary of state in launching these spectacular initiatives? Had not America already done enough for Europe?
Would it not be better, in the end, for the United States to return to its old
policy of peaceful isolationism, rather than setting out on a high-risk project
like meddling in the mutual antagonisms of the warlike European nations?

The U.S. government's resolute intention to intervene in order to change
what many regarded as a likely development toward Communist victory in
Europe would soon be given—in piquant fashion—a more thorough justification. In the summer of 1947, the journal *Foreign Affairs* published an
anonymous article featuring an in-depth analysis of the aims of the new
foreign policy. This article is the best source for our knowledge about the ra-
tionale of the new doctrine. It soon became generally known that the author, who had used the pen name "X," was none other than George
Kennan, close colleague of the secretary of state. The article started out by
emphasizing the mainsprings of Soviet foreign policy in Marxist ideology,
with its theory of the inevitable collapse of capitalism due to internal contradictions. But capitalism would not perish without a proletarian revolution: "A final push was needed from a revolutionary movement in order to
tip over the tottering structure." The very fact that their victory was predestined, however, meant that Soviet leaders could show patience when it
came to administering that final push: "The theory of the inevitability of the
eventual fall of capitalism has the fortunate connotation that there is no
hurry about it." This suited the leaders well, moreover, because they had
been preoccupied ever since the revolution with consolidating their power
inside the country. With suppressed loathing, Kennan described how Stalin
had established "organs of suppression" and concentrated all power in his
hands—in brief, how he had made himself dictator.

Kennan then turned to international relations. Between capitalism and socialism, the Soviets believed, an implacable antagonism reigned. One day the final confrontation would come. As a result, dealing with the Soviet leadership was both easier and more difficult than dealing with aggressive individual leaders like Napoleon or Hitler:

> On the one hand it is more sensitive to contrary force, more ready to yield on individual sectors of the diplomatic front when force is felt to be too strong, and thus more rational in the logic and rhetoric of power. On the other hand it cannot be easily defeated or discouraged by a single victory on the part of its opponents. And the patient persistence by which it is animated means that it can be effectively countered not by sporadic acts which represent the momentary whims of democratic opinion but only by intelligent long-range policies.

The Russians, in other words, should be met with the same combination of long-range resoluteness and short-term flexibility that they themselves displayed. It could never be forgotten that the ultimate purpose of the Soviets was to overthrow capitalism and to defeat democracy. A purposeful policy was therefore required, as was a readiness to act. The most important sentence in the article read: "In these circumstances it is clear that the main element in any United States policy toward the Soviet Union must be that of a long-term, patient but firm and vigilant containment of Russian expansive tendencies."

It was very difficult, in fact, to tell how strong the Soviet adversary really was. What powers could the war-weary people of Russia muster? What would happen after Stalin? Could the magical powers of Communism already worn off, so that the glory with which the Red Army had covered itself was like the radiance still visible from a star long dead? To rely on the possibility that an overexpansion of the Communist regime would lead to a loss of control over the newly conquered nations and, perhaps, a fall of the Soviet Union was, however, too risky. Instead, the United States had to be prepared for the worst. And if at any point the Soviet Union took measures seeming to indicate a desire for conciliation, the United States would have to understand—in view of Soviet ideology—that it was just a question of tactical and temporary concessions, which ought to be taken in the spirit of caveat emptor. For the United States, the Soviet Union would always be "a rival, not a partner." The United States had to accept the challenge. It was the right thing to do, if the nation meant to be true to its ideals: "To avoid

destruction the United States need only measure up to its own best traditions and prove itself worthy of preservation as a great nation. Surely, there
was never a fairer test of national quality than this."[31]

The United States had now decided. The key actors identified a choice
and mobilized the political ability and courage to go against the prevailing
norm of isolationism. The prospects that the Soviet Union would collapse
from its own ambitions was too rash; a policy of resignation would be too
dangerous—and too immoral. The Americans were determined not to
watch with arms folded while Communist expansion rose like a flood over
the democracies of Europe. They meant to contain this expansion, by
means of a patient but resolute resistance to the ambitions of the Soviets to
widen their rule.

With great determination, the United States then proceeded to implement the Marshall Plan. Supranational forms of cooperation were developed further, and the creation of the OEEC (Organisation for European
Economic Cooperation) became the next step toward the economic integration of Europe. During a four-year period (1948–52), sixteen European nations obtained assistance under the American aid program, which ultimately came to 13 billion American dollars. The U.S. intervention gave
another course to history. A half-century later, it would be the fate of world
Communism, which after World War II had been so victorious, to be cast on
the rubbish heap of history, while the democracies of Europe, which after
the war had seemed destined to perish, would be economically and politically stronger than ever.

Accountability and Counterfactual Analysis

Politics and political science are similar in that just as responsible political
action requires one to think in terms of alternatives, so does a rationalist approach involve the reconstruction of different strategies between which actors can choose. Nothing is simply given. Something other than what is
presently happening can take place, and something other than what actually happened could have taken place. Good political analysis is therefore
always counterfactual, whether the purpose is to offer an explanation or to
furnish a basis for making a decision.

Counterfactual analysis was long thought unscientific. In the aforementioned debate on historicism in nineteenth-century Germany, one position
was that the object of history as an academic discipline was to ascertain

what it was that had actually happened and nothing else—"wie es eigentlich gewesen."[32] Adherents of the school of source analysis rejected any reasoning in terms of alternatives (i.e., "what would have happened to x, if something different took place than what actually occurred?"), on the grounds that such an approach could only lead to unchecked speculation, without any reliable basis in fact. Serious social scientists did not engage in "if-thinking." Historians had to follow rigorous positivist rules in regard to the presentation of empirical evidence.[33]

It may be interesting to note, in light of our discussion of whether history is predetermined, that this positivist line took shape in polemic with Hegel, Fukuyama's great inspiration. According to Hegel, truth could be attained only by reducing the multiplicity of events to rational concepts. Ultimately, reality could be deduced from so-called *Allgemeinbegriffe*—universal concepts organized in an ascending hierarchy.[34] On the one hand, then, we have Hegelian idealism, according to which history is a successive manifestation of underlying rational principles. On the other, we have positivist empiricism, according to which history is nothing but the events that one can prove actually took place. Neither camp takes any interest in alternative histories: in the one view, namely, such things could not have happened; in the other, they cannot be shown to have been possible.

Revived counterfactual analysis, by contrast, involves the investigation of "possible worlds." In economic history, for example, this analytical approach has made a breakthrough, under the name of the "new economic history." It shares with Hegelianism a rationalist and deductive approach: "[T]he fundamental methodological feature of the new economic history is its attempt to cast all explanations of past economic development in the form of valid hypothetico-deductive models."[35] There is also, however, a great difference: the basic idea of the new economic history is precisely that history is not predetermined. Events could indeed have taken another turn. A paradigmatic example is the work of Nobel Prize winner Robert Fogel on economic growth in the United States: "[I]f the U.S. had not developed the rail road system but continued with the canals, the national income of 1890 would have been just five per cent lower than it actually was."[36]

How can we carry out counterfactual analysis, then, without falling into the old trap of arbitrary speculation? Or put politically, how can we analyze policy in such a way as to open up options for decision makers?

A great deal of ink has been spilled on these methodological questions, and counterfactual analysis is still controversial. I disagree, however, with those who claim that counterfactual analyses are all equally "absurd," because they are all equally hypothetical.[37] On the contrary, we must resort to counterfactual analysis if we are to be able to engage in scientific explanation at all. How can we otherwise establish what caused such events as—to take some classic counterfactual examples—the outbreak of World War I, the American New Deal in the 1930s, Hitler's assumption of power in Germany, or the defeat of Japan in 1945? Take the last-mentioned query. One possible view on the matter might be that "even if the United States had not dropped the A-bomb on two Japanese cities in August 1945, the Japanese would still have surrendered roughly when they did."

The titles of the chapters in an anthology edited by Niall Ferguson point out some of the questions that have prompted researchers to undertake counterfactual analysis:

1. England without Cromwell: What if Charles I had avoided the Civil War?
2. British America: What if there had been no American Revolution?
3. British Ireland: What if home rule had been enacted in 1912?
4. The Kaiser's European Union: What if Britain had "stood aside" in August 1914?
5. Hitler's England: What if Germany had invaded Britain in May 1940?
6. Nazi Europe: What if Nazi Germany had defeated the Soviet Union?
7. Stalin's War or peace: What if the Cold War had been avoided?
8. Camelot continued: What if John F. Kennedy had lived?
9. 1989 without Gorbachev: What if Communism had not collapsed?[38]

If we mean to carry out serious counterfactual analysis, we must follow a few simple rules of thumb, as a group of experienced social scientists have ascertained in the course of cooperative research financed by the American Social Science Research Council.[39] I summarize these rules somewhat freely below. They may be formulated as follows:

1. *Narrowly specified relations.* Social effects may be indirect and very long-term. If we try to calculate effects of this kind, we will quickly find ourselves in a realm of arbitrary speculation in which scarcely anything can be proved. For example, Pascal's famous counterfactual claim about Cleopatra's nose becomes meaningless if formulated in the following fashion: "if Cleopatra had had an unattractively large nose, World War I might not have occurred." A prudent rule of thumb is therefore to refrain from formulating such hypotheses. There is a price for this, however. Scien-

tifically speaking, after all, Pascal is doubtless quite right that Cleopatra's nose could have changed history; the problem is simply that the effects 2,000 years later are so difficult to prove. It is advisable to be a cautious general, when marching off toward the counterfactual frontiers of knowledge. One ought to be hesitant about exploring relations that are indirect, intricate, and long-term.

2. *The nature of the connecting principle.* The connecting link between cause and effect may not be as obvious as it may intuitively appear. This becomes clear, for example, upon a review of the different analyses made of the Cuban missile crisis. Liberal revisionist scholars argue that "if Kennedy had made a secret overture to Khrushchev before choosing the blockade, Khrushchev would have responded positively." Their conservative opponents rejoin that the Russians considered Americans "too soft, too liberal, and too rich to fight." A tougher language of force, accordingly, would have induced the Soviets to change their policy earlier: "If Kennedy had displayed greater resolve at the Bay of Pigs, at the Vienna summit, and in Berlin, Khrushchev would not have sent missiles to Cuba." When undertaking counterfactual analysis, then, the researcher must give careful thought to the nature of the connecting principle. One must thoroughly think through, for example, whether a hard or a soft strategy will work best in a specific situation, rather than just thoughtlessly (or ideologically) assuming that the one or the other is always superior.

3. *A minimal rewriting of history.* Successful counterfactual analysis means rewriting history as little as possible. The idea is that, in principle, possible worlds (1) should start with the real world as it was otherwise known before the counterfactual argument entered the picture; (2) should not require us to unwind the past and rewrite long stretches of history; and (3) should not unduly disturb what we otherwise know about the original actors, structures, technologies, and so forth. A counterfactual statement like the following, for example, is of course meaningless: "If Napoleon had possessed atomic weapons, he would have won the battle of Waterloo."

4. *Consistency with well-established theories.* Counterfactual analysis should be consistent with scientific knowledge and ought not to posit far-fetched effects on the basis of preposterous principles of causality—for example, "If Oswald had not shot Kennedy, then someone else would have done so because Kennedy was astrologically fated to die from assassination" or "If North Korea had conquered South Korea in 1950, the economy of the South would have grown even more rapidly than it actually did because of

the wisdom of the Great Leader Kim Il Sung." The problem lies, of course, in the difficulty of knowing anything within a branch of study like the social sciences, in which no natural laws can be cited. Once again, caution is advised: to hew to a minimalist strategy rather than devoting one's energy to the construction of grandiose but doubtful schemes.

5. *Consistency with well-established statistical generalizations.* In the absence of natural laws, social scientists resort to empirical generalizations. They can point to frequencies and probabilities. Those undertaking counterfactual analysis are well advised to avoid contradicting such statistical patterns. Bruce Russett, for example, argues that "If more countries had been democracies, we would have had fewer wars." The best way to advance this argument is to try to convince skeptics—with the help of careful statistical analysis—that the collinearity problem created by the confounding of variables does not explain away the democracy effect.

6. *Projectability.* Sound counterfactual analysis requires sound theories that provide lawlike generalizations fitting the missing data points in the analysis. But how can we judge whether these lawlike generalizations are robust enough to support counterfactual inferences? The iron test of any counterfactual analysis is its ability to predict—that is, "If my argument is correct, then what else is true?" Computer simulations and artificial-intelligence models can help to broaden the material; this may be especially helpful when one faces the small sample size (as, for example, when one studies what causes revolutions to break out). Counterfactual reasoning offers an exploratory theoretical device that helps compensate for the dearth of cases and events.

A large measure of dispassionate distance is needed if one is to live up to these demands. The scholar or decision maker must be the master of the material or situation, not its slave. The challenge is to make the possible world real. And if one is to meet this challenge, one must be capable of discerning alternatives in history.

This capacity is something that Secretary of State Marshall, his advisor Kennan, and their colleagues possessed in a high degree. They refused to fall for the idea of determinism on which their Communist adversaries sought to ride, and they identified an option for action over the medium term. They understood that economic reconstruction would issue in political stabilization, and launched a concrete program to that end. "If the United States provides economic support to Europe," they reasoned, "the threat from Soviet Communism will subside." But what if, by contrast, the Americans had chosen after the stresses of World War II to retreat into isolationism, in itself an understandable reaction? What if they had simply stood there with arms folded and watched while the Russians invaded Western Europe? In that case, we could rightly have held them responsible for betraying democracy.

A Communist victory in Europe after 1945, then, has served as our critical case of counterexample to a determinist conception of history. It was not, after all, just the Marxist doctrine of historical development that pointed to the inevitable triumph of socialism. There were also a number of objective circumstances—of an economic and political kind—that indicated that the states of Europe would fall victim to Soviet aggression. Yet that is not what happened. The intervention of certain farsighted actors ensured that what many people thought to be the probable did not become the actual.

CHAPTER 3

Nation-States Need Not
Go to War

The War of All against All

Blaming history is the first way to evade responsibility. Pleading the ubiquity of force is the second. Law, it is said, resides in the barrel of a gun. War is the continuation of politics by other means. How, then, can the will of politicians prevail, when force reigns over the world? "We can do nothing!" the politicians proclaim. "In political affairs, the victory goes to the stronger."

War is the ultimate expression of this view, and it has only gotten worse over time. "Why did wars occur at all?" asks Charles Tilly in his study of war during the last thousand years. He himself supplies the answer: "The central, tragic fact is simple: coercion *works;* those who apply substantial force to their fellows get compliance, and from that compliance draw the multiple advantages of money, goods, deference, access to pleasures denied to less powerful people." Seen over the long term, European wars have claimed ever great numbers of victims, even as they have become less common. The number of wars in which great powers have taken part has fallen substantially over the last 500 years, as has the duration of such wars. The intensity, however, has increased. The number of battle deaths per state increased from just under 3,000 per year in the sixteenth century to more than 223,000 in the twentieth. The average number of states involved in great-power wars rose from 9.4 in the sixteenth century to 17.6 in the eighteenth, only to fall back to 6.5 in the twentieth century. This rise and fall indicates the emergence of general war among most or all of the great powers—and then its subsequent counterbalance, during the nineteenth and twentieth centuries, by the tendency of Western states to start or intervene in local conflicts outside the West. The number of war victims, in other words, has increased to an appalling degree: "As a result of these changes, the sheer volume of great power deaths per year soared from 9,400 during the sixteenth century to 290,000 during the twentieth," to which all the civilian deaths must be added. If these are counted as well, the figures must be multiplied many times. The trend toward increased civilian casualties has, of course, been greatly strengthened by the weapons of mass destruction found in modern technological society.

Taxes and state budgets are a reflection of reality here. In the time before the nation-state arose, no princely house had a national budget in the modern sense of the word. There was, to be sure, a tax system of a sort, in the form of various duties for financing the expenditures of the court. Princes also borrowed money, often in their own name and against real collateral. Faced with the ubiquity of war, however, the new nation-states began introducing modern tax and budget systems in the sixteenth century. The financing of war led to a revolution in national systems of accounting. Public expenditures increased, as did public indebtedness. Such indebtedness did not lead, it bears noting, to any diminution in the level of state activity. On the contrary, the effect was to promote the development of modern bureaucracy, on account of the need to keep track of revenues and expenditures.

European politics became synonymous with the politics of war. It was military technology that decided the success or failure of states. "War wove the European network of national states, and preparation for war created the internal structures of the states within it. The years around 1500 were crucial." The use of gunpowder changed the character of war. The next development was the cannon; over the next 150 years (1500–1650), those royal houses that could afford cannons were victorious. Eventually the pattern became complete. The provision of armaments and the collection of taxes became the nation-state's most important task.[1]

That nation-states resort to arms as soon as they see their interests threatened is a notion backed by timeless experience. Indeed, this notion was given exaggerated anecdotal expression in one of the classics of political science. In the winter of 1502–3, the story goes, the Florentine government sent Niccolò Machiavelli to the camp of Duke Cesare Borgia, in the hope of ascertaining the latter's plans. Upon completing a repast together, the two men sat before an open fire and conversed over a bottle of Chianti. At one point their talk turned to the question of whether a political project that was unsupported by force of arms could be imagined. Both men burst out into laughter. Such a notion struck them—so unworldly it was—as intensely comical. In a wicked world one must oneself employ namely wicked methods. That prince who shows goodness in all his actions will be lost among peers who do not share his scruples. Interests, not ideals, are the stuff of politics. If we fail to understand this, we shall never see the realization of our desires—be they ever so noble. We cannot talk ourselves to the unification of Italy, Machivaelli would write ten years later. We must be ready to best our opponents without scruple, and we must be prepared—banishing all doubt—to create alliances with our former enemies, if such be necessary to reach the goals that we desire.[2]

The heir to Machiavelli in the history of political ideas is Thomas Hobbes. From Epicurus, Hobbes borrowed the phrase "the war of all against all"—along with the materialistic, mechanistic, and utilitarian outlook of the ancient philosopher. International affairs, he averred, were propelled by the interests of nations. This idea has since served as the basic principle of the so-called realist school. Strikingly enough, Hobbes did not derive his deductive theory—according to which people's instinct for self-preservation and power leads them ineluctably to destroy one another—from any special study of international relations; it proceeded, rather, from his observations of the domestic political sphere. The shadow of the English Civil War lay over the thoughts of Thomas Hobbes. The lust for power, he warned, turns men to wolves and pits them against each other. For any solution to be possible, man must relinquish his rights and freedoms to *Leviathan*, Hobbes's designation for an unbridled state power. His discourse on this point was less a historical analysis of the origins of state power than an exhibition of the social-contract notions prevalent in his time. We introduce the state and see what becomes different thereby. The state of nature, like democracy, is marked by self-will and civil war. For this reason, we must submit to the dictates of Leviathan. We must sacrifice our freedom for security, if we are to survive at all. While Epicurus shunned the wicked world of politics, preferring to philosophize with his friends in the garden, Hobbes came to the very opposite conclusion: he embraced the evil world of politics, deeming it the only alternative to a yet greater evil—the slaying of human beings by one another. Only an absolute ruler, he averred, can provide us with the security we need.[3]

In our own time, the idea that war is unavoidable as long as nation-states exist has been embraced by the ideologues of totalitarianism. Lenin's contribution to Marxist theory was to interpret imperialism as the "highest stage" of capitalism—the form taken by the system since the time of Marx. In accordance with the Hegelian schema, capitalism had now "swung over into its opposite." Capitalism had been born in competition, but through its very success had now issued in monopoly. Under monopoly capitalism, finance capital had assumed a new role. Previously a mere handmaiden of industry, the large banks were now launching ever more aggressive attempts at dominating the market. There were no longer any national boundaries for capital for the proletariat. The rivalry had become international. Capital was exported on a massive scale, and new investments were made on distant continents; temporary cartels were formed, only to be replaced by a yet more ruthless exploitation of markets and colonies. It was a historical law that war must come. The outbreak of World War I served to confirm Lenin's theory, although he must have been surprised at the support given by the German Social Democrats for the Kaiser's war policy. For the longest time, in fact, he refused to believe that this report was anything but a rumor spread by the German general staff in order to discredit socialism.[4]

The Nazis and Fascists, for their part, viewed the state as a biological being—and one possessed of an irrepressible need for self-assertion. Irrationalism pervaded the whole of Adolf Hitler's thinking. Argument, fact, examination—all were merely tools for achieving the real goal: mobilizing the martial energies of the people. Questions of truth were secondary; what mattered was power and victory. Instinct was a surer guide to the right policy than dry, rational analysis. Violence was seen as the highest expression of political will—an idea that nourished a belief in what the German minister of propaganda called "the total war": a final, decisive trial of strength fated to take place between the peoples. Mussolini's Fascists paid the same enthusiastic homage to raw force and talked about "the beauty of unreflected action."[5]

If this, then, is the nature of states, what are we to do? Hobbes's solution would seem the only tenable one for international relations. Leviathan must be invested with unlimited power. Supranational organizations will be incapable of holding states in check unless they are endowed with such authority. The warlike nation-state must be crushed. The only solution to the problem of war is federalism.

Thus can be summarized the notion that spread within the resistance movement against Nazi occupation in Europe. The federalists' viewpoint acquired renewed strength against the background of the wars waged by the totalitarian states. Their dream of a united and peaceful Europe was an old one. The many wars that broke out in connection with the emergence of nation-states in the 1500s prompted many thinkers—even then—to urge the various royal houses to seek peace and cooperation. In place of the abdicating Catholic Church, some other cooperative organization would be needed that could set limits on the ability of sovereign states to make war on each other. A good many utopians would repeat this conclusion in the course of bloodbaths during the subsequent centuries. Between the Napoleonic Wars and World War I, demands for European unification began to assume a more concrete form. In a variety of appeals, such figures as the philosopher Immanuel Kant, the freedom fighter Giuseppe Garibaldi, and the writer Victor Hugo called upon the states of Europe to come together. It is true that when war broke out in 1914, many assumed that the idea of a unified Europe had received its coup de grâce; yet the horrors of that conflict soon gave the notion a new lease on life. The European movement grew strong in the 1920s and may be said to have culminated in the autumn of 1929, when the French foreign minister, Aristide Briand, presented a plan for a European union to the League of Nations. Yet this event also signified an ending. The rise to power of Nazism and Fascism, and the political developments following thereupon, stripped the pan-European idea of its pertinence.

Rather, it was in the resistance movement, as mentioned above, that the federalist idea lived on. In an internment camp on the island of Ventotene, outside Naples, men of the resistance under the leadership of Ernesto Rossi and Altiero Spinelli hatched a dramatic conspiracy. They called for the reshaping of Europe, so that future generations might be spared the devastation of war. In 1941, the *Ventotene Manifesto* was published. The original had been written on cigarette paper and hidden in a tin can with a false bottom; it was then smuggled back to the mainland by Rossi's wife. This document resulted, two years later, in the formation of the Italian federalist movement.

The *Ventotene Manifesto* begins with an analysis of how the character of the nation-state had changed. Originally, the authors averred, the nation-state was an expression of the right of all people to join together in pursuit of common interests; thus, it had been a powerful instrument for progress. That such an account of the history might be thought a bit sanitized is clear, I presume, from the discussion above. But now conditions were different. The nation-state had come to be seen as a being standing over and above the individual; an organism endowed with a will of its own, developing independently of any such injuries as it might inflict on the individuals it comprises; and a master to be served abjectly by its citizens. The modern state was nothing but a war machine. It is true that such a designation might be thought equally fitting for the nation-states of an earlier epoch, but this is scarcely a decisive objection to the authors' argument: as we saw above, the wars of the twentieth century were unquestionably worse than those of earlier times. A condition of peace was now regarded, the authors continued, as nothing but a temporary respite from war; civilian society had no function any longer save to contribute to an increase in military strength; the sole role of women was to mother future soldiers. Through recurrent wars, the new, totalitarian state forced the harshest sacrifices on its citizens.

The internal organization of the state had been altered. Free organizations were no longer tolerated. In the totalitarian state, corporative bodies were subjected to the will of the state and transformed into instruments of oppression. The production of ideology was standardized. The whole of social life was made to serve the war policy of the totalitarian state.

Yet resistance lived on. Nazism and Fascism would meet defeat at the hands of the Allies. The future belonged to the resistance movement.

The authors understood that the fall of Germany would not automatically usher in a peaceful Europe. In all ages, namely the upper classes had opposed internationalism and drawn advantage from the nation-state—this, too, perhaps a dubious claim. "The classes which were most privileged under the old national systems will attempt, underhandedly or violently, to quench the thirst, the sentiments, the passions groping towards internationalism, and they will ostentatiously begin to reconstruct the old state organs." Feelings of patriotism were not to be underestimated. If nothing was done, the warlike nation-states would soon stage a comeback. "The question which must first be resolved . . . is that of the abolition of the division of Europe into national, sovereign states."

The attempts made hitherto to promote peace through international organizations had been far too modest. In the absence of supranational authority, lasting peace could not be attained: "The uselessness, even harmfulness, of organizations like the League of Nations has been demonstrated." Future efforts must therefore focus on building a supranational Europe. "All matters . . . would find easy solutions in the European Federation."

The dividing line between progressive and reactionary forces in the future would run between those who wished to retain the system of nation-states and those whose prime purpose was "the creation of a solid international state." Such a state would have to be freed from bureaucracy, militarism, and the dominance of the Catholic Church; nor could it be allowed to dominate the organizations of civil society.

With a Leninist fervor, the task before the faithful was laid out: "The revolutionary party cannot be amateurishly organized"; it must be "made up of men who are in agreement on the main problems," who are devoted to the cause "day by day, with discipline."[6]

The *Ventotene Manifesto* bears the mark of the time in which it was written. The horrors of the war were immediate; Nazism, Fascism, and totalitarianism were the sworn enemy. The basic tone of the manifesto was unmistakably socialist, and the Communist variant of totalitarianism—with its fervent, enlightened vanguard—met with uncritical acceptance. Yet the analysis it contained of the problems associated with the nation-state bears relevance beyond the issues of the time. The exhortation to build a European federation summed up the hopes and longings of centuries for peace and furnished the basis for the remarkable process of integration seen in Europe over the following half-century.

These ideas were given powerful expression the next year, when Rossi and Spinelli succeeded—in the midst of Nazi occupation and raging war—in gathering men of the resistance from Denmark, France, Italy, Norway, Holland, Poland, and Czechoslovakia (together with anti-Nazis from Germany) to a series of secret meetings in neutral Switzerland. These meetings also issued in a manifesto, with much the same content as that written at the prison camp in Italy:

> European peace is the keystone in the arch of world peace. During the lifetime of one generation Europe has twice been the centre of a world conflict whose chief cause was the existence of thirty sovereign States in Europe. It is a most urgent task to end this international anarchy by creating a European Federal Union.
>
> Only a Federal Union will enable the German people to join the European community without becoming a danger to other peoples.
>
> Only a Federal Union will make it possible to solve the problem of drawing frontiers in districts with mixed population. The minorities will thus cease to be the object of nationalistic jealousies, and frontiers will be nothing but demarcation lines between administrative districts.

Only a Federal Union will be in a position to protect democratic institutions and so prevent politically less developed countries becoming a danger to the international order.

Only a Federal Union will make possible the economic reconstruction of the Continent and the liquidation of monopolies and national self-sufficiency.

Only a Federal Union will allow a logical and natural solution to the problems of the access to the sea of those countries which are situated in the interior of the Continent, of a rational use of those rivers which flow through the several States, of the control of straits, and, generally, of most of the problems which during recent years have disturbed international relations.

Nazism and Fascism had triumphed across Europe. Yet from the windswept prison island went the call of the conspirators that the time had now come to build a new, peaceful, and therefore federal Europe. There was no other way out. For it lies in the nature of nation-states to go to war. Wars are unavoidable as long as nation-states remain. There can always, to be sure, be periods of temporary peace. But history has shown that, sooner or later, nation-states will take up arms against each other again.

L'Europe des Patries

European integration as it actually developed after the war was very different from what the federalist manifesto had envisaged. With the landing of the Allies in Normandy, the resistance movement was faced with other tasks. Its time was now taken up with practical and immediate problems. When the war was over, the former resistance groups did indeed come together at conferences, and an all-European movement was formed. But just as they had feared, the nation-states were soon consolidated once more. Yet peace persisted all the same. Europe acquired a new experience. The expectations of the federalists were apparently mistaken. Nation-states need not go to war. There was thus cause to reconsider the question that, of all those bearing on human relations, may be the most fundamental of all. The critical case in this chapter, then, is European integration after the war. The puzzle to be solved is the following: Why did the nation-states of Europe cease to make war on each other during the second half of the twentieth century?

In order to answer this question, I will focus on certain critical points during the postwar process of European integration.[7] It is necessary to go into detail at these points, if one wishes to fully understand how key actors reasoned about their possibility to rule and thus to take responsibility. This, then, will be the topic for the following pages.

The integration process has been characterized by a delicate balance between the principle of federalism and that of the sovereign nation-state. What the actors themselves call the one or the other does not, as usual, always serve to make the matter clear. The origins of European federalism in the resistance movement against Fascism have tended to endow the word *federalism* with favorable connotations. At least on the Continent, almost everybody therefore wishes to claim the word as their own—even those who actually prefer to work for peace on the basis of nation-states.

We turn first to the foremost pioneer of European integration, Jean Monnet. He was a French businessman, an international civil servant, and a visionary. His experiences, analyses, and recommendations would prove of the greatest importance in changing the nature of relations among what had hitherto been the warlike nation-states of Europe.

Even as a very young man, Monnet had entered the service of peace. After a stint representing France in Allied organs of cooperation during World War I, he took part in the preparatory work for the Treaty of Versailles; then, in 1919, he was appointed financial adviser to, and deputy secretary-general of, the League of Nations. The death of his father prompted him to resign his public duties in order to devote himself to the family cognac distillery. At the approach of World War II, however, the French government called on his services once again. He was charged with coordinating the transport of civilian and military necessities across the Atlantic. He then bore similar responsibilities as a representative for the British government in the United States. Later Monnet took a post in the French Résistance government, and after the war became head of postwar planning.

The economic and political problems were colossal. The reconstruction of Europe was an extraordinary challenge. And the atmosphere of international relations had become ice-cold. Due to tensions between East and West, the threat of war was acute once more. In his memoirs, Monnet gave vivid expression to the despair he had felt over the fact that, in human affairs, wars and self-inflicted misery seemed never to end. And when, in the spring of 1950, he embarked on his yearly walking tour in the Alps, he found that the problem of all the constant wars was pounding through his head more than ever. He wrote down his thoughts each night, telling of "the anxiety that weighed on Europe five years after the war: the fear that if we did nothing we should soon face war again." A new threat had appeared on the European horizon: instead of the old rivalry between Germany and France, a war between the American and Soviet superpowers was feared. This did not mean the old threat had been completely eliminated: "In the confused state of Franco-German relations, the neurosis of the vanquished seemed to be shifting to the victor: France was beginning to feel inferior again as she realized that attempts to limit Germany's dynamism were bound to fail."

What then was to be done? Monnet is a brilliant example of how politics as rational action can be acquired through realism, imagination, and purposefulness. To begin with, Monnet felt obliged to assume the continued existence of nation-states for a long time to come. Germany's standing as an independent nation had been recognized. "German sovereignty had just been re-established. Could it now be called into question again, even partially?" All attempts at holding Germany in check, mainly at French instigation, had come to nothing. "But if the problem of sovereignty were approached with no desire to dominate or take revenge—if on the contrary the victors and the vanquished agreed to exercise joint sovereignty over part of their joint resources—then, a solid link would be forged between them, the way would be wide open for further collective action, and a great example would be given to the other nations of Europe." The initiative for a realistic peace mission would have to come from France. Only that country could speak on behalf of Europe. Great Britain, with its traditions of splendid isolation, was not to be relied on in this respect. West Germany was still in a weakened state. It fell to France to secure the peace, through a radically new way of visualizing future relations between European nation-states. It was time for what Monnet called "a bold, constructive act."[8]

In connection with a meeting in Paris in May 1950, in which Robert Schuman, the French foreign minister, was to confer both with his West European colleagues and with the American secretary of state, Monnet submitted a memorandum to the top leaders of his country. In it he stressed the key role of France and underscored the need for action. Europe could not continue, Monnet argued, to place its fate wholly in the hands of the United States. Just as Secretary of State Marshall had done when presenting his plan for a European recovery,[9] Monnet stressed that the United States expected Europeans to take responsibility for their own welfare. Europe was not like the United States, Monnet continued. The citizens of the United States were first and foremost Americans and only secondarily residents of a particular state. In Europe it was the other way round. Europeans had no experience with suprastatal arrangements. For a common identity to emerge, an experience of cooperation would first be needed—in the economic realm not least—together with a constitutional structure that sovereign nation-states would not regard as a threat.[10]

Monnet then submitted a concrete proposal, and Schuman was not to disappoint him. At a press conference in connection with the aforementioned meeting, Schuman presented the sensational declaration that has since borne his name. He started out by saying that the overriding purpose of the proposal was peace: "World peace can not be safeguarded without making efforts proportionate to the dangers which threaten it. The contribution which an organized and active Europe can bring to civilization is indispensable to the maintenance of peaceful relations. For more than twenty years, France has acted as the champion of a united Europe, and has always had the defence of peace as an essential goal. When Europe has not shared this goal, we have had war."

Next came the political moves. The French government proposed, in accordance with Monnet's memorandum, that the entire production of coal and steel in Germany and France be placed under a common directing authority, within an organization that would be open to other European states. This directing authority would consist of independent persons—an equal number of whom would come from each country—appointed by the respective governments, who would also jointly choose the chairman.

The task of the authority would be to work for modernization and quality improvements, for uniform conditions in coal and steel both in the French and German markets and within any other countries joining the agreement, for the development of common export products, and for a general harmonization of living and working conditions in the participating countries. Such economic integration would serve to secure peace: "The fusion of production formed in this way will mean that any war between France and Germany will become not only unthinkable but materially impossible."[11]

As Sverker Gustavsson has pointed out, this proposal had a constitutionally "impure" structure. This was not a mistake, however, but a rational actor's most deliberate and sophisticated move to attain something that could change the tragic repetition of wars between European nation-states.

On the one hand, the European Coal and Steel Community would have no constitutional basis of its own. The foundation would be interstatal. The construction was presumed to rest on a treaty between the participating countries, to be approved by the respective parliaments. On the other hand, a suprastatal authority would keep watch over the treaty and, where necessary, adjudicate between competing claims. "The suprastatal arrangements rested on an interstatal foundation." According to Gustavsson, arrangements are usually said to be suprastatal if they meet three criteria. "First, member states are able to bind each other through majority rule. Second, no further decision within each country is necessary. Common decisions have direct effect. Third, decisions of the suprastatal authorities enjoy, when interpretations are in dispute, precedence in principle over decisions made by member states. Interstatal arrangements are the opposite on every score. Each member state has a veto. International agreements must be adopted within each nation to have effect there, and they enjoy no precedence in principle." By the second and third criteria, then, the Schuman Plan qualified as suprastatal. "But where the first criterion is concerned— that of majority rule—the Schuman Declaration is silent."[12]

The solution proposed by Monnet and the French government was not of a purely federalist character, inasmuch as the directing authority that it established was not to be chosen through general elections in the member states. It was out of the question that the nation-states involved would agree in such a fashion to transfer the requisite power and authority to the common organization. The point was rather to endow the organization with sufficient power as to make it into a tool—one independent of chauvinist popular opinion—in the hands of the national governments.

As expected, the proposal was rejected by Britain but welcomed by Belgium, Italy, the Netherlands, Luxembourg, and West Germany; of particular importance was the enthusiastic support shown by Konrad Adenauer, the German chancellor. One year later, the European Coal and Steel Community was founded. Monnet was made the first chairman of the directing authority.

The reaction among federalists was one of confusion and surprise. Their view further elucidates the strategy of the pioneers to take control and responsibility for the policy of avoiding wars. To be sure, the federalists saw the Coal and Steel Community as a welcome step in the direction of peace in Europe. They felt disquiet, however, at the fact that the nation-states would apparently be keeping their sovereignty and at the fact that the organization was not furnished with a democratic constitution. Peace was great, but was it necessary to sacrifice democracy to attain this goal? A resolution from the federalist executive committee praised the "great initiative" of the French foreign minister but emphasized as well the importance of providing the directing authority with a democratic anchor: "It cannot be stressed too strongly that such a decisive role can be entrusted only to a democratic European political authority."[13] Altiero Spinelli, for his part, felt obliged to remind Europeans of the meaning of supranationalism. The establishment of federal organizations should entail "transferring to them certain prerogatives of national sovereignty." It was the citizens, not the governments, who ought to be the principals of a new, peaceful, and federated Europe: "The drafting of the pact of federal union should be carried out by an Assembly in which the participating countries are represented by delegates who speak for the peoples and not for the governments."[14]

The new Europe was on its way. It had been possible, with the aid of some deliberate obscurity on the constitutional question, to surmount the obstacles that had previously paralyzed efforts to ensure peace. The shadow of the Cold War had facilitated the common project. The fear of world Communism had made it possible at long last to establish cooperation among the leading nation-states of Europe. "Tomorrow's federal Europe should erect a monument of gratitude to Stalin."[15]

The 1950s were marked by growth and confidence—and by ceaseless negotiations as well, which will not be analyzed further here. The reconstruction led to European prosperity. Ten years after the war, living standards had become higher than ever. An affluent Europe was also less fearful of Communism. Various international conflicts, to be sure, took place in this period (as in Suez, Hungary, and Berlin); yet the Soviet Union had left Austria and Finland, Greece had been stabilized, and Yugoslavia had established friendly ties with the West. Negotiations among the six members of the Coal and Steel Community continued, and in the summer of 1955 the six foreign ministers reached an agreement in Messina to work for an arrangement in which cooperation would extend to the entire economic sphere. In March 1957, the Treaty of Rome was signed, establishing the European Economic Community (EEC). A common market would be established through the removal of all obstacles to the free movement of goods, services, capital, and labor; common policies would be instituted in the areas of agriculture, fisheries, transportation, and trade with outside countries; social and economic policies would be coordinated; and a cooperative scheme on the peaceful use of nuclear power would be introduced. At the same time, the principle of the nation-state reigned supreme: decisions would made unanimously—that is, each member state enjoyed the right of veto.

In 1961, four more states expressed interest in joining the EEC (Denmark, Ireland, Norway, and Great Britain). But the optimism was suddenly shattered. How history is not predetermined, or linear, but can be changed by the influence of key persons was dramatically demonstrated when France elected a president who came from the realist school: Charles de Gaulle. For de Gaulle, nation-states remained the fixed foundation of international affairs; their place had not been taken by ideologies or parties occasionally in power. He felt disdain for "Eurocrats," with their federalist inclinations and indistinct mandate; indeed, he had criticized the Coal and Steel Community on the grounds that it lacked a democratic basis and made no provision for democratic accountability; de Gaulle's respect for the will of the people would be revealed when, in 1969, as a consequence of a lost referendum, he chose to resign. De Gaulle thought that Europe ought to become a third balancing power in the world, alongside the United States and the Soviet Union. But it was not a supranational Europe he desired, but rather a Europe of cooperating nation-states (a *confédération*, maybe even just a *groupement*). For de Gaulle, Europe was a league of friendly nation-states—*l'Europe des Patries*. The distinctiveness and sovereignty of the individual states ought to be preserved. Nor was this Europe limited to a handful of countries in the western part of the continent. De Gaulle's vision was of a Europe stretching "from the Atlantic to the Urals." Ideologies flowered, wilted, and died; nation-states remained. No one knew how long Communism would last. But the states lay where they lay. With a perspicacity few understood at the time, the French president urged that Europe be prepared in the future to take its East and Central European sisters into its embrace.

In talks on television, and in less common conferences with the press, de Gaulle repeated his message. Europe had to take its fate into its own hands; it could not remain a U.S. satellite. This vision prompted him to question the role of the United Kingdom in European cooperation. At a press conference in January 1963, therefore, he made clear his intention to veto British membership in the EEC. De Gaulle expressed his admiration for the British people but took the view that Britain was too closely bound to other English-speaking countries—above all the United States—to be fit for membership in the Community. British membership would lead to a complete change in the structure of European cooperation, the recent start of which had been so auspicious. In the wake of the addition of Great Britain, moreover, several other states would join as well, and the relationship vis-à-vis the United States would be changed. All these many states would eventually form an Atlantic community under American leadership, which "would soon swallow up the European Community." Such an American-led community was perhaps what many countries desired, but "that is not at all what France wanted to do and is doing, which is a strictly European construction."[16]

Was the integration project about to fail? With de Gaulle's intervention, developments had swung powerfully toward the nation-state pole. European cooperation came to a standstill. France put a brake on continued integration. In the course of seven months during the mid-1960s, in fact, France sent no representative to the Council of Ministers. This "empty chair crisis" served to mark French displeasure with the excessively far-reaching ambitions of vanguardist Eurocrats. The crisis was solved through the so-called Luxembourg Compromise, whereby each state was expressly given the right of veto over questions bearing on "vital national interests." France was to interpret this right broadly; the entire agricultural sector, for example, was interpreted as such an interest. The "compromise"—if indeed that is the right word to use—was yet another triumph for the principle of *l'Europe des Patries*. It was when Pompidou succeeded de Gaulle as French president that the prospects improved for continued movement in a supranational direction.

The 1970s, however, proved to be a mixed decade. Great Britain, Denmark, and Ireland joined the Community; Greece, Spain, and Portugal would do so later. At the same time, developments were marked internally by sharp conflicts of interest and externally by the stresses induced by the oil crisis. The nation-state principle of the realist school acquired a powerful new spokeswoman in the British Prime Minister, Margaret Thatcher, who in this respect proved the heir of de Gaulle. In a public speech in 1988, she laid out her position with her customary clarity:

My first guiding principle is this: willing and active cooperation between independent sovereign states is the best way to build a successful European Community. To try to suppress nationhood and concentrate power at the centre of a European conglomerate would be highly damaging and would jeopardize the objectives we seek to achieve. Europe will be stronger precisely because it has France as France, Spain as Spain, Britain as Britain, each with its own customs, traditions and identity. It would be folly to try to fit them into some sort of Identikit European personality.

There were two things the prime minister wished to make clear. To begin with, a federation such as the United States was no model for a European community. Europe consisted of nation-states, which would never consent to a supranational federation. In addition, Thatcher was opposed to all those regulations that the Eurocrats in Brussels loved to devise. In Britain she had vanquished socialism; she had no wish to see it reappear in a new guise. "We have not successfully rolled back the frontiers of the state in Britain only to see them reimposed at a European level with a European superstate exercising a new dominance from Brussels."[17]

It seemed that the nation-state principle had triumphed. To all appearances, the de Gaulle–Thatcher line had stopped any further development in a supranational direction. But then developments took a surprising new turn when bold, imaginative, and, some even say, unscrupulous actors found ways to take command. The early 1990s saw new steps toward integration in spite of the fact that the threat that had driven the nations of Europe together—the Soviet Union—had disappeared. How did the politicians reason at this point?

The first threat to the countries of Europe had been the possibility of renewed conflict between Germany and France. But after 1945, when Germany lay in ruins, the fear was rather that the continent would become a battlefield for the superpowers—the United States and the Soviet Union. Then, when the Soviet Union fell, an economic threat served as the most important motor for European cooperation. The view was that if the governments of the continent failed to tame inflation, Europe would never be able to achieve its dreams. A new leader in the vein of Jean Monnet assumed responsibility for the European integration. Jacques Delors, a Frenchman, lacked the elite education otherwise mandatory for a member of the French governing class; he had worked for many years as a banker before taking the step over to Monnet's commission on postwar planning and thence to Mitterrand's government, in which he served as minister of finance. His biographer describes him as "indeed a federalist, but [one who] knew full well that the earlier federalist dream of a 'United States of Europe' was no longer plausible. Any new Europe would be a complicated juxtaposition of different jurisdictions of a model quite unprecedented in the annals of federalist development." As the master had done, so Delors continued. He endeavored to push developments in the desired direction, while avoiding any showdown over constitutional questions. As his biographer writes,

> The "Monnet method" was consciously elitist. For everyone to benefit, European construction had to proceed in the shadows of democratic accountability as ordinarily understood . . . How fundamental issues of democratic deficit might have been addressed was itself quite unclear. Little consensus existed about how to do so and profound issues of political philosophy remained open. Should the legitimacy of Community Europe be built on a transnational European political culture focused upon the European Parliament? Or should it follow from a full "Europeanization" of national parliamentary lives and political cultures? Neither option had been pursued far enough to understand its implications.[18]

Such obscurity was no more accidental now than it had been earlier. And the focus on immediate, concrete goals was just as resolute as ever. Economic growth with monetary stability was possible, if member states exploited the potential of free trade to the full. Delors collected all earlier decision into a white book, *Completing the Single Market*, with 280 measures. The member states, which now were twelve, should combine into a common market. All member states, including the British, had signed the Single European Act. (Delors was careful when addressing Thatcher to put the stress on Europe as a market for the sale of goods and services, rather than as a hotbed of socialism.) Compared with the Luxembourg Compromise, the Single European Act provided for a greater use of majority voting in the Council of Ministers. It thus signified a move in a federalist direction.

Cooperation thereupon intensified. In the Dutch city of Maastricht, in December 1991, the governments of the member states agreed to introduce changes in the basic treaty. The European Union, with its three "pillars," was formed. It consisted of the European Community (in the form it had reached in 1991), a common policy to be developed in the areas of foreign and security policy, and cooperation on justice and interior affairs. The member states also agreed to introduce a common currency. Four years later, the Union took in three new members (Sweden, Finland, and Austria); a number of Eastern and Central European countries had applied for membership as well—much as de Gaulle had predicted decades earlier.

Yet setbacks were a constant threat. Denmark rejected the Maastricht Treaty in a referendum, and France—which had been considered the most pro-EU country—approved the treaty only by a very narrow margin. One year later, however, the Danes voted yes to a partially renegotiated treaty. General assent to a common currency was still lacking.

In Germany, a legal battle broke out over the Union. A jurist presented a document to the constitutional court, in which he questioned the compatibility of the Maastricht Treaty with the democratic principles enshrined in the constitutions of the member states. The court set the objection aside. The member states, it found, were still "masters of the treaties" ("Herren der Verträge"). Sovereignty had not been handed over to any new state; it had only been "lent out" for the common use of the cooperating nation-states. If the treaty were violated, the German Bundestag would always be able to re-call its delegation.

Resolute and ingenious attempts, in other words, were made to solve the problems that were constantly arising. In the course of the 1990s, new agreements were reached on intensified cooperation in the areas of social and employment policy.

At the turn of the millennium, the situation changed dramatically. In 2004, the EU was enlarged to include ten new nation-states from Central and Eastern Europe at the same time that the constitutional discussion was intensified about the "democratic deficit" of the union. As a response to this criticism, a constitution for the EU with more majoritarian-decision rules was proposed and presented to the various member states for approval. Very much against the tradition of the EU, the people were thus asked to give an opinion—with the result that the proposal was rejected in referenda in France and Holland in the spring of 2005, after which a referendum in Great Britain already under way was cancelled.

Against this background, the present situation (in January 2006) is, for obvious reasons, unusually difficult to judge. Has the European integration now come to a stop? Even if this is what some journalists and politicians maintain, it seems highly unlikely from the longer perspective we have adopted in this chapter. The EU has developed through a series of successes and setbacks. The process has been declared dead many times before, only to start again with new energy and inspiration thanks to initiatives of new actors working in the tradition of Monnet. Or in the, perhaps somewhat extreme, words of Andrew Moravscik, "Looking back in 50 years, historians will not see the referendums as the end of the EU—not even as the beginning of the end. The union remains the most successful experiment in political institution-building since the second world war."[19]

Does this study of the EU refute the thesis that nation-states must go to war? Has it proved that war is possible to avoid? If the requirement is to avoid war for a few decades, the answer is obviously yes. Forever? That is more doubtful, even if it seems highly unlikely today that France and Germany ever would start fighting each other again after their EU marriage. The EU has been a peace-building success. It shows that war is not inevitable. My view is neither the hard-boiled "realistic" concept that politics is a war of all against all nor an "idealistic" concept that politicians can do anything to promote good values. The historical experiences of Europe have been built into the institutional design of the EU, and its investigators acknowledged the fact that politics is about the ever-present possibility of existential threat, rather than its ever-present actuality.[20]

Now this is not, it bears final noting, the only way of realizing this most ardent of human desires (see Figure 3.1). The traditional method for achieving this is a balance of power. War can be avoided, according to the realist school, if states keep their armaments in sufficient repair.

Balance will keep war at bay.[21] Integrationists call for cooperation, of which there are two variants: uniting and acting together. The creation of the European Union is the story of how the latter course proved the salvation of a lacerated continent, but at the cost of a democratic deficit. There are also those, finally, who believe there is a third way, namely, that democratic states do not make war on each other.[22]

In the following section, I will further explore this cost of a democratic deficit in the EU. Some say that it was exactly the price Europe had to pay to reach the goal of peace. Others, like the just-quoted analyst Andrew

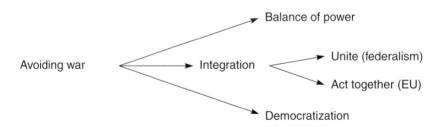

Figure 3.1. Avoiding war.

Moravscik, maintain that it is this very talk about democracy that creates the present problem for the EU.

Accountability and Legitimacy

There is no better example of trustee democracy (as opposed to participatory democracy, to use a distinction from Chapter 1) than the development of the European Union. It has been pushed forward by the enlightened elite, who have feared the verdict of the people, because supranational arrangements, even for such benign values as peace, are never supposed to be approved by ordinary citizens. Therefore, referenda must be avoided.

Monnet's success derived from the fact that he had something concrete and constructive to offer for the medium term. He is often described as a visionary, but his skill in persuading politicians to adopt his ideas lay more in the fact that he skillfully avoided discussing long-term consequences with undue clarity. It was when the politicians started to solve the democratic deficit around the turn of the millennium that it at last became impossible to avoid the constitutional issue. Monnet instead pointed to the functions whereby cooperation might come about. He talked about coal and steel, not about sovereignty and nation-states. In place of international law came functionalism.

But this pragmatism did not exclude passion. Monnet's overriding goal for humanity was peace. He did not believe, however, that federalism in our time would lead us there. Every realistic analysis must reckon rather with the fact that nation-states are the central actors, and will so remain for the foreseeable future, and that it is they, represented by their governments, that must be convinced of the necessity for a new approach to relations between states. Nation-states must be persuaded to bind their strategic resources together in such a fashion that it simply becomes impossible for them to make war on one another again. Governments will have to realize, if only out of an instinct for survival, the advantages of such an arrangement. The best must not become the enemy of the good. If now a supranational federation cannot be built, that does not give us leave to resign and to leave nation-states free to sleepwalk their way into a new war. Patience and good arguments are needed, to be sure, to induce national governments to reconsider. But the mission is not an impossible one. There is no natural law saying that force must govern in international affairs. Nation-states need not go to war.

Giandomenico Majone has developed Monnet's elite argument further. The Italian professor does not lament the expert influence in the EU; on the contrary, he is keen that expertise be given the lead. Let us therefore take a look at his arguments. Majone reminds us, to begin with, that majoritarian democracy—with its ideal of accountability—is not the only democratic model. In political reality, in fact, it is sooner the exception than the rule, and one largely limited to Great Britain and to countries of British tradition. The more common arrangement is the one to which Arend Lijphart has given a variety of designations through the years, but which in his later usage is known as "consensus democracy," and in the present study is given closer treatment in Chapter 5. Majone, who cites Lijphart directly, prefers quite simply to refer to "the non-majoritarian model of democracy." In such a system, governmental institutions are not directly accountable to citizens. Democratic legitimacy is achieved instead through the quality of the decisions made—a result of expert direction, of governance by "the competent." Just as in the United States, moreover, minorities are protected from "the tyranny of the majority" by a system in which power is shared, dispersed, and limited in a variety of ways. The point of governance by expertise is precisely that such an arrangement renders decision makers independent of the capacious influence of election campaigns—thus "insulating the regulators from the potentially destabilizing effects of the electoral cycles." When politicians must ensure their reelection, by contrast, they tend simply to issue irresponsible promises rather than make the serious and responsible decisions needed for the long-term.

In majoritarian democracy, legitimacy is regarded as a procedural question: are the leaders appointed and dismissed in democratic order? In non-majoritarian democracy, by contrast, the focus is on "substantive legitimacy," and "[r]eliance upon qualities such as expertise, professional discretion, policy consistency, fairness or independence of judgment is considered to be more important than reliance upon direct political accountability." What is the quality of the decisions taken? Are they compatible with each other and with the long-term program? How knowledgeable are the decision makers? How well demarcated are the limits within which leaders must act? It is the answers to these questions that determine the legitimacy of government.

The legitimacy of the system, in other words, is achieved differently in the majoritarian and non-majoritarian models. In the former, citizens see the system as legitimate because they are able, in general elections, to judge the success of the policy pursued (what I in this book call "accountability"). In the latter, citizens consider the system legitimate if the substantive quality of the decisions made by their leaders is high—that is, if the consequences of these decisions are as favorable over the long-term as possible (what I in this book call "responsibility").

Majone would argue, in keeping with the latter model, that the best way to enhance the Union's democratic legitimacy would be to require decision makers to furnish reasons for their decisions. Such transparency would enable citizens to judge the quality of the policies pursued. The need to justify one's actions systematically would furthermore activate a range of other mechanisms for controlling regulatory discretion—that is, peer review, policy analysis, judicial review, and public participation and debate. There is no doubt, in Majone's estimation, that the legitimacy of the Union would be more effectively enhanced were the principle of deliberative democracy implemented—that is, if leaders were required to furnish thorough and well-considered reasons for their decisions—than if decision makers were held accountable through general elections.

Majone follows the Swedish economist Knut Wiksell in distinguishing between two different forms of political activity: efficiency and redistribution. In Majone's view, majoritarian democracy is suited only for the latter. As a historical matter, redistribution and majoritarian democracy have been interwoven. In view of the cultural variety of the member states as well as their differing legislative traditions and economic levels, Majone considers the EU an unlikely candidate as an agency of redistribution. He points out that there is a widespread sense within the nation states that redistributive majoritarian democracy has gone too far. The EU should instead see to it that efficiency is enhanced that overall incomes grow. For the latter purpose, rules are needed—efficient, well-thought-out, universally applying rules. Again and again, Majone asserts that what the EU needs is less in the way of popular elections and more in the way of expertise. The European Central Bank—with its independence from popular influence—is an embodiment of Majone's ideal form of governance: it enjoy, legitimacy not because its directors follow political instructions or heed the wishful thinking of the populace, but because they furnish reasons for their actions and pursue policies with beneficial results. If Europe is to live in prosperity and peace, judicious men must not be subjected to electoral temptation or required to satisfy populist demands. Like high magistrates or prominent scientists, Majone argues, the leaders of the EU must be free to reach agreement on tenable rules for the ordering of social life. His political heroes are Plato's guardians.[23]

Fritz Scharpf is another representative scholar who has made influential contributions to the theory of governing the EU. The democratic deficit is undeniably embarrassing, he admits. Confidence in politicians just continues to fall. "In the few years since the Berlin Wall came down in 1989, the triumph of democracy has given way to a deep political malaise almost everywhere in the West." Yet we cannot give up. In a manner reminiscent of Majone's ideas about "substantive legitimacy," Scharpf argues that the legitimacy of the Union can be increased if the quality of the decisions is improved. Scharpf seeks to complement an analysis of accountability and institutional reform with a discussion of the content of policy. There are two ways to increase the legitimacy of the Union. Scharpf speaks of "input-oriented legitimization"— that is accountability—as distinct from "output-oriented legitimization," by which he means a forceful policy that inspires confidence among the citizens of the Union. The content of this policy includes full employment, advanced social policy, and human rights. Instead of the "the democratic principle of government *by* the people," this is called "the republican principle of government *for* the people."

Or, with another formulation, there are two ways to promote the legitimacy of the EU: accountability through the democratic principle of electing and dismissing by the people, and responsibility through the "republican" principle of delivering good policies for the people.

Scharpf does not argue for a federal state either. His solution for the democratic deficit is not that the nation-states unite, but rather that they act together (see Figure 3.1 above). They can do this by pursuing a proactive, "republican" public policy. The nation-states must above all see to it that their economy is put in order and that their welfare arrangements are not structured in such a fashion as to come into conflict with the fundamental goal of full employment. The national economies must be competitive, yet the competition between states must be fair, that is, in line with Union rules. The different states must implement their national solutions in a manner compatible with their Union obligations and refrain from applying "beggar-my-neighbor" strategies. In his moralizing conclusion, in which he even cites Kant's categorical imperative, Scharpf explains that while this may sound contradictory—that states are to compete and not compete at the same time—it is in fact no more remarkable than forbidding the use of drugs in international sports competitions. He points out that the Union has excellent instruments like the Commission and the Court for determining which rules of competition should apply. In juridical terms, European integration has proceeded far. Now it is high time to intensify political cooperation, through coordinated but voluntary action. An offensive public policy is necessary if the EU is to acquire popular support.[24]

It may thus be said that Scharpf has formulated a theory for the intensified European cooperation of our time. He goes around the question of democratic accountability and argues instead that the Union can attain legitimacy by conducting a successful economic policy. Legitimacy is achieved through responsibility rather than through accountability.

Earlier I quoted Moravscik's optimistic statement that the "no" referenda in France and Holland do not mean the end of the EU.[25] As he sees it, what has come to an end is instead idealistic federalism, according to which the proposed constitution was a way out of the democratic deficit. These federalists deluded the politicians into believing that the EU needed a constitutional reform. But the truth was instead the opposite: the success of the EU depended on the fact that the Union had not been especially democratic but extremely instrumental in providing a good life for its citizens.

The no-voting result was composed of three groups. First, there was ideological extremism: the center supported the constitution, while the extreme Right and Left voted "no." Second, there was a protest vote against unpopular governments. Third, and most important, there was a reaction against the insecurity felt by poorer Europeans. Business, the educated elite, and wealthier Europeans favored the constitution, whereas those fearful of unemployment, labor market reform, globalization, privatization, and the consolidation of the welfare state opposed it.

But what were these groups protesting against? The proposed constitution did not mean any substantial change in these areas, nor has this been maintained by any of its critics. It was a conservative compromise, according to Moravcsik:

> The proposed constitution sought to marginally improve the EU's efficiency and transparency, while retaining its basic structure . . . [I]t was not the substance of the emerging constitutional settlement that triggered opposition. The objectionable aspect was its form: an idealistic constitution. Since the 1970s, lawyers have regarded the treaty of Rome as a de facto constitu-

tion. The new document was an unnecessary public relations exercise based on the seemingly intuitive, but in fact peculiar, notion that democratisation and the European ideal could legitimate the EU.

Politicians should have followed the pragmatic path from Monnet and Delors and legitimated the EU through trade, economic growth, and useful regulations, not through constitutional arrangements, "for there is no 'democratic deficit' in the EU—or not much of one. Once we set aside ideal notions of democracy and look to real-world standards, we see that the EU is as transparent, responsive, accountable and honest as its member states." Still, leading intellectuals with "the court philosopher of continental social democracy, Jürgen Habermas" in the head position, Moravcsik continues, called on European leaders (that is, Habermas's former student Joschka Fischer) to take new initiatives after the referenda to make the EU more accountable to its citizens. "Yet anyone except a philosopher can see that this is the sort of extreme cure that will kill the patient." Europe wanted continued prosperity and a political body that could deliver exactly that. "In western democracies, popularity is inversely correlated with direct electoral accountability. The most popular institutions are courts, police forces and the military. Parliaments are generally disliked." So, over the next few decades, "the EU should return to its successful tradition of quiet and pragmatic reform." That had been the de facto constitution of the EU since its beginning, and that is also its future. Europe has moved beyond those who insist "that the answer to failed democracy is more democracy . . . The constitution is dead, long live the constitution."[26]

This argument by Majone, Scharpf, and Moravcsik is open to objection, though, on both empirical and normative grounds. As an empirical matter, to begin with, it is hard to see how it would be easier to pursue common policies in Europe than to conduct common elections there. Differences in living standards, between the richest countries and the Central European members, for example, are scarcely less striking than the differences between the states that serve to prevent a common demos from emerging.

Normatively speaking, furthermore, the "republican" idea is questionable. Trustee democracy—with its intellectual roots in Plato's ideal of guardianship—is hardly enough for well-educated European citizens. The expert is the antithesis of the democratic representative. This new idea that the Union's democratic deficit is redressed not through strengthened accountability but through efficient and coordinated public policy on an interstatal basis may prove counterproductive; indeed, it may serve to facilitate the return of some old notions: to wit, a nineteenth-century conception of the relationship between the elite and the people. The EU has demonstrated its strength by delivering peace. This important goal has prompted EU citizens to accept the democratic deficit. Ought they then continue, now that peace seems to have been secured on their continent, to accept the democratic deficit in the future, on the grounds that the Union can deliver prosperity? That would be to declare Plato the victor of the struggle within Western civilization over the best form of government. The constructive, pragmatic, and reformist Scharpf would not go so far; as mentioned, after all, he calls for legitimization both through accountability and through the "republican" principle of good public policies for the people. But Majone and Moravscik, who do not shy away from sterner implications of their thinking, would doubtless object less.

It is sometimes said that with the emergence of the European Union, democracy is entering its third stage. The first grew forth in ancient Greece, with the establishment of the democratic city-state; government by the few was replaced with government by the many. The second stage ensued when representative democracy, as opposed to the direct form thereof, took root. The question now is whether we are witnessing a third stage, wherein democratic governance is established beyond the nation-state. In that case, the republican solution is not enough; good results are not sufficient. If we are not to abandon all hopes for a democratic legitimacy, we must always keep the establishment of accountability in view.[27]

The integration of Europe is impressive evidence that man is the author of his own history. It shows as well that there is no law of nature that nation-states must go to war. This success has furthermore appeared, improbably enough, on the continent that had been the bloodiest in history and in which there was talk of the risk of a third world war. It was the nation-states of this very continent that started building a union for peace. The categorical theory enunciated by thinkers from Hobbes to Lenin must therefore be reconsidered. My "first argument," as introduced in Chapter 1, that politicians have a real choice, seems to be confirmed in the EU case. It has been possible to break with the tragic tradition of violence between states in Western Europe. Concerning my "second argument," that these choices are shared by ordinary citizens, this hardly seems to be the case. In-depth analysis has demonstrated that in the shadow of the prevailing pragmatism, the people have been excluded from the decision-making process; goals and purposes of strategic actors have shifted over the years, and basic concepts have been given a new meaning. Accountability has been substituted by responsibility, democracy by "republicanism." The rule by experts has also been shown to be a desirable model for policy areas outside the monetary field. Consensus, legitimization through results, and deliberative democracy make for a dangerous triumvirate today and form the foundation for a new view of popular government, against which I argue in this book.

These proposals have served to undermine accountability also within the national political arena. Elected leaders respond by saying that they no longer have any power. Power has moved elsewhere, they say—into the hands of supranational organs. Politicians have foresworn responsibility, in other words, and the EU has become just another level of authority on which the blame can be laid. Seeking to achieve legitimacy through responsibility rather than through accountability calls to mind the paternalist outlook of an earlier time—before the breakthrough of democracy—when leaders were in the habit of rejecting popular demands on the grounds that the people did not understand what was good for them.

CHAPTER 4

Globalization Has Not Wiped Out the Freedom to Choose

The Globalization Trap

Borders are dissolving. Trade is increasing. Currencies and capital flow without restrictions. Citizens move ever more freely between countries. The result is ruthless exploitation as never before, as national governments look helplessly on. For how, under these new circumstances, can they carry out policies of their own? Of all the excuses that politicians use when foreswearing responsibility for developments in society, the world market appears to be the favorite. In the mid-1990s, two European journalists, Hans-Peter Martin and Harald Schumann, were able to give this political predicament a catchy designation in their bestseller, *The Global Trap.* In this book, they portray politicians as essentially powerless prisoners of the global market. As a result of globalization, the authors aver, "the whole of politics becomes a spectacle of impotence, and the democratic state loses its legitimacy. Globalization turns out to be the trap for democracy itself."[1]

With journalistic verve, the authors make their presentation sharp and concrete by illustrating their thesis with the personal fates of people they have encountered in the course of world-spanning interviews. The book begins by describing the welcome given by Mikhail Gorbachev, deposed Soviet president, to participants at a conference held at a luxury hotel in San Francisco. The subject of the conference is the expected 20/80 society. It transpires that, in the future, it will be enough for 20 percent of the population to work; the rest can spend their time watching television and taking in other simple entertainments. We then meet Michel Camdessus, head of the International Monetary Fund, who approves a massive loan (under enormous pressure) to the government of Mexico; a director for a firm that issues credit ratings for countries and who is said thereby to exercise greater power than any minister of finance ("The man from Moody's rules the world"); a government advisor who warns of an impending ecological disaster when the earth can no longer feed its population, on account of the exploitation and skewed distribution produced by globalization; an unemployed electrician in the Third World who reacts listlessly and without comprehension to the global interconnections that have made his firm bankrupt; the German chancellor who in campaign speeches declares his support for a "social" market, but who yields to finance capital at the slightest sign of trouble; a burnt-out computer programmer on a delayed flight wondering about the meaning of life; a disillusioned man who does not wish to bring children into an economically uncertain world and who would rather flee the rat race and move with his girlfriend to a life on a Greek island; and an upper-class woman in South America who entrenches herself behind fences and security systems to keep away the poor and criminal. Everywhere Martin and Schumann see the signs of *globalization* and *fragmentation*:[2] international finance capital governs the lives of people, which leads to powerlessness, environmental destruction, and a devastating division into rich and poor, which will most likely issue in civil war. The North–South Dialogue ceased a long time ago. Now the question is instead, "Who will give the order to shoot to keep them out?"

The process began in the late 1970s. It was at that time, the authors aver, that a qualitatively new period began—when politicians started deregulating currency and capital markets. The state of affairs in the world today is not, accordingly, the result of any conspiracy by anonymous actors on the financial markets. Globalization is rather the result of measures undertaken by politicians themselves. They have consciously foresworn all responsibility and allowed the market to rule the roost instead. Right and Left seem no longer to matter. Ideologies have converged in the neoliberal view that it is freedom for capital that gives increased wealth to the world. Elected representatives of all camps have seen it as desirable that political obstacles to the operation of markets be removed: "[O]ptimum use of capital can be made only if it is free to move across national boundaries. Their magic word for this is efficiency. Guided by the pursuit of maximum profits, the world's savings should always flow where they will be best employed—and this will naturally be where they show the highest return." Keynes has given way to Hayek. Society has gotten harder and colder. "Downsizing" and "lean production" are the new watchwords; Martin and Schumann prefer the label "deregulation: method in the madness."

Not even in the environmental field have politicians been able to take measures to counteract the devastating impact of globalization—this notwithstanding the fact that, as best Martin and Schumann can ascertain, both citizens and politicians consider this question to be more important than any other: "At present, as we well know, an interest in environmental questions is seen as more important than concern for jobs or social peace, and yet not many of today's headlines suggest that the ecological health of the planet has in any way improved."

The solution can only be a return to traditional welfare policies and responsible resource management. Between the market and democracy reigns antagonism: the greedy market tolerates no political restrictions, while politicians cannot accept their loss of the initiative. The world after 1989 did not become what we had hoped: "The end of the communist regime, however, brought not the end of history but an enormous speeding up of social change." It is these rapid changes that are now bringing misery to the peoples. The only country sufficiently powerful to impart a new direction to these changes, and to restore the balance between politics and the economy, is the United States. But the authors hold out no hope that such will take place, so saturated with neoliberal doctrine is the world's most powerful nation. "The global trap finally seems to have snapped shut. The governments of the world's richest and most powerful nations appear to be prisoners of a policy that no longer allows for any change of course. Nowhere do people feel this more acutely than in the homeland of the capitalist counter-revolution itself: the United States of America."

That leaves us with the EU. The democratic deficit exhibited by that body, however, makes it less than attractive in the eyes of the authors. Yet it is on Europe that we must pin our faith all the same. "A democratic European Union!" goes the brief and rather desperate slogan launched by the authors in the last pages of the book. But this not wholly original prescription goes no further than what might be termed a pious hope, summarily set down in a number of points. The authors' strength lies in the spicy reports they provide on the state of the world as they understand it; they show no capacity, however, for analyzing how the necessary and desirable democratization is to take place—this notwithstanding the fact that it is precisely the difficulty of pursuing responsible and accountable policies that forms the very core of the concept of "the global trap." Two elements in their thinking leave a lingering impression on the reader: their deep pessimism regarding the ability of elected leaders to wield effective power; and their suggestive account of how voters abandon impotent politicians with contempt, turning to right-wing populists instead.

The discourse on globalization is a large one in social science. The development of the world economy during the last quarter-century has inspired economists and political scientists to take up, in a new perspective, the discussion of such fundamental concepts as free trade, the market, the state, wealth, equality, and peace—and the relationships among these factors. Scholars disagree on these matters, as usual. They quarrel, for example, over what globalization really means. But it is also possible, as usual, to reach certain conclusions—if, that is, the sweeping judgments are broken down into more precise statements, which can then be tested against the empirical evidence. Does the thesis put forward by Martin and Schumann find support, then, in the picture that emerges from the research? There is a difference, of course, between academic research and popular social science. It lies in the nature of the thing that Martin and Schumann resort to simplification in order to reach a larger public—and in this it must be said that they have succeeded, to an extent that flat-footed researchers in the academy must envy. The question is instead whether this simplification has been done in a defensible manner—that is, whether the picture it paints accords on the whole with the results found by scholars.[3]

A first critical point to address is whether the last quarter-century truly represents a qualitatively new period in the history of world trade. Many debaters have thoughtlessly repeated this assertion. Indeed, the claim has become something of a cliché—"pop internationalism," to use Paul Krugman's apt and sarcastic term for the notion entertained by commentators unaware of the history, who believe that a new, apolitical era has opened up, in which the competition between Europe and the United States will not differ appreciably from that between multinational corporations like Coca-Cola and Pepsi.[4] Scholars who have actually done the historical research, however, find that "the contemporary conventional wisdom about the novelty of globalization is challenged."[5] Over the course of the last 150 years, the dependence of economies on foreign trade has ebbed and flowed, in a sort of wave motion, and this last period of growth is by no means the most expansive one. Alongside the striking differences between countries—with the highest ratio of merchandise trade to gross domestic product being in the small European nations, with Japan and the large European powers on a middle level, and with the United States having the lowest proportion throughout this period of time—the major finding is that economies were at their most open between 1870 and 1914. If we turn from trade to capital flows, moreover, the impression is further strengthened (as can be seen in Figure 4.1). After a high degree of internationalization during *la belle epoque,* a strongly protectionist reaction set in (with the 1930s as the low point), after which time the economies have started working their way back up again. We have not yet reached, however, the level of international economic integration seen in 1914.

The researchers who carried out these calculations, Paul Hirst and Grahame Thompson, summarize their findings as follows: "[T]he level of integration, interdependence, openness or however one wishes to describe it, of national economies in the present era is not unprecedented. Indeed, the level of autonomy under the Gold Standard in the period up to the First World War was much lower for the advanced economies than it is today."[6] A similar formulation is found in another study: "All these measures of transnational-securities trading and ownership are substantially greater in the years before the First World War than they are at present. More generally, every available descriptor of financial markets in the late nineteenth and early twentieth centuries suggests that they were more fully integrated than they were before or have been since."[7]

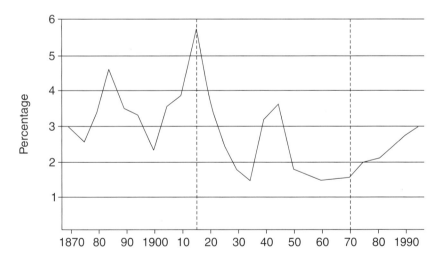

Figure 4.1. International capital flows among the G7 economies, 1870–1995 (as percentage of GDP). *Source:* Paul Hirst and Grahame Thompson, *Globalization in Question,* 2nd ed. (Cambridge: Polity Press, [1996] 1999), 28. Published with permission of Polity Press.

Clarifying these historical circumstances is not just interesting in itself. It also has bearing on the main thesis put forward by globalization theorists—that politicians become powerless when the economy is internationalized. Namely during the 1870–1914 period, nation-states were strengthened as never before: societies were integrated through universal suffrage, welfare policy was begun, and public expenditures started to increase (not least in the area of defense). Increased internationalization need not issue, apparently, in the marginalization of politics.

It bears emphasizing, finally, that a strong state is not necessarily—despite what Martin and Schumann assume—a normatively attractive thing. As we saw in the preceding chapter, the strengthening of nation-states (notwithstanding internationalization, be it noted) had a dreadful consequence: states took up arms against one another a hundred years ago. Nation-states may go to war. Indeed, it was this that brought *la belle epoque* to a tragic end.

To this extent the matter may seem clear: it is not the case that world trade in our time has become uniquely open or that different economies have been laced together to an unprecedented degree. Yet the present circumstance does display, as certain scholars have pointed out, a novel feature that is of the greatest importance for political accountability. One thing has happened that is indeed qualitatively new: the *welfare state* has made its appearance. This has necessitated the broadening of the tax base. Welfare states were built during a period stretching from the 1920s through the 1960s—which is to say, after the collapse of free trade. The welfare state was a national project; it aimed at redistribution and equalization within each country. When borders are dismantled, the preconditions for such a project are altered.

Does this mean, then, that the globalization trap is real all the same? No, that is not the conclusion of the authors in question. They take the view, rather, that there is a lot politicians can do about the consequences of globalization. We saw in the preceding chapter how Fritz Scharpf, among others, has developed this reasoning in connection with the European Union. The way member states can achieve their welfare goals, according to Scharpf, is not by combining into a federation (for which the requisite support in terms of public opinion is lacking), but by coordinating their policies on the basis of the nation-state. This reasoning is also applicable in the globalization debate. Or put differently: even if the economy was more internationalized before World War I than it is today, something qualitatively new has taken place nonetheless—in that the conditions for conducting a nationally based welfare policy have changed. The conclusion is that nation-states must coordinate their policies in order to achieve welfare, employment, and sustainable development.[8]

The term *globalization* itself, moreover, has come under question in the research. This term is usually thought to refer to a situation in which large corporations and other actors have left their national economies behind. Now, the idea goes, companies move freely between states, locating wherever conditions are most favorable. But this picture is rejected by researchers in the field. Exchange between countries has certainly increased, but the trade in question is "inter-national," not global. Truly transnational companies are still relatively rare. Most companies continue to organize their operations on a national basis. Even in the case of the large multinational corporations, production is still largely based at home—to a two-thirds extent in the case of American companies, for example—and the boards are still dominated by nationals of the home country. If one is searching for transnational actors, one will be better off looking at non governmental organizations (NGOs), like Greenpeace or the Red Cross; they symbolize the globalized world better than the companies do. Indeed, the increased eagerness of companies to locate a portion of their operations in regions that offer tax and other economic incentives appears to be having an interesting consequence: firms are locking themselves into the advantages offered by special regions or states. Internationalization makes companies more dependent on politicians, not less.

The term globalization is furthermore misleading in that the world economy is in fact far from global—it does not span the entire world. Trade and investment flows are instead concentrated to the triad of Europe, Japan, and North America, and there are no signs of any substantial broadening beyond these areas.

The dominant view in research, then, is that politicians still retain control, albeit under altered conditions. Consequently, they cannot evade responsibility by pleading that they can do nothing about a globalized world market.

It is revealing that the champions of the powerlessness theory who are most often cited—like Reich and Ohmae—restrict their analysis to the economic side of internationalization, and the presumed powerlessness of politicians is merely an implied conclusion, indeed little more than a suggestion. In a widely noted book with the striking title *End of the Nation State,* Reich contents himself with pointing out that the growth zones of the future will not coincide in their geographical outlines with national borders.[9]

It bears recalling, however, that there is something called regional policy, whereby politicians seek to counteract (or for that matter to reinforce) the redistribution taking place.

Economies are becoming internationalized. But the ability of politicians to wield influence—heretofore largely bound up with the nation-state—is not exhausted thereby. Politicians now face altered conditions, but the powers at their disposal have not been weakened in the manner assumed by global-ization theorists; on the contrary, they may actually have been strength-ened. In order to describe the intricate relationship between reality and our perception of it, certain authors have cited the words of President Kennedy, who is said to have once declared that the opposite of the truth oft is not the lie—deliberate, contrived, and dishonest—but the myth—persistent, per-suasive, and unrealistic. So it is with the myth of the globalized world economy. "The persistence of the globalization myth seems to be based on a lack of information and confusion about international restructuring."[10]

Or to cite Hirst and Thompson once more, we should be on our guard against the suggestive panorama painted by globalization theorists, to the effect that, in the world today, business is free simply to serve consumers, while influence is no longer wielded by nation-states or by armies: "The question, however, is whether such a global economy exists or is coming into being. As we have seen, there is a vast difference between a strictly *glob-alized* economy and a highly *inter-nationalized* economy in which most com-panies trade from their basis in distinct national economies." They conclude:

1. If, as we have argued in earlier chapters, the international economy does not correspond to the model of a globalized economic system, then nation-states have a significant role to play in economic gover-nance at the level of both national and international processes.
2. The emerging forms of governance of international markets and other economic processes involve the major national governments but in a new role: states will come to function less as "sovereign" entities and more as components of an international "quasi-polity"; the central functions of the nation-state will become those of providing legiti-macy for and ensuring the accountability of supranational and subna-tional governance mechanisms.
3. While the state's claim to exclusive control of its territory has been reduced by international markets and new communication media, it still retains one central role that ensures a large measure of territorial

control: the regulation of populations. People are less mobile than money, goods or ideas, and in a sense they remain "nationalized," dependent on passports, visas, residence and labor qualifications. The democratic state's role as the possessor of a territory is that it regulates its population, and this gives it a definite and unique legitimacy internationally in that it can speak for that population.[11]

What, then, is the role, more precisely, of politicians in today's internationalized world? The judgments of different researchers form a rich spectrum on this point, from concrete specifications to functions stated in a highly abstract manner. The former arguments have to do with levels. Politics in the future will not relate to the nation-state exclusively but will have a role to play both regionally and supranationally—even if it is believed that the nation-state will possess superior capabilities for governance in the future as well. In the same way, large companies operate across a range of levels. And without an anchor in local networks and traditions, multinational corporations cannot be successful either ("glocalisation,"[12] in other words, is a necessity).

In the more philosophically oriented part of the debate, many participants feel free to leave the empirical economic history behind, in favor of grand declarations—such as that history is predetermined and globalization is irreversible. At this level of abstraction, the debate concerns "whether globalization is some kind of autonomous force."[13] As we saw in Chapter 2, however, it is difficult as a general matter to uphold the idea that development moves forward of its own accord, impervious to attempts by citizens and politicians to influence its course. Even those authors who, without presenting any serious data or other material, assume that we have left "modern" times behind and are now entering the "postmodern" age, with globalization as the foremost feature, generally take the view that politics will continue to be important, albeit in a different way than what we have seen hitherto. "History has not ended."[14] It is taking new forms, but these do not mean that politicians are "losing control."[15] The absence of definitions and evidence in the debate that postmodernists themselves call "the global babble"—over whether or not globalization "really does mean anything new"—means that one scarcely becomes any wiser on this question by reading such articles.[16] Even so, these authors find themselves able to conclude that politics and accountability will continue to be meaningful conceptions in the future global state they imagine.

The historicist manner in which a leading scholar like James Rosenau reasons is typical of the genre. He theorizes that we are in the thick of an enormous societal transformation, in which globalization and new technology are coming to full realization (although we may not have entered this stage completely as yet). This trend is clashing with equally powerful localizing dynamics. The resulting encounter serves to dissolve the tension between foreign and domestic spheres, and a new space for political control comes into being: "the Frontier." It is sooner along the Frontier than in the international arena (as we have conceived of it hitherto) that the real challenge awaits political leadership in the world. For in the future, there will be an even greater need for political leadership.[17]

It may thus be said that, in this historical-philosophical discussion, the extent to which politicians are able to make choices and to influence events is deduced from pure theory. Certain other theorists posit a high degree of freedom of choice. As the reader doubtless noticed, there is a decided tilt to the Left in *The Globalization Trap:* it is the world of neoliberalism that comes under criticism, a world in which politicians have become helpless prisoners of the market. But a different and more offensive Left can also be found in the globalization debate—a Left that argues to the contrary that politics is primary. Globalization is no reality, they claim—just a neoliberal dream. Against such a dream these authors put forth another: a defense of—or, if you will, a return to—the Social Democratic welfare state. In reality, then— as opposed to neoliberal fantasy—there is no globalization that has irrevocably wiped out the freedom to choose.

The debate over globalization is not the first to take up the question of whether "history" or "development" has brought us to the point where "politics has come to an end." We have heard such claims before in political science—most especially, during the last few decades, in the debates on "the End of Ideologies"[18] and "modernization."[19] According to the claims made in these well-known discussions, conflicts between citizens had been overcome in the successful democracies, and the tendency was for politics to be replaced by administration. Economic growth was thought to be the motor in this modernization. All states, upon reaching the higher stages of economic development, become alike. Similarly, champions of the globalization theory claim today that the future will be dictated by globalization, and politicians have only to accept the consequences, whether or not they will. From a methodological standpoint there is cause to point out that in all three debates, the procedure has been to compare countries at different stages of economic development, according to the "most different" rather than the "most similar" principle.[20] Such a research design, with both very rich and very poor countries, is ill-equipped to detect such differences as may exist between countries at the same stage of economic development. Differences of this kind may be presumed to have a political or, if one prefers the designation, an ideological explanation. The variation between comparable countries shows that politicians have a freedom to choose at each step on the developmental ladder. In other words, the failing of the globalization theory is that it presumes what is to be proved: to wit, it leaves no room for any counterexamples that might show that at each phase of the modernization process, politicians have a range of alternatives from which to choose—for example, to adapt to or to resist the supposedly inherent dynamics of the world market.[21]

How, then, are we to assess Martin and Schumann's polemic? Their thesis that politicians have no control and that the world market rules is one of the most common and popular in the blame avoidance debate. But is it true? Without any doubt, they have fastened onto one of the most important social changes of our time; however, they have exaggerated the tendency and in critical respects have given a misleading picture of the processes they discuss. Whether our era is to be called unique or not, national governments still have an important role to play. Politics has not come to an end; its preconditions, rather, have been altered—in interesting ways that offer new possibilities. Politicians need not, and of course should not, react passively to any such mass unemployment and environmental destruction as may follow in the wake of globalization. In addition, the authors' incessant drumbeat—to the effect that political governance and accountability have been thwarted by economic developments—merits the designation of populism sooner than that of popular social science. The conclusion cannot be escaped that *The Global Trap* is an exercise in demagogy. Economic internationalization is the core of truth in the globalization theory; to this observation have been added, however, so many excessive, showy, superficial, and downright inaccurate claims that the theory must be rejected. The categorical thesis that politicians are powerless prisoners of the world market, and so cannot be held accountable by citizens, does not bear up under scrutiny.

Agenda 21

Globalization should be distinguished from internationalization. Scholars are agreed that the economy has become internationalized and that the world market is of growing impact for nation-states. But from this it does not follow, as I have argued, that politicians have become prisoners of globalization. Rational actors can find ways out of the trap. There is room for political maneuvering also in an internationalized world.

Let us take a look at that area in which, if Martin and Schumann are to be believed, our concerns are most deeply engaged—that of the environment. Water and air pollution are international in character; rivers and winds do not halt at national boundaries. The polity, however, is not—if we should trust the globalization theorists. Politicians are not supposed to be able to handle international questions of this kind. Environmental politics should then be the most likely case for the globalization theory to be right. But in spite of that, politicians have in fact adopted positive measures to improve the international environment. Our critical case in this chapter, illustrating how choice in democracies is possible, may thus be formulated as follows: How did it happen that national governments started implementing more far-reaching environmental policies on the international scene in the 1990s? During this decade, politicians launched policies that, according to the globalization theory, were impossible to pursue. The politicians went against the world market.

If politicians are powerless in the face of economic internationalization, the logical question is whether cooperation across borders can be accomplished in the political sphere, in the same way as in the economic. Can not politics be internationalized, too? The environmental area provides a good illustration of the new role that scholars see states as playing—"less as 'sovereign' entities and more as the components of an international 'quasi-polity.'" The leaders of the world ought accordingly to be willing, in an attempt to institute common environmental policies, to reach out their hands to one another.

Our counterexample is exactly this argument, taken from the assessment that Boutros Boutros-Ghali made upon becoming secretary-general of the United Nations in 1992. In Boutros-Ghali's view, the globalization of the economy had made a corresponding "global leadership" necessary. His method of working was to convene international conferences, with the aim of concluding agreements among the national governments. As a jurist, he tended to think about politics in terms of rights. Citizens must be ensured the right to peace, to a good environment, to social development, and to equality between the sexes. The means for ensuring such rights would be treaties between states, wherein the signatories commit themselves to working for common goals:

In response to globalization, the United Nations has defined human rights for the international community. It has fostered the progress of international law. It has transformed the law of the sea. Through a series of global conferences, it is promoting international consensus on disarmament, the environment, population, social development, migration, and the advancement of women . . . As secretary-general I have placed great importance on international conferences as a way of raising the world's consciousness about these problems. International conferences are not a new idea; they have played a part in diplomacy since antiquity. But the conferences convened since 1992 represent something new and different. They are linked. They are cumulative. They foster global consensus on interlocking global issues. They generate specific commitments. And they provide a comprehensive framework for international action in fields that are drastically affected by the negative side of globalization.[22]

Boutros-Ghali put forward, in other words, a thought-out strategy for countering the real or supposed effects of economic globalization. It was not at all the case, he argued, that politicians must be bound by the borders of nation-states. Through international cooperation, they can surmount such barriers and take back the initiative (if, indeed, they had ever really lost it).

Martin and Schumann themselves mention Boutros-Ghali's ideas about what can be done about globalization. In a manner typical of their quick and sweeping presentation, however, the words they place in the mouth of the secretary-general on this issue are not attributed to any source; nor are they analyzed in any detail.[23] Rather than paying any attention to Boutros-Ghali's purpose in launching his initiative—namely, to induce nation-states to demonstrate that they still have freedom to choose—Martin and Schumann simply cite his concern over the consequences of the internationalized economy as additional support for their thesis about the inescapability of the global trap. Let us therefore analyze the question more closely, by taking a look at the first United Nations Conference on Environment and Development (also known as the Earth Summit), held in Rio de Janeiro in 1992, and by investigating the subsequent fate of the program there adopted: Agenda 21.

Twenty years had passed since the Conference on the Human Environment had taken place in Stockholm, also under the auspices of the United Nations. These were twenty lost years, in the view of some: the environment had only gotten worse during the 1970s and 1980s. In the mid-1980s, therefore, a UN commission was convened under the leadership of Gro

Harlem Brundtland, former prime minister of Norway. Its charge was to prepare a world conference on a global strategy for "sustainable development" on our planet. After some years of work, it presented its report, *Our Common Future.* "We live in an era in the history of nations when there is greater need than ever for co-ordinated political action and responsibility," the Brundtland Commission declared. During the 1950s, the risk for new wars and the need for economic reconstruction in the wake of World War II had given rise to cooperation between nations. Now, the commission argued, the worsening environment called for common efforts of a similar kind. "The present decade has been marked by a retreat from social concerns. Scientists bring to our attention urgent but complex problems bearing on our very survival: a warming globe, threats to the Earth's ozone layer, deserts consuming agricultural land."

The commission placed the difficulties faced by developing countries at the center of its analysis. The problem was not just the continued environmental destruction resulting from the exploitation of natural resources, especially by large multinational corporations. Equally devastating was the abiding or even worsening economic fracture between rich and poor countries. One could say, to use terms that would later become common, that the Brundtland Commission warned of both globalization and fragmentation. Indeed, it is precisely the globalization argument that we find in its report—as usual, in the form of blank assertions rather than empirical data. Through the activities of transnational corporations, the commission averred, politicians had been deprived of both power and responsibility, particularly in developing countries. "Transnational corporations (TNCs) play an important role as owners, as partners in joint ventures, and as suppliers of technology in the mining and manufacturing sectors in many developing countries." There was an unhappy "asymmetry in bargaining power between large corporations and small, poor, developing countries."

The world must therefore start protecting its natural resources—"the global commons." Wealthy countries bore an especial responsibility. Economic growth had to be increased everywhere, in both rich and poor nations. Above all, countries had to cooperate much more closely than hitherto: "The Commission therefore regrets but cannot ignore the recent decline in multilateral co-operation in general and a negative attitude to dialogue on development in particular." Far-reaching changes in the forms of political cooperation were therefore necessary, if the goal of sustainable environmental development was to be achieved. This was a long-term commitment. The commission warned against any belief that such changes could be carried out quickly: "We have no illusions about 'quick-fix' solutions."

The twentieth century had brought fundamental change to the relationship between man and nature, wrote the commission in its "Call for Action." At the beginning of the century, human beings lacked the power to alter planetary systems in any radical fashion. But "[a]s the century closes, not only do vastly increased human members and their activities have that power, but major, unintended changes are occurring in the atmosphere, in soils, in waters, among plants and animals, and in the relationships among all of these." The course events were taking had to be changed. Citizens and politicians would have to take responsibility for the future environment. At a coming international conference, common plans for an ambitious new environmental policy would have to be worked out. "But to keep options open for future generations, the present generation must begin now, and begin together, nationally and internationally."[24]

On the basis of the commission's report, the UN General Assembly decided to convene a conference on development and the environment. A preparatory committee worked on the issue from 1990 to 1992, and Maurice Strong was appointed secretary-general for the conference. It was decided, at the urgent request of the new Brazilian government, that the conference would take place in Rio de Janeiro; the Brazilian government was anxious to improve the country's reputation after more than twenty years of military rule and long-standing criticism for the destruction of the Amazon rainforest.

The Rio Conference took place on 3–14 June 1992. It turned out to be the largest high-level intergovernmental meeting ever held, with representatives from 181 countries. At the concluding summit meeting, heads of state and government from approximately 120 countries took part. In his opening speech, UN Secretary-General Boutros-Ghali declared that the Rio Conference was historic for three reasons: the citizens had become conscious of how truly vulnerable was our earth, the politicians were working with a time frame far longer than our own lifetime, and the UN had now been given a new and extraordinary task. In the face of these environmental questions, there was, according to Boutros-Ghali, an opportunity—indeed a necessity—for member states to cooperate effectively. It would be one of his most important tasks, he declared, to follow up on this conference. The following accords were concluded:

- The Convention on Climate Change, which was juridically binding on the signatories;
- The Convention on Biological Diversity, likewise binding on the signatories;
- The Rio Declaration on Environment and Development, which formulated fundamental principles for a responsible policy on the environment
- The Forest Principles, which aimed at a program for the sustainable use of the world's forests;
- Agenda 21, a concrete long-term action program looking forward to the twenty-first century, comprising no less than forty chapters.

Agenda 21 was to a great extent based on the report of the Brundtland Commission. It saw environmental policy in a broad international, economic, social, and development-oriented context. Environmental destruction was not an inevitable process impervious to change. Everyone had a responsibility to ensure that change took place in the way the natural resources of the earth were handled:

> Underlying the Earth Summit agreements is the idea that humanity has reached a turning point. We can continue with present policies which are deepening economic divisions within and between countries—which increase poverty, hunger, sickness and illiteracy and cause the continuing deterioration of the ecosystem on which life on Earth depends. Or we can change course. We can act to improve the living standards of those who are in need. We can better manage and protect the ecosystem and bring about a more prosperous future for us all. No nation can achieve this on its own. Together we can—in a global partnership for sustainable development.

Negotiations had proceeded, and not without conflict: for example, between the countries of Europe, which sought a stabilization of carbon dioxide emissions in the year 2000 at the level of 1990, and the United States, which favored a single strategy for all greenhouse gases; between Israel and the Arab countries, in regard to environmental protection for occupied peoples; and between Saudi Arabia and certain other oil-producing countries on the one hand, and a variety of other states on the other, on the question of protection of the atmosphere. There were also conflicting views on the storage of radioactive waste and on norms for environmentally dangerous military products. The conference concluded, however, in an atmosphere of general satisfaction over the fact that world opinion had been aroused on behalf of environmental improvement, and over the fact that it had actually proved possible, notwithstanding everything, to reach agreement on so many large and important questions. The participants were strongly aware, however, that the critical thing now was to implement the program. They furthermore understood that this had to be a long-term commitment.[25]

To oversee efforts in the wake of the Rio Conference, the Commission of Sustainable Development (CSD) was established. Five years after the conference in Rio, moreover, the so-called Earth Summit +5 was held in New York. The purpose was to review what had happened after Rio and to adopt the Programme for the Further Implementation of Agenda 21. The view at this follow-up meeting was that a degree of progress had been achieved since Rio—but only in certain areas and in certain countries. Agenda 21 was being implemented far too slowly, and the global environment was continuing to deteriorate in many respects. Nor had the follow-up conference succeeded in re-creating the enthusiasm for environmental questions that had marked the meeting in Rio. An analysis of the conference concluded that the next Earth Summit, to be held ten years after Rio, in 2002, would have to be better prepared if progress was to be made. The world would have to take environmental questions even more seriously.[26]

Those wishing to investigate what transpired in the years immediately following the Rio Conference have an excellent source to which to turn. In response to the environmental interest manifested at Rio in 1992, the United Nations Environment Programme (UNEP) started producing a series of papers in 1997, under the title of *Global Environment Outlook.* The first issue, *GEO-1,* sought quite simply to describe "the state of global environment." The publication offered, in cooperation with a number of research institutes the world over, a careful empirical survey of the environment and of environmental policy. It is a rich source bulging with information, notwithstanding the modest insistence of the authors that it was impossible to cover every region in detail: "Rather it should give the reader—whether a policy maker, a corporate leader, a student, an activist, or an interested citizen—a 'feel' for the priority environmental concerns in each region and the overall health of the planet, as well as giving a direction for possible environmental response strategies." The main message was the same as that at the follow-up conference in New York: considerable progress had been achieved on certain issues and in certain regions, but it was not enough if the environment was to be improved. "If there is one conclusion to be drawn from *GEO-1*, it is that despite progress, the pace at which the world is moving towards a sustainable future is simply too slow."

There can be no question here of reviewing the entirety of this ample report; we must content ourselves with sampling the findings and looking at the general conclusions. The report documented the environmental status in different parts of the world of land, water, forests, biodiversity, the atmosphere, the marine and coastal environment, and the urban and industrial environment. It pointed, for example, to the rapid degradation of land in Africa, West Asia, and parts of Latin America. It furthermore emphasized that all regions had experienced problems relating to either ground water or surface water or both. Every day, 25,000 people died as a result of poor water quality, and waterborne diseases still represented the largest single cause of human sickness and death worldwide. Sixty percent of the world's population lived within sixty kilometers of the coastline, and one-third of the world's coastal regions were at high risk of degradation (the risk being greatest for the coasts of Europe, followed by those in Asia and the Pacific). Problems of air pollution were pervasive; in Eastern Europe, air quality was considered the most serious environmental problem. Acid rain and trans-boundary air pollution, once problems only in Europe and parts of North America, were becoming apparent in parts of the Asia-Pacific region and Latin America. The impact of current patterns of production and consumption on personal health and well-being was high on the priority list for both North America and Western Europe. Data in support of these characterizations were presented in a good many tables and diagrams; variables and regions were respectively divided into exact values and individual countries.

A subsequent chapter analyzed the environmental measures taken by various nations. Many countries had achieved economic affluence through unlimited access to such environmental resources as air, water, land, soils, and so on, while giving little thought to the impact of growth on the environment. When environmental consciousness gradually emerged, governments turned first to prohibitions and regulations. Although, in the view of the authors, significant improvements in environmental protection had been made in many parts of the world with the help of such strategies and policies, they recommended that economic incentives be used to influence behavior. "Few, if any, economic incentives have actually replaced regulations because most have been introduced with the primary objective of increasing government revenues rather than altering behavior towards environmentally friendly activities." The future lay in an approach that combined various policy instruments to achieve environmental goals without constraining economic growth and development. Many governments realized this, and the report mentioned several good examples: Germany, Sweden, and the Netherlands were said to be the most progressive in this regard. The authors placed considerable emphasis on the function of communal management systems in the developing world. Individual property rights could play an important role in stimulating a sense of responsibility for the environment. One example of customary rights over land use was found in Papua New Guinea. Private water rights in India provided an incentive for the efficient management of an increasingly scarce resource. In New York City, the number of taxis was controlled with tradable licenses. In Singapore, a scheme that charged drivers for using roads in the city center during peak hours had resulted in a 73 percent reduction in traffic. A long list of "cleaner and leaner" production methods was presented. The report called for a new attitude toward consumption; after all, if there came to be as many cars per inhabitant in China as in the United States, some 20 percent of the former country's arable land would be covered by roads and parking spaces. And if the entire population of the world were to consume at the level of the rich world today, rapid ecological collapse would be the inescapable consequence.

A variety of outcomes, however, was possible. With the help of integrated modeling techniques, the authors were able to carry out a number of simulations, and in so doing to distinguish three scenarios. The first scenario (or the "baseline") entails the continuation of current trends, policies, strategies, and attitudes; business as usual prevails. According to the second (or "Variant 1 BAT"), the Best Available Technology is used all over the world. The third (or "Variant 2") involves the use not just of the best available technology but also of renewable energy sources as well; in addition, fundamental changes in human diet and consumer attitudes take place. The consequences for the environment of the three different options vary drastically. The point of these simulations was precisely to show that the peoples of the world had a choice, and that this choice was of the greatest importance. The fate of the peoples lay in their own hands. They could not evade their responsibility. "While many may attribute the current degradation of the world's resources to poverty and burgeoning population growth, the inefficient use of resources, high levels of consumption, waste generation, and industrial pollution are equally to blame." The final words read as follows:

The results of the analysis indicate that technology transfer and fundamental changes in attitude can lead to significant changes in future energy
consumption, land use, and carbon dioxide emissions, and subsequently in
positive changes in land cover and temperature change in the future . . .
Although this analysis is only a first attempt to explore the possible impacts
of certain policy strategies, it clearly demonstrates that reduction of human
pressures on the global environment is indeed technically possible if the
willingness to change is there.[27]

A long series of studies and reports have since confirmed the description
of the environmental situation provided by *GEO-1* and the Earth Summit
+5: progress has been made, although too slowly, and in many parts of the
world the environment continues to worsen; to understand what has happened, it is necessary to look at specific areas; national campaigns and local
initiatives have been decisive for success; greatly increased efforts are, however, needed across the board; and although many NGUs are important
partners for achieving a better environment, the accords reached by the
governments in Rio remain the foremost inspiration and lodestar for the
work of environmental improvement.[28]

Five years later, it was time for yet another assessment; in August–September 2002, the World Summit on Sustainable Development took place in
Johannesburg (Earth Summit +10). There was the hope that with the
holding of this second follow-up conference, the world would be taking environmental questions more seriously, yet this hope can hardly be said to
have been fulfilled. As at the previous meeting, reports were presented to
the secretary-general by issue area. Once again, the picture was a split one
in regard to both issues and countries. New problems had arisen that posed
an obstacle to advancement—the effect of AIDS on social development in
many countries being one of the examples cited. The authors found it hard
to conceal their disappointment that "progress towards the goals established
at the UNCED has been slower than anticipated, and in some respects conditions are actually worse than they were 10 years ago."[29] The conclusion of
the secretary-general was that the initiative taken by the UN in this area
was now even more important than earlier; the seriousness of the situation
made it still more urgent to hew to the course that had been staked out,
whereby the governments of the world would cooperate to alleviate the in-
jurious effects of globalization. Politicians, the secretary-general stressed,
could not avoid their responsibility: "Political will is the key to success be-

cause effective new initiatives will require major changes in the way policies and programmes for sustainable development are designed and implemented."[30] Most recently, the terrorist attack in the United States on 11 September 2001 had "highlighted the fact that we are living in one world, and that no part of that world can afford to ignore the problems of the rest of the world."[31]

Both progress and retrogression could be observed in as good as every environmental area. Where the forests of the world were concerned, there was some good news: an increase in the area of planted forests had successfully counteracted deforestation. Raw materials were being used more efficiently, and recycling—particularly of paper—was becoming more and more widespread.[32] When it came to the seas and oceans, the finding was that "significant progress has been achieved over the past decade in promoting an integrated approach to coastal management." Yet a large number of coral reefs had been destroyed, through both human and natural influences. Fishing stocks had also declined, even if—poor consolation—the proportion of overfished stocks was growing at a slower rate than during the mid-twentieth century.[33] The state of health in the world had improved, and the average life expectancy was higher, thanks to improved sanitation, nutrition, drugs, and vaccines. AIDS, however, cast its shadow over world health, affecting conditions in many parts of the world dramatically for the worse.[34] The widespread loss of biodiversity continued, and the status of biodiversity in most countries—in terms of species, habitats, and ecosystems—had not significantly improved. The list of species threatened with extinction was rapidly lengthening.[35] The expert group for the protection of the atmosphere stated that global warming had not ceased, notwithstanding a significant reduction in air pollution, particularly in Europe.[36] Agricultural yields had increased greatly, as a result of improved technology.[37] But changes in patterns of production and consumption were slow, and the experts warned of "increased stress on the environment owing to increased production and consumption."[38] Energy consumption was rising at a worrying rate, although technical gains had been noted (so that energy use was now more efficient), while new breakthroughs had been seen in the application of advanced fossil fuel technologies to the long-term goal of near-zero emission of air pollutants, including greenhouse gases.[39]

Fragmentation continued to mark global developments—that is, the situation had improved in the industrialized world but was deteriorating in developing countries. (Reports made particular mention of the worsening situation in the developing world in regard to forests, health, the atmosphere, and agricultural yields.) This difference between rich and poor countries also showed up in finance and trade: official development assistance had fallen during the 1990s, and the heavy debts owed by poor countries served to constrain them from pursuing sustainable development. At the same time, freer trade had been shown to have good effects: increasingly, "market forces rewarded good environmental performance rather than cost savings at any price," while the growing market for "environmentally friendly products" had offered new trading opportunities for developing countries. Moreover, the authors considered themselves able to reject the assertion that polluting industries had been migrating from developed to developing countries (even if there had been exceptions).[40]

Policies of environmental protection, then, are moving forward in the industrialized world but meeting difficulty in developing nations. This circumstance forms the background to a scientific study, *Implementing Agenda 21*, which examines environmental strategies in nine high-consumption societies: Australia, Canada, Germany, Japan, the Netherlands, Norway, Sweden, the United Kingdom, and the United States. What importance have the governments of these countries placed on Agenda 21 in domestic politics? In summarizing their findings, the researchers divided up these countries into three groups. The first group, which they classified as "enthusiastic," consisted of the Netherlands, Norway, and Sweden. They characterized Australia, Canada, Germany, Japan, and the United Kingdom as "cautiously supportive." Countries in this second group were basically positive; however, the measures they had taken on behalf of environmental goals were uneven. The United States, finally, was described as "disinterested" in the concept of sustainable development. "In the United States, Agenda 21 has virtually no political salience." The authors were anxious to emphasize that results were not necessarily better in the three enthusiastic countries than in the others; the classification served only to illustrate that in the former, environmental policies had become more "central and visible" and that the governments of these countries had "worked more conscientiously with policy implications and experimented with more innovative approaches than their governmental counterparts in the other countries." The main finding was that, in general, governments had truly tried to integrate environmental questions into their political life, not least by drawing NGOs into the political process.

The authors then proceeded to a careful analysis of what characterized the three groups of countries in other respects: for example, the enthusiastic nations all have relatively small populations, are heavily dependent on economic interaction with surrounding countries, and have a compact political elite but also an exceptionally open and highly mobilized civil society. The authors' basic tone was optimistic. They were impressed by the impact of the UN's environmental program: "In the first place, it is important again to underline the relatively rapid integration of the notion of sustainable development into political life in the developed states. It is not common for a new normative idea to gain widespread cross national acceptance—not just as a device employed by particular specialist constituencies—but as a concept that passes over into mainstream political usage in a great variety of national contexts. Yet sustainable development has achieved just such recognition in little more than a decade."[41]

What implications, then, does this analysis of the UN's environmental program have for the globalization theory? The similarity between environmental policy and the case treated in Chapter 3—European integration—is striking: politicians need not give up just because a problem has an international dimension. They can cooperate across national boundaries to achieve common purposes. By acting together, they can achieve goals beyond the reach of any individual nation. But it must also be said that in a good many cases, the environmental objectives set out by the world's governments in Agenda 21 remain remote. Many observers are disposed to dismiss the Rio Conference and its successors as "just another UN talkshop." That seems, however, to be a hasty conclusion. Changing a process—like environmental destruction—that has been going on for more than a hundred years is a big step to take: it requires a policy as sustainable as the society at which it is aimed. "Output," in the form of political decisions on various levels, must always precede "outcome," in the form of actual changes in the environment. The important role played by the Rio Conference and its successors was to place environmental questions on the political agenda. The Brundtland Commission's warning against believing in quick solutions was altogether justified. To continue the comparison with European integration, a little thought experiment might be worthwhile: what kind of results would an assessment of the latter project have yielded had such an assessment been carried out already within five or ten years of the start? A careful analysis of the many stages in these two processes is necessary for a valid comparison.

Can we expect a political intervention in the domain of globalization of the same strength as we have seen in the domain of European integration? This is, after all, far from certain. In view of the cool interest displayed by the United States in these matters, together with the limited prospects enjoyed by developing countries for making progress in this area, international environmental policy today is poised between success and collapse. Accordingly, the globalization theory—with environmental policy serving as the critical case—stands out as the strongest of the arguments reviewed in this book to the effect that politicians have no control over the course of events. Even if the UN environmental policy is a good example of how decision-makers may try to shoulder their responsibility, this blame-avoidance argument cannot be refuted with the same confidence as the others. In this problem area, the argument that politicians have a freedom to choose needs to be surrounded with qualifications. Concerning the argument that the voters share the decisions, it should, on the other hand, be underlined that in the more successful and "enthusiastic" countries, the local participation in this field has been extraordinarily high.

Accountability and the Market

As a result of the deregulation in recent decades, globalization theorists argue, politicians have abandoned their responsibility. Instead it is the market that rules the roost. Keynes has given way to Hayek, as we could read in Martin and Schumann. Neoliberalism provides politicians with an alibi for unhappy social conditions: they can say it is not their fault but rather that of the market. How should we assess this constraint for the politicians' freedom of action?

In short, the argument that citizens cannot hold politicians accountable because of globalization is nothing less than a fundamental misreading of free-market ideology. Hayek himself, in fact, took the diametrically opposed position. According to him, politicians bear a great responsibility.

The life work of Friedrich Hayek, originally Austrian economist and winner of the Nobel Prize, combined economic analysis with a deep and original theory of moral philosophy—a theory that, on the surface, can seem full of contradictions and paradoxes. On the one hand, he doubted the ability of politicians to control events. He believed, for example, that the consequences of Keynesianism would be altogether different from what politicians believed. Such was his thesis in *The Road to Serfdom,* the famous book in which he warned that the efforts at socialist planning undertaken in the 1940s would lead—notwithstanding the hopes of policymakers that such would eventuate in a good and equal society—to an outcome desired by no one: an economic dictatorship, and in time a political one as well.[42] People ought instead, as far as is possible, be left free to manage their own material affairs. Every form of political "constructivism" tends to undermine its own objectives. On the other hand, Hayek himself argued energetically for the order he desired. He himself became a constructivist, prescribing for others how common affairs are to be ordered. The antirationalist proved at last a rationalist. Accordingly, historians of ideas portray Hayek's views as contradictory. The attempt to combine rationalism and antirationalism is "foredoomed to failure and issues in a confusion of categories. It is an impressive failure none the less."[43]

However, Hayek's ideas must be understood on two levels—one theoretical, the other more political.[44] At a theoretical level, Hayek doubted man's capacity to realize his desires with the help of political measures. It is impossible for one person to gather all the information needed to direct social processes. Those who try to do so invite effects that are the very opposite of what they intend. Thus had politics in the twentieth century assumed its characteristic pattern, whereby "unintended consequences"[45] flowed from the actions of well-meaning politicians. Politicians cannot, therefore, take responsibility for the achievement of goals that require detailed leadership and planning. The task of politicians is rather to maintain a universal system of rules, which in turn creates a "spontaneous order." Hayek's doctrine of spontaneous order was founded on the view that human reason is embodied in cognitive and perceptual structures that have grown forth over millennia. He had an evolutionist theory of knowledge. The spontaneous order that embodies human reason is a social institution governed by biologically inherited or culturally transmitted rules. "Progress can not by its very nature be planned."[46] Although Hayek himself criticized the notion of "economic man" as excessively constructivist, his own political theory may nonetheless be regarded as an "invisible-hand explanation" of sorts, according to which good political results arise as the "essential side-effects" of conditions that are not consciously sought.

Hayek's concrete political conclusion was to call for an order of society in which rules operate in a general manner with as little detailed political regulation as possible. The Social Democratic welfare state, therefore, struck him as a failure—an object lesson in the overweening social ambitions of man.

If we distinguish between these two levels, then, many of the apparent paradoxes in Hayek's thought disappear. The responsibility of politicians pertains to the system level. In Hayek's world, politicians have not capitulated from their responsibility. They have delegated responsibility. This means they are still responsible for ensuring that such an order offers the best possible conditions for individual action. At the level of theory—in relation to the system itself—Hayek was a rationalist and a moralist. The purpose of the arrangement he proposed was to better society. The recommendation to deregulate, he might say, represents a kind of hypothesis—to the effect that people's preferences will be better satisfied by an arrangement of this kind. Politicians are not to remain passive in the face of such changes; it is their responsibility to ensure that the promised improvements actually take place.

It would no doubt be an exaggeration to say that all neoliberals embrace Friedrich Hayek's advanced moral philosophy. I would sooner describe the latter as the best possible formulation of the views on responsibility held generally by adherents of the free market. If we mean to avoid making demagogical claims, we certainly cannot say that neoliberals regard politicians as having no responsibility. They do have a responsibility, but it is for the system as a whole. If the effects of deregulation prove to be different from those expected by its champions, the latter would be logically compelled to reconsider their position. The famous defection of Robert Nozick, for example, may be explicable in such terms. The foremost guru of neoliberalism abandoned much of his libertarian doctrine when a development he had expected did not materialize—that is, when a greater measure of compassion and charity vis-à-vis pauperism in large American cities did not emerge.[47]

In the debate on globalization, scholars very clearly reject the idea that an increased reliance on market mechanisms frees politicians from responsibility. In the end, after all, it is the politicians who determine how much market there will be. Politicians delegate certain tasks to the market; if these tasks are not properly performed, the delegation can be revoked. The sovereignty of nation-states has not been replaced by a globalized world market:

> The argument from the state's incapacity to produce sovereignty is the most fundamental of all, since this is not merely a commodity to be traded, but the essential constituent of the international market itself. Change in sovereignty thus shows up in all other aspects of state performance. That said, much of contemporary discussion of the "end of sovereignty" is misplaced . . . Sovereignty has never been static and, under its rubric, states have delegated and devolved a range of powers; they have also arrogated new ones, and continue to do so. The sovereignty game, to this extent, has

always been fluid in its constitutive rules, and globalization encapsulates this latest phase. Globalization, however, cannot be construed as a force apart from the practice of sovereignty, reshaping it from the outside. Instead, the changing practices of sovereignty register in the development of globalization, and signal the transitions taking place. Sovereignty and globalization actively refashion each other, and should not be thought of as each other's negations.[48]

It may be that politicians are in some measure trapped by globalization. But if they are, one author writes, they themselves—and not any anonymous market forces—are responsible for this. There is, however, the crucial and optimistic rider that politicians can also escape from this trap: "[T]he fact is that they are hoist with their own petard: the liberalization, privatization and deregulation that brought this vulnerability to market forces was in part their own doing. Conversely, it is logical to conclude that it is they—US President and Congress—who have the power if anyone has to reverse the process and tip the balance of power back again from market to state."[49]

So the critical case of globalization and environment does not change my general conclusion that there are alternatives in politics between which we can choose. The world market can certainly be a formidable adversary, and global environmental deterioration is an enormous challenge. It is furthermore true that the globalization theory offers—notwithstanding its many exaggerations and errors—the strongest argument available to those who would stress the difficulties faced by any politician who might seek to govern and to take responsibility. All the same, I would repeat that the delegation from politics to economy can be taken back, if unwanted effects occur. The political control of national economies has—with successes and setbacks—been built up over centuries. World market regulation is still in being; Agenda 21 was formulated only as a first step in the construction of such an international regime for environmental politics. It is not to be expected, of course, that such political ambitions should not meet with opposition or even obstruction. At every stage there are options, however. Globalization has not wiped out the freedom to choose. The market is possibly a rival to politics, but it is not an equal. Politics is the superior sphere, and politicians cannot escape the fact that, at the end of the day, it is they who bear ultimate responsibility for the state of things in the world.

CHAPTER 5

Power-Sharing Does Not Exclude Accountability

Power-Sharing

Blaming collaborators is a popular tactic in the exercise of evading responsibility. Because politics means collective decision making, others are involved, and when things go wrong, it is tempting to say that the fault is theirs.

The logic of this argument is a tricky one, though. On one hand, there is the view that cooperation is necessary: I have no freedom to reject my potential collaborators' foremost claims, because that will exclude all cooperation. On the other hand, sharing politics with others is a way to prevent unfortunate outcomes, especially abuse of power. Mutual surveillance is a counterbalance to political decay, such as bribery and corruption.

Consequently, power-sharing has in all times been regarded as a popular remedy against bad politics. "I do not, gentlemen, trust you." In their famous book, *The Calculus of Consent,* James Buchanan and Gordon Tullock use this quotation from one of the American Founding Fathers[1] as a device for presenting their constitutional ideals. In the view of the authors, man pursues his self-interest in politics as surely as in the economy. This was a truth that political scientists seemed to have forgotten. Instead, their analysis of collective-choice processes had often been grounded on the implicit assumption that man seeks in politics not to maximize his own utility but to pursue the "public interest" or the "common good." A return to the Framers' more realistic assessment of human nature—or put differently, to a correct interpretation of the American Constitution—would mean not concentrating power but dispersing it among many different decision makers.[2]

The Hobbesian view of human nature taken by Buchanan and Tullock forms the core in the theory of public choice, which in the half-century since their work was published has become one of the most influential branches in the social sciences.[3] This becomes evident upon consideration of just a few of the best-known works in this tradition. Kenneth J. Arrow has made the point that there exists no rule for decision making that can satisfy certain elementary democratic criteria for how individual values are to be converted into collective choice. This observation is commonly cited as yet another argument against placing all power in the same hands.[4] In addition, Anthony Downs's "economic" theory of democracy has provided the tools for generations of political scientists to criticize the idea that a desire to satisfy the public interest is what motivates policymakers.[5] Finally, William Riker's critique of majoritarian democracy furnishes an eloquent defense for the view that passing majority opinion ought not to be allowed an immediate or unchecked impact on policy.[6]

The separation of powers recommended by these skeptics can easily be transformed into a blame avoidance argument: if power is divided, the responsibility for its exercise must be divided, too. "If I had been able to decide the matter myself," the accused politician pleads, "none of this would have happened. It's not my fault. My partners are the ones to blame!"

The Calculus of Consent cites another classic of modern political science at one point: *A Preface to Democratic Theory*.[7] In the latter work, Robert Dahl subjects the Framers' fear for despotic politicians to an analysis of unsurpassed keenness and clarity. His focus is on the ideas of James Madison; indeed, Dahl refers to the variant of democracy based on power-sharing simply as "Madisonian democracy." Let us tarry here awhile; with Dahl's help, we shall seek a deeper understanding of the reasons why power should be divided among a plurality of centers.

In Dahl's interpretation, the central proposition in Madison's political philosophy is the following: "If unrestrained by external checks, any given individual or group of individuals will tyrannize over others." Madison also provided an explicit definition of tyranny: "The accumulation of all powers, legislative, executive, and judiciary, in the same hands, whether of one, a few, or many, may justly be pronounced the very definition of tyranny."

With historical examples from Greece and Rome and with psychological postulates about the nature of man, Madison sought to persuade his listeners of the risk for the abuse of power ("tyranny") if power were concentrated. He had no difficulty doing this. On this point the Founding Fathers were agreed. That human beings had a "a passion for power" seemed to them evident. Given only the chance, they would abuse their power to their own advantage.

Such an abuse could issue from either the majority or minority. The concentration of power must therefore be avoided. The power of those in leading positions must be checked, in order to ensure that they cannot act against the rights of citizens or undermine the common interests of society. As Dahl points out, much analysis remains to be done, of course, if these sweeping statements are to be converted into empirically well-founded proposals. But of one thing Madison was certain: "Frequent popular elections will not provide an external check sufficient to prevent tyranny." The majority, namely, was not always in the right. Individuals could be oppressed in the name of the people as well. But how can a system for arriving at decisions be devised that is compatible with the idea of political equality, and which at the same time protects the rights of minorities? Madison was not, as Dahl demonstrates, always successful in his attempts to wrestle with this fundamental dilemma for all democratic theories. But however he examined and reexamined the problem, he always came back to the necessity for power-sharing. The stress in his recommendation lay on external checks. Madison did not deny that people were equipped with internal checks against the abuse of power; he discussed thoroughly, for instance, how restraint dictated by conscience, attitudes, and basic personality varied across different social groups. But these internal checks were insufficient. The goal—constructing "a non-tyrannical state"—presumed the dispersion of power into many hands.[8]

The foremost champion in our time of the idea of power-sharing is the Dutch-American political scientist Arend Lijphart. Lijphart's designations for such a system have varied over the years ("accommodation" and "consociationalism" being two examples); more recently, he has dropped "power-sharing" in favor of "consensus democracy."[9] In the spirit of Madison, Lijphart urges that all power not be placed into the hands of a single group—not even the majority. All must have a share in it; none may be excluded. *Consensus democracy* as opposite to *majoritarian democracy* is the best way to avoid the abuse of power.

Lijphart has many other and, in his own view, perhaps even more important arguments for his theory of consensus democracy. They all lead to the same conclusion: the corrective for political ailment is power-sharing. If all have a share in power, the result is a policy more in line with everyone's interests. We get "a kinder, gentler democracy," with less egoism and more concern for the common good.[10]

According to Lijphart, power-sharing can be accomplished through four different institutional means: "grand coalitions," "decentralization," "minority veto rights," and "proportional representation." The risk for abuse of power is reduced if the following criteria are met: all have a share of governmental power; power is delegated from the central level to those most nearly affected; minorities have a veto over questions of special concern to them; and winner-take-all rules do not apply in elections to parliament, so that losers are ensured representation as well. A party that is left in the undisturbed possession of power, and which due to overrepresentation may hold power for a long period, provides the richest soil for the abuse of power. Or in the words of Lord Acton, "Power tends to corrupt and absolute power corrupts absolutely."[11]

Of Lijphart's four institutions for power-sharing, proportional representation is the most fundamental. His reasoning is as follows. Because all persons seek in the first instance to satisfy their own interests, and are prepared to do so even at the expense of others, it is critical that all be able through their chosen representatives to take part in government; that way, they can ensure that no injustices are committed. Each party should therefore be represented in parliament in proportion to its electoral size. No party should be overrepresented, and no threshold for representation should apply. The likely consequence of this will be that so many parties are represented in parliament that none has a majority on its own. If the votes needed to form a government are to be gathered, then, there will have to be cooperation. Instead of a squaring off between government and opposition, a coalition government—best of all, a grand coalition—is both necessary and desirable. A government of this kind can stay united only if minorities enjoy the guarantee that on questions critical to them, they will not be summarily run over. In the same spirit, power ought to be decentralized—spread across a variety of levels and areas within the political system. Cooperation and consensus along these lines are the best way to prevent the abuse of power.

Furthermore, Lijphart explicitly claims—albeit with caution—that the proportional method counteracts political corruption. He is not unaware that some are persuaded to the contrary. The division between a majority endowed with power and a minority in opposition is thought by some to be the best guarantee for the necessary oversight; general elections mean that those who have abused their power can be dismissed; the regular opportunity that majoritarian democracy provides to throw the bums out is the best way to ensure accountability. But however plausible this sounds, Lijphart objects because empirical studies speak sooner for his model. Bribery, corruption, and the abuse of power are less prevalent in consensus democracies than in majoritarian ones. Recurrent elections appear to be a less effective method for fighting corruption than the perpetual mutual oversight that takes place in a system in which all have a part in power. The studies Lijphart cites are statistical in nature: they involve the calculation of correlation coefficients and averages from data for perceived corruption in a large number of countries. Contrary to the hypothesis put forward by advocates of majoritarian democracy, there is no significant relationship between corruption and form of democracy. "Moreover, the weak relationship that does appear is actually negative: consensus democracies are slightly *less* likely to be corrupt than majoritarian systems . . . This relationship becomes a bit stronger, but is still not statistically significant, when the level of development, which is strongly and negatively correlated with the level of corruption, is controlled for."[12]

Originally, Lijphart's theory was not a normative but an explanatory one: as he saw it, the world actually functioned more according to the consensus model than to the majoritarian model. He based his argument at first on the experience of divided societies like his homeland, the Netherlands; by and by, however, he transformed his argument into a general one. Governments and oppositions worked together. Parties collaborated.[13]

In later works, however, Lijphart not only contends that majoritarian democracy furnishes a bad explanation for how most countries function, but also finds majoritarian democracy deficient as an ideal. Where cooperation prevails, he argues, the interests of all groups are served better than in a system where the winner takes everything and the loser gets nothing at all. The opposition ought not to be shut out; the government should rather share power with it. None may be excluded; all must be able to take part. If a society is fragmented, representatives of the fragments within it should form an "elite cartel," so that all groups can take part in decisions and none is favored at the expense of another.[14]

According to Lijphart, moreover, consensus democracy produces good economic results. Majoritarians argue that the concentration of power facilitates the making of clear and quick decisions. Lijphart objects, however, that quick decisions are not always wise ones, and that the alternation between winning teams characteristic of majoritarian systems can lead to sudden and damaging shifts in economic policy. "Policies supported by a broad consensus . . . are more likely to be successfully carried out and to remain on course than policies imposed by a 'decisive' government against the wishes of important sectors of society . . . [F]or maintaining civil peace in divided societies, conciliation and compromise—goals that require the greatest possible inclusion of contending groups in the decision-making process—are probably much more important than making snap decisions."[15]

The theory Lijphart has developed over the course of almost forty years has changed political science fundamentally—in the direction of greater realism. As early as the 1970s, Bingham Powell noted that the theory of consensus democracy "has been among the most influential contributions to comparative politics in the last decade."[16] But the theory is controversial as well. From the standpoint of this book, the most important objection is how well voters in a consensus democracy can hold their leaders accountable. The answer is not very well. If everyone has a part in decision making, who, then, is to be held responsible? If all leaders remain in power irrespective of electoral outcomes—with the only reaction to the judgment of the voters being some minor rotation of persons among the different ministries—has not the population then been reduced to subjects, the sole role of whom is to ratify the policies of their leaders? It is significant that Lijphart does not discuss accountability more exhaustively in his work. It is another concept, rather, that is central for him: "responsiveness." By "democracy," then, Lijphart has in mind a system in which the government reflects popular opinion, rather than one in which the people hold their leaders accountable and, ultimately, dismiss them.

According to Bingham Powell's interpretation of Lijphart's theory, consensus democracy implies its own hypothesis about responsibility:

[T]he proportional influence vision implies its own hypothesis about responsiveness. This vision would stress the superiority of multiparty electoral competition and rules that directly reflect the choices of citizens into the composition of the legislature, fairly and without the distortions that so frequently accompany majoritarian arrangements. The legislature suffers from neither over-weighting some parties at the expense of others nor forced cohabitation within individual parties or pre-election coalitions that can freeze bargaining opportunities. Authorization of policymakers will be dependent on this fairly and equitably reflective body, and thus dependent on the expressed preferences of the voters themselves. Parties that have gained substantial voter support will be indispensable in forming governments and policy making coalitions; those that have done badly will play a proportionately lesser role.

The hypotheses of the alternative visions thus counterpose alternative strengths and weaknesses. The putative strength of the majoritarian vision is a strong and direct connection between votes, legislative seats, and governments; its potential weakness is the distortion in representation of voter preferences that is often necessary to create pre-election identifiability and/or post-election majorities. The putative strength of the representational vision is the multiplicity of choices and their fair reflection in legislative representation; its weakness is the dependence of policymaker coalition formation on elite bargaining.[17]

Thus, many scholars maintain that the choice between majoritarian and consensus democracy is not clear-cut. The question should ask which democratic value one holds higher: the accountability of majoritarian democracy or the responsiveness of consensus democracy. For Lijphart, a fair representation of the people's will is the democratic ideal. In a majoritarian system, this will can be distorted by overrepresentation of the largest party. Such a party easily becomes too powerful—even despotic. The best way to counteract tendencies of this sort, and to ensure that leaders are truly responsive to the people's will, therefore, is to institute power-sharing: to allow all the different groups to take part in government, with the result that each can keep watch over the others and none is able to take advantage of another. Pippa Norris offers the following summary: "[T]here is no single 'best' system: these arguments represent irresolvable value conflicts . . . In constitutional design, despite the appeal of 'electoral engineering,' there appear to be no easy choices."[18]

As being against such a relativist (not to say watered-down) conception of the matter, I would argue that the meaning of words cannot be changed so casually. Lijphart's use of terms puts one in mind of the constitutional ideals of conservative parties a hundred years ago, when they sought to block the introduction of parliamentary government. Conservatives believed that alternations in power and the dismissal of old governments would lead to spasmodic shifts in policy, which would be dangerous. And to the extent that they saw anything positive in the word "democracy," they had in mind the idea that the government ought to reflect, in its composition, all the different groupings in parliament. As for which groups were to be represented in parliament—that is, which franchise rules were to apply—that was another matter. A good government, in the conservative view, was precisely a responsive government—one in which the various interests in parliament were balanced.[19] The democratic movement, however, was a revolt against this constitutional philosophy. According to the Left parties in favor of parliamentary democracy, the government should precisely reflect "the majority of the people," not "as many people as possible," and the voters should have the right to change government and dismiss a disliked minority.

Behind Lijphart's plea for consensus democracy and proportional representation, classical philosophers appear. In a path-breaking pamphlet from 1857, Thomas Hare recommended proportional representation with the somewhat curious argument that the very multiplicity of candidates in proportional elections guarantees a higher intellectual and moral standard, because it is only those who have nothing but money to offer who need to pay bribes. This pamphlet, as well as a work published two years later on the superiority of the proportional method not least from a moral standpoint, made a strong impression on John Stuart Mill.[20] He had the following to say on behalf of proportional representation: "Consider next the check which would be given to bribery and intimidation in the return of members to Parliament. Who, by bribery and intimidation, could get together 2000 electors from a hundred different parts of the country?"[21]

In the famous seventh chapter in *Considerations of Representative Democracy,* entitled "Of True and False Democracy," Mill posed the question: What in fact is a majoritarian democracy? It is a system, he said, in which there is "representation of the majority only." By contrast, the proportional method leads to the "representation of all." In a majoritarian democracy, members of parliament are recruited on the basis of their economic and social roots in a locality. Those chosen are often narrow-minded persons interested only in furthering their own interests and those of their district. Eminent men committed to the good of the nation get shut out. "Of all modes in which a national representation can possibly be constituted, this one [the introduction of proportional representation] affords the best security for the intellectual qualifications desirable in the representatives." Distinguished persons have their support scattered here and there across the country and so are penalized by majority elections: "Hundreds of able men of independent thought, who would have no chance whatever of being chosen by the majority of any existing constituency, have by their writings, or their exertions in some field of public usefulness, made themselves known and approved by a few persons in almost every district of the kingdom; and if every vote that would be given for them in every place could be counted for their election, they might be able to complete the number of the quota."

Another argument for power-sharing through proportional representation is that the recruitment of eminent persons encouraged by it would serve to heighten the quality of other parliamentary representatives, too. True to his utilitarian ideas about the value of free debate and the salutary effects of competition, Mill explained that such an electoral reform would force the majority to acquire more distinguished representatives as well: "And it is not solely through the votes of minorities that this system of election would raise the intellectual standard of the House of Commons. Majorities would be compelled to look out for members of a much higher calibre . . . The slavery of the majority to the least estimable portion of their number would be at an end."[22]

Third, politics in proportional systems, compared with majoritarian systems, has been found to be less marked by special economic interests and the abuse of power. This effect seems to arise because individual candidates do not stand out as strongly in a proportional system as in a majoritarian one; as a result, they are less vulnerable and dependent. In a comparative study of political corruption, Arnold Heidenheimer singled out proportional representation as a corruption-reducing factor, because it "reduce[s] the personalized relationship between candidate, party and voter."[23]

It has furthermore been said that the corruption that can also be observed in countries with proportional representation is simply one side of the coin, the other of which is autonomy, decentralization, and the dispersion of power. As an argument for proportional representation, this undeniably seems a bit illogical. Instead of presenting the dispersion of power as a method for counteracting its abuse, the argument turns the question on its head and portrays the abuse of power as the price to be paid for its dispersion: "the value judgment 'there should be no corruption' clashes with a wide distribution of power and indeed the democratic requirement that all actors should be autonomous."[24] But power-sharing has no value in itself. It is a method for avoiding the abuse of power.

Power-sharing is thought to transform the preferences of individuals and thus to refine self-interest into a common interest. Just as the invisible hand of the market induces an individual to serve the common interest, too—an interest that was no part of his original intention—proportional representation leads the individual member of parliament to take account of the interests of the entire country, and not just of his own district. Indeed, such a fostering of public spirit was, for Mill, the major argument on democracy's behalf; "proportional representation" was thus indissolubly bound up with "representative government":

> Still more salutary is the moral part of the instruction afforded by the participation of the private citizen, even if rarely, in public functions. He is called upon, while so engaged, to weigh interests not his own; to be guided, in case of conflicting terms, by another rule than his private partialities; to apply, at every turn, principles and maxims which have for their reason of existence the common good . . . Where this school of public spirit does not exist, scarcely any sense is entertained that private persons, in no eminent social situation, owe any duties to society, except to obey the laws and submit to the government. There is no unselfish sentiment of identification with the public. Every thought or feeling, either of interest or of duty, is absorbed in the individual and in the family . . .
>
> From these accumulated considerations it is evident, that the only government which can fully satisfy all the exigencies of the social state, is one in which the whole people participate; that any participation, even in the smallest public function, is useful; that the participation should everywhere be as great as the general degree of the improvement of the community will allow . . . But since all cannot, in a community exceeding a single small town, participate personally in any but some very minor portions of the public business, it follows that the ideal type of a perfect government must be representative.[25]

Modern scholars also embrace this ideology of power-sharing through proportional representation. For example, in a discussion of the advantages and drawbacks of both majoritarian and consensus democracy, Vernon Bogdanor starts out by rejecting six "false" arguments against proportionalism. The first fallacy, which the author finds to be "the most foolish," is that proportional representation is too hard for voters to understand. The author makes things too easy for himself, however, when he rather flippantly dismisses the interesting question on the transparency of the electoral system with the argument that were the majoritarian claim true, it would mean that voters in countries with majority elections like the British are stupider than voters in the many countries that apply proportional representation.

The second argument Bogdanor refutes is that proportional representation encourages political extremism and dictatorship. Bogdanor finds it doubtful that proportionalism was responsible for the collapse of democracy in Germany and Italy and points to the use of British majoritarianism in many African countries with nondemocratic regimes. Such a comparison does not, however, gainsay the fact that the ungovernability of the Weimar Republic paved the way for Hitler.

In the same way, it is hard to agree with Bogdanor's claim that proportional representation does not serve to encourage the proliferation of parties.

Nor is Duverger's well-known thesis about the correlation between two-party systems and majority elections refuted by individual examples of countries with proportional representation that have a small number of parties.

Just as dubious is Bogdanor's fifth argument, that proportional representation does not make it harder for voters to select governments. It would seem undeniable, after all, that governmental alternatives are often less clear in systems with power-sharing and that voters don't know what government they are going to have when they vote for a particular party.

Bogdanor's sixth argument, finally, calls into question the idea that proportional representation undermines the link between voters and members of parliament. That, the author concludes a bit evasively, may be the case in some countries with proportional representation, but not in all.

Where majority elections are concerned, the real problem—for Bogdanor as for most other observers—is that they lead to a misrepresentation of opinion. On the other hand, the author concedes, proportional representation has its drawbacks, too—especially when it comes to the disproportionate influence it can give to a small party when no large party is able to form a government on its own. He thus contradicts what he himself claims in his fifth argument. The choice has to do, in other words, with whether the drawbacks of the one system are greater than those of the other. Bogdanor concludes that it would be wrong to imagine that a small party holding the balance of power can exercise whatever influence it likes. Critics exaggerate this danger. The risks—or, if you will, the drawbacks—of proportional representation are less severe than those involved in majority elections.

Bogdanor's final and decisive reason for power-sharing is to claim, in the spirit of Mill, that if all have a share in the exercise of power, the effect will be to foster public spirit. Introducing proportional elections in Britain, for example, would allow "greater identification with government. It would give almost every voter a direct stake in the election of his or her local MP and provide a choice going beyond that of party nominees. It would consequently have an educative effect upon voters, encouraging them to think of political issues in other than simplistic party terms. Governments would be forced to take a wider range of opinion into account before formulating their policies, and this would encourage the growth of a spirit of accommodation."[26]

That all have a share in the exercise of power could also be motivated by the increasingly heterogeneous character of nations. In the modern multicultural society, proportional representation counteracts the abuse of power by impelling citizens to consider the common good. Such is the thesis put forward by Lani Guiner in *The Tyranny of the Majority,* a striking title for a book based on an event during the Clinton administration. Guiner had been active in the black civil-rights movement, but she failed to secure a post to which Clinton had appointed her because of a campaign directed against her. Using anecdotal accounts of children confronted with various situations in which a choice must be made, she tries to show that proportional justice corresponds to a fundamental human instinct. She takes her philosophical point of departure, not unexpectedly, in a quotation from James Madison: "If a majority be united by a common interest, the rights of the minority will be insecure." She describes her credo in the following way:

> In the end, I do not believe that democracy should encourage rule by the powerful—even a powerful majority. Instead, the ideal of democracy promises a fair discussion among self-defined equals about how to achieve our common aspirations. To redeem that promise, we need to put the idea of taking turns and disaggregating the majority at the center of our conception of representation. Particularly as we move into the twenty-first century as a more highly diversified citizenry, it is essential that we consider the ways in which voting and representational systems succeed or fail at encouraging the Madisonian Majorities.[27]

It is the absence of power-sharing in developing countries, scholars claim, that explains the prevalence of corruption there. There are no countervailing forces against the governing group.[28] The resulting concentration of power fosters "narrow self-interest and even corruption," which can be broken only if "the dedication to the goals of 'good government' is stimulated by a modified and politicized version of the invisible hand."[29]

That corruption arises at all is thought to reflect the fact that when power is concentrated, an inevitable process of decline from virtue to narrow self-interest sets in. This is an idea that scholars have been able to date back as far as the eighteenth century.[30]

Power-sharing is the notion that fits best with the idea of democracy, which says that all shall have a share in governance. It is true that proportional representation makes it harder for politicians to form governments; however, this drawback—in the view of a leading scholar like Bingham Powell—is more than outweighed by the fact that "the proportional vision" and its design enjoy a clear advantage in creating a policy congruence between citizens and policymakers.[31]

In England, homeland of John Stuart Mill, however, a concentration of power in the hands of the majority has been allowed—a fact that adherents of proportionalism have criticized for more than a century. According to them, "radical improvements in the political mores would result from the adoption of their proposals, for instance the moral regeneration of the voters and particularly the reduction or even elimination of bribery and corruption."[32]

The abuse of power is best corrected by sharing it—first and foremost, through a system of proportional representation, which encourages everyone to keep watch on everyone else. Such has been the belief of champions of power-sharing, from Mill to Lijphart. But what has the political reality of the matter been?

Mani Pulite

Italy has been the Promised Land of proportionalism. Historical experience has made the Italians particularly anxious for a constitution that disperses power into many hands, to ensure that the risk for the abuse of power might be counteracted. All the same, far-reaching corruption came to light in Italian politics at the beginning of the 1990s. The intended mutual oversight—whereby, it was presumed, the different parties would keep watch over each other—had obviously not at all worked as it ought. It was in the very area where the principle of power-sharing was thought to have its greatest strength that it proved itself strikingly deficient. The Italians responded to this political-moral crisis by engineering, quite consistently, a transition to the opposite of consensus democracy—to majoritarian democracy. The hope was that, by this means, politics would be cleaned up. The question for the counterexample in this section may thus be formulated as follows: How is the political corruption in Italy to be explained, in view of the fact that it was precisely in order to avoid such an abuse of power that the constitution had been structured in accordance with the principles of proportionalism and power-sharing? Instead of calculating the kinds of statistical aggregates, with the far-from-clear patterns they display, on which Lijphart based his argument about corruption and forms of democracy, I shall now attempt to uncover through a detailed case study how the mechanisms behind the abuse of power may function and what the Italians tried to do about it.

The experience of Fascism under Mussolini prompted the parties and the victorious powers to work for a constitution after World War II that would, in the most effective way possible, counteract the concentration of power and the overrepresentation of a dominant party.[33] It was thus ensured that as many parties as possible would have a chance to be represented in parliament, so that no interests would be set aside. The intention behind the constitution, according to one scholar, was "to revive an extreme form of proportional representation for parliamentary elections in order to prevent any single party from ever again becoming too powerful."[34] The threshold was set so low that a party needed to get only 2 percent of the vote to be represented in parliament. As a result, nearly a hundred parties made it into parliament in the first election.

By instituting power-sharing, the framers of the Italian constitution sought to guarantee a just and fair reflection of the popular will. All power ought not to be placed in the hands of a single party. But did the new constitution in fact accomplish this? There were those who had their doubts already from the start, among them the prime minister himself. Even if the largest party did not always achieve a majority on its own, it could always secure power through skilful negotiation with other parties. As the leader of the party—the Christian Democrats (DC)—that had garnered the most votes in the election, De Gasperi saw great opportunities before him to take and hold power for a long time. In this judgment, he was to be proved perspicacious. And did such an arrangement not entail great risks precisely for the abuse of power? "De Gasperi privately feared that this absence of a potential alternative government would hinder the development of a healthy parliamentary system, because he knew that his own party, since it lacked any fear of losing office, might become unresponsive to popular wishes and succumb to the inevitable corruption of being permanently in power."[35]

The constitution had provided the conditions for Italy's distinctive variant of parliamentarism, the special features of which can be summarized in a few key words (italicized below).[36] The leaders of the parties were the masters of the country. It was negotiations within this "elite cartel," rather than expressions of the popular will, that decided the political course taken. The Italian word for this was *partitocrazia.*

Governments were short-lived. Negotiations at any time might lead—through a formal reconstruction of the government—to a shuffling of positions within the cartel; afterward, however, the same politicians generally returned, albeit in new posts. And throughout, the Christian Democratic Party remained the supreme director of the political play. Bribes and benefits were a part of the negotiating game. Between 1945 and 1996, Italy had fifty-five governments, each one lasting on average eleven months; only three governments lasted longer than two years. *Malgoverno* was the Italian word for this.[37]

Cooperation and consensus together were the guiding star of politics. Criticism was dismissed on the grounds that concessions were necessary for cooperation. Rarely has the art of evading blame been more finely developed than in the consensus democracy of postwar Italy. Certain scholars reject, however, such a designation for Italy, on the grounds that the governing cartel did not constitute a proper grand coalition, because—due to the resistance of the Americans and the papacy—the Communists were not allowed to enter the government.[38] It was only after the fall of world Communism that the party, now transformed into an ordinary left-leaning group, was able to take up posts in the government. In any case, whether or not Lijphart's scheme is quite adequate for classifying Italy, the elite cartel was a fact; and the absence of alternatives was experienced as more and more distressing. Politicians in the broad middle of the political spectrum could always feel secure of a place in the government, irrespective of electoral outcomes. "[C]enter governments, for all the attacks and vituperation to which they are exposed, are never called to electoral accountability and do not have to do anything about it. That is, the fact that the center is a no-alternance formula gives its politicians irresponsible power and allows them the luxury of instability, disagreement, 'immobilisme.'"[39] The system became a "blocked democracy" *(democrazia bloccata).*

The sharing of power was not restricted to government posts. The parties shared the higher positions within the state administration as well. This was a way for the governing party to assure itself of other parties' support. An example was the distribution of seats on the governing board of Italian television *(lottizzazione)*. This led in turn to the development of a parallel polit-ical system—alongside government and parliament—whereby politicians through appropriate alliances were able to penetrate most sectors of society *(sottogoverno)*.

Corruption and bribery grew widespread. Both voters and organizations were bought with money or political benefits. The courts, the police, and the social-insurance system were politicized. Cooperation with organized crime deepened, and the Mafia became a political power factor of the first rank. Proceeds from drugs and weapons became the currency of intercourse between parties and lobbyists. In 1992, two judges were killed. Their names were Falcone and Borsellino; they had symbolized the fight against the Mafia. More and more, Italian democracy took on the character of a polit-ical barter system *(clientilismo)*.

Political violence was also rife, in the form of outright terrorism from both Left and Right. Fascists and Communists both felt restive about what they considered the excessively close cooperation with the political elite being conducted by the parties that most nearly represented their interests. In 1969, the Fascists carried out their first big attack, exploding a bomb in a Milan bank; seventeen people were killed. Similar attacks soon followed in various parts in the country, targeting railways and train stations in partic-ular. These attacks claimed a large number of victims: the bomb at Bologna's central station, for instance, killed eighty-five people. The idea was to sow chaos and confusion in society, to pave the way for a coup d'état. The biggest political scandal up to that point took place in 1981, when a lodge known as "Propaganda 2" (or P2) came to light. P2 was a hidden power center that worked with criminal methods; it consisted of highly placed persons like government ministers, top bureaucrats, members of parliament, officers, bankers, diplomats, judges, journalists, and police. The government fell, and for the first time the Christian Democrats had to yield the post of prime minister. They stayed within the government, how-ever, and indeed regained the top post within a short time. The violence of the extreme Left was just as bloody. A notorious terrorist organization, the Red Brigades, was formed in this period; its roots were in the student move-ment. It carried out about a hundred terrorist attacks, including the murder in 1978 of the leader of the Christian Democrats, Aldo Moro. All this formed part of the *violenza politica*.

The survival of Italian democracy seemed to hang by a thread. The very titles of a few works on Italy bear witness to the difficulties: *Republic without Government?, Surviving without Governing, A Difficult Democracy, The Politics of*

Bargained Pluralism, The Crisis of the Italian State. Perhaps Italian democracy was actually an anomaly? Authoritarian regimes had long ruled, after all, in neighboring countries of southern Europe: in Portugal, Spain, and Greece. Perhaps this tendency toward authoritarianism existed in Italy as well, under the surface and behind the scenes?

At long last the bubble burst.[40] Mario Chiesa, a Socialist politician, was arrested in Milan in February 1992—just as he was taking bribes. In collaboration with a large charitable institution, he had offered companies contracts in exchange for political support and money. The arrest had been carefully prepared. In the course of the investigation, the scandal grew into the biggest in the political history of modern Italy. The result was the fall of the First Republic and the end of consensus democracy. What was revealed was a "kickback society" *(tangentopoli),* and not just in Milan but in all of Italy. The tracks led higher and higher up into the political elite. Party leaders and prime ministers figured among those shown to be deeply involved in criminal activities: for example, Craxi (who fled ultimately to exile in Tunisia) and Andreotti.

The investigation, christened "Operation Clean Hands" *(Mani pulite),* was led by Antonio Di Pietro, a Milan magistrate. Di Pietro was a tough, charismatic workaholic from a simple background, and he nourished a burning hatred for the arrogant, unscrupulous, self-satisfied Italian power elite. He was soon to become "the most popular man in Italy," as the recurring phrase goes in his biographies. As a young man, he had, like so many others in the same situation, made his way as a guest worker to Germany, where he polished cutlery at a factory in the daytime and worked at a sawmill at night. Upon returning to his homeland, he started working with the police and studying law at night. He passed the bar in 1978 in record time. He then embarked on a career as a judge, distinguishing himself with his eagerness and energy. He was not always thought a good colleague, however; his determination sometimes drove him to keep legal cases and witnesses for himself and to pursue questions on his own.

How was it that Operation Clean Hands succeeded in unraveling the entire fabric of corruption, and in bringing all of *tangentopoli* into the light? It was because of Di Pietro's minute preparations and his uncommon severity. Di Pietro had learned from Falcone, the murdered magistrate, how to use computer technology to trace bank transactions; in this way, he obtained evidence for the link between politicians, the Mafia, and common crime. The murder of Falcone the same year whipped up the atmosphere further.

With his methods of interrogation, his threats, and his frightening behavior, he was described as "merciless, bellowing, like a real hyena."[41] Di Pietro resembled "the classical inquisitor, putting you in extreme psychological distress."[42] Those arrested were placed in the notorious San Vittore prison in Milan, where brutal, unhealthy, and unsanitary conditions sooner called to mind the Middle Ages, or some impoverished dictatorship in the Third World. Those under suspicion were given to understand that they would remain in prison until they confessed. Even if they stayed silent and so were released due to lack of evidence, they would immediately be arrested again—and again and again—until the confession came. Journalists filed daily reports about how ever more prominent politicians were being led off to prison, to the accompaniment of mass rejoicing. The atmosphere resembled that in Paris during the French Revolution. At least twenty-seven persons committed suicide. In the elegant salons of the elite cartel, politicians turned pale at the mere mention of San Vittore.

To the very last, the politicians tried to wriggle off the hook. Political cooperation, they pleaded, requires giving and taking. Politics means making decisions, and that means building coalitions and assembling majorities. It was naive to believe that such things can be done for free. Everyone was therefore guilty, because politics is a system that unavoidably makes them so. As every farmer understood, getting work done involves dirtying one's hands. "Clean hands" was an unrealistic, childish ideal; it made it impossible to get anything done. Nor should Italians' understanding of the conditions of politics be underestimated: had not the parties received the confidence of the voters through an unbroken string of years, notwithstanding the fact that their position was now weakened as a consequence of hysterical accusations?

There was one politician in particular whom Di Pietro was after: Bettino Craxi, Socialist leader and former prime minister. Long did the latter seek to escape blame. In a parliamentary debate, for example, he had the following to say: "Parties have relied on, and continue to rely on, the use of funds that come in irregular and illegal forms . . . I don't believe that there is anyone in this Chamber, any politician responsible for important organizations, who can stand up and swear the contrary of what I have just said: sooner or later the facts will show that he is perjuring himself."[43]

However, after having being imprisoned under uncommonly grim conditions in San Vittore, one of Craxi's friends (and financiers) gave up, confessing that he had paid out money to various Socialist leaders; he denied, however, ever having given money directly to Craxi. This confession led to new arrests, and these in turn led to so many troubling revelations about Craxi's activities that he resigned as Socialist leader.

The political crisis was now a fact. Consensus democracy had been compromised. A reform movement was born: its aim was to pull out the rot by the roots—that is, to change the electoral system. Its leader was Mario Segni, son of a prime minister and himself a defector from the DC. Segni's view has been summarized as follows:

> Pointing to the abuses being revealed by the *Mani pulite* investigations, [Segni] contended that had Italy had an electoral system that allowed the electorate to 'vote the rascals out,' the worst excesses of *tangentopoli* would have been avoided. Italian politics had degenerated into moral squalor because the electoral system had guaranteed permanent majorities for the DC and its allies. Feeling themselves to be politically immune, the bosses of the DC and the Socialists (PSI), and their hundred of imitators at local level, had behaved as if they were above the law.[44]

In a referendum in 1993, more than 80 percent of the voters endorsed a changeover to majority elections. Seventy-five percent of MPs would be chosen by majority vote from single-member constituencies; the remaining 25 percent would be chosen by a more proportional arrangement. Thus was the First Republic buried. It was replaced by a majoritarian system: that of the Second Republic. (All the same, no individual party achieved a majority this time either, so the formation of coalitions—in the manner of the First Republic—had to continue.) It was an unusual regime change that had taken place—accomplished without any coup d'état, without demonstrations on the street, without decisions by representative bodies. "The First Republic dies, not in parliament but in the courtrooms of Milan. It falls, not at the barricades but at announcements of criminal suspicion. Never before has such a thing been seen: a revolution led by a prosecutor. In the name not of new ideals but of old principles: those printed in the criminal code."[45]

The men of the old regime were consumed. Of the members of parliament who had been elected in 1992, one-third were now under legal investigation. Over 2,000 people had been arrested. The traditional parties were more or less wiped out: the PSI, the Social Democrats, and above all the DC. The last-mentioned party split up and dissolved; its heirs today number at least three—formed from factions on its left, its center, and its right. Of the MPs chosen in 1994, finally, 71 percent had never sat in parliament earlier.

A right-wing politician, Silvio Berlusconi, then became prime minister. He enjoyed support from a range of political groups, including from an alliance that many regarded as fascistic. Berlusconi was highly critical of the *Mani puliti* investigation, among other things because it had put him and his corporate empire under suspicion as well. By means of a decree, the government sought to reduce the power of the investigators to arrest suspects and detain them without trial. Such methods, the government averred, were unworthy of a constitutional state. The *Mani pulite* investigators threatened to resign, and a popular storm forced the government to withdraw the decree. There is one further feature of the tale, finally—and a piquant one. When he first formed his government, Berlusconi had in fact offered—in a manner reminiscent of the declining years of the First Republic—the post of minister of justice to Di Pietro, who had indignantly declined.

Is it the fate of Italy always to be afflicted, then, with the degenerate form of an electoral method? Majoritarian democracy was compromised by Fascism and the favoring of a single strong party. Proportionalism similarly acquired, during the First Republic, the worst possible reputation on account of how—in direct defiance of expectation—it had promoted corruption and bribery. The return of majoritarian democracy, finally, put wind once again in the sails of authoritarian elements. Italian reality seemed remote from good values: accountability, a fair and just representation, and the like.

A pronounced regionalization of politics has also emerged. Many politicians have started calling for a division of Italy into independent republics; others recommend a federal solution. Economic gaps between the different regions are extremely marked; however, the entrenched distrust of politicians serves to undermine solidarity and prevent any kind of equalization. It is not simply that the rich regions of northern Italy increasingly refuse to turn over tax revenues to the poorer regions. The poor areas themselves wish to break free from the morally dilapidated system that had been controlled for so long by the elite cartel in the large metropolitan centers. The crisis in Italy has undermined the country's sense of nation, its identity.

In the election of 1996, the Left bloc—known as the Olive Tree alliance—obtained a majority. Various left-leaning groupings then governed Italy, and reshufflings of the different parties within the government continued to take place, just as they had done under the First Republic. In 2001, finally, the Right returned to power, and Berlusconi was again prime minister. The trials continued, although the mass media no longer kept watch at San Vittore so closely. Di Pietro was still on the front pages of the papers. At long last, however, criticism of his methods of interrogation prompted him—for the sake of "calm in the country and confidence in the institutions"—to resign not just from the investigation but also from his post as magistrate. He did this "without any struggle at all, on his tiptoes cautiously, with a final sense of duty, with death in his heart, and with no future prospects whatsoever."[46] His modesty was not so great, however, to keep him from breaking the news of his resignation in spectacular fashion, in the middle of a TV broadcast; and his future prospects were not so poor as to prevent him from later becoming a senator for the Left.

The circus around the electoral system in Italy continues. When I wrote these pages in September 2005, the news was that Prime Minister Berlusconi had suggested a new shift of the system—this time back to proportional representation, obviously because the opinion polls predicted that with the prevailing majoritarian system he was likely to lose in the upcoming election. In spite of this manipulation, he lost in Spring 2006 after an extremely close election followed by a period of hesitation over whether to accept the election results.

What does this case study tell us then? Proportional representation is no guarantee for a clean government; the truth seems rather to be the opposite. Blaming collaborators is not acceptable; as a matter of fact, such attempts were in the end strongly rejected by the Italian voters. Choice was indeed possible. Italy changed from a consensus to a majoritarian system. It is another story if this was enough to restore a healthy polity. Democracy under the Second Republic is as yet a fragile flower, budding in the shadow of a heavy tradition of corruption and authoritarian tendencies.

Accountability and the Ethics of Conviction and Responsibility

The fundamental mission of a politician is to bring to fruition the program he or she has presented to the voters. In order to do so, cooperation with other politicians is necessary. Sometimes such cooperation can be arranged only through compromise and logrolling—that is, by breaking some promises. What, then, are the moral constraints for such breaches of faith? The classical wording of this dilemma was formulated by Max Weber, when in the revolutionary winter of 1919 he held the two lectures "Politics as a Vocation" and "Science as a Vocation." Although the tone of these lectures was high-minded, Weber did not by any means deny the necessity of deviating from one's convictions in order to get things accomplished in politics. No indeed, it was precisely this that the two lectures concerned. The question was simply when such deviations are permitted.

It was in the first-mentioned lecture that Weber made his famous distinction between *the ethic of conviction* and *the ethic of responsibility.* Following the ethic of conviction means letting oneself be guided solely by the intrinsic value of one's goal. As for what the results are of such a course of action, those are not the actor's responsibility: "The world is stupid and base, not I. The responsibility for the consequences does not fall upon me." The objective for applying the ethic of responsibility, on the other hand, is exactly to look to the consequences of acting in one way rather than another. Is the goal better reached through cooperation and compromise, or by keeping some distance? After all, pushing one's own point of view in what Weber calls "sterile excitation" may serve to counteract the achievement of one's purpose or lead to worse results than might otherwise have been attainable.[47]

Can the behavior of the Italian politicians, then, be defended by reference to the ethic of responsibility? No: bribery and corruption are, of course, never permitted. The moral decay under *tangentopoli* was light-years away from the deep moral commitment of Max Weber. Any attempt to enlist Weber's political philosophy on behalf of one's efforts to evade responsibility by blaming one's partners is insolence. A few distinctions will serve to make clear that there is no possible basis for such an attempt.

A first obvious distinction must be made between acting for one's own gain or for one's political program. Weber approved—as an indispensable political instrument—the strategic calculation of what is the right formulation, the right occasion, the right move. In addition, he argued that politicians ought ideally to combine a passionate commitment to their cause and a chilly distance regarding choice of method. The method chosen must serve to promote the cause, not the person. The corruption seen in Italy was inexcusable from every standpoint, including—or rather not least—that of an ethic of responsibility. The corruption in question was simply economic bribery—a way for the individual to enrich himself. As Donatella della Porta puts it in an incisive study of how the system worked in Italy at the beginning of the 1990s, "Cartels of businessmen reach agreements on a series of public decisions which they must demand from the politicians: they collect money and hand it over to political cartels, in turn these offer privileged access to public decisions, and they distribute the money between politicians."[48] Weber's analysis, by contrast, concerned how one can garner support for one's political program by acting strategically.

Strategic action of this kind involves a strict morality. Following the ethic of responsibility rather than that of conviction does not mean casting all morality overboard—quite the contrary. A second distinction must be borne in mind: that between a consequentialist ethic like Weber's and, conversely, amorality. The passion demanded by the ethic of conviction can deprive a leader of the detachment needed for successful action and may even lead to violence. By contrast, the ethic of responsibility involves giving rational consideration to the means, ends, and consequences of social action; such an approach naturally lacks, however, the passionate involvement that vitalizes politics. Both kinds of morality are needed. It is said in the discourse on Weber that "some kind of practical reconciliation must indeed take place between these two ethics." It is not a question of choosing the one or the other but of "establishing how these ethics can be reconciled in practice . . . The political leader must, for Weber, combine passion and responsibility in order to pursue politics as a vocation, and this very often may involve a compromise."[49] Or in Weber's own words,

> [I]t is immensely moving when a *mature* man—no matter whether old or young in years—is aware of a responsibility for the consequences of his conduct and really feels such responsibility with heart and soul. He then acts by following an ethic of responsibility and somewhere he reaches the point where he says: "Here I stand; I can do no other." That is something genuinely human and moving. And every one of us who is not spiritually dead must realize the possibility of finding himself at some time in that position. In so far as this is true, an ethic of [conviction] and an ethic of responsibility are not absolute contrasts but rather supplements, which only in unison constitute a genuine man—a man who *can* have the "calling for politics."[50]

Before us we see, in other words, a politician who is highly focused on the question of what boundaries are to be set for strategic action aimed at implementing as much as possible of his program. The humanly touching element here is the fact that the answer is not given—that the politician feels hesitation, that he feels distress at being torn between the reasons for and against a given course of action. It is otherwise both with the ethicist of conviction and with the amoral cynic: neither need feel any hesitation—nothing is allowed, or everything is allowed. But it is very clear that, for Weber, it is the politician himself who bears the ultimate responsibility for the positions he takes. What Weber stands for is the very opposite of any attempt to shift the blame on to others.

Does the ethicist of conviction, then, feel any responsibility? Weber's use of language may be criticized for its lack of any clear distinction between responsibility and result—which is the third distinction to which I would call the attention of the reader. H. H. Bruun points out that a person devoted to the ethic of conviction will reject all other criteria for judging an action than those that are based on its intrinsic value: "If forced to choose between ethically 'clean hands' and the attainment of political goals . . . he will always sacrifice the goal in order to preserve the ethically correct character of his conduct." But such a person also considers himself to be responsible—not for the consequences of his actions, but for his inner conviction of what is right. He, too, "feels responsible in a certain sense, viz, to an 'inner' goal or an 'inner' axiological principle." Brunn proposes, therefore, that we speak of an "active ethic of responsibility," whereby actors engage in consequentialist reasoning about the effect of their actions on the outer world, as opposed to just "passively" taking responsibility for ensuring that their actions do not violate their inner convictions.[51]

Researching the consequences of one's actions is mandatory. It requires great knowledge, and not merely of an empirical kind. One must also be able to foresee the effects and side effects of various courses of action. To this extent politics resembles science. Weber was concerned with *"informed* choice, and science has a role in enabling informed choice. Part of making an informed choice involves not merely selecting means to a preselected end but selecting the ends themselves, particularly in light of . . . 'the inescapable factualness of our historical situation.' "[52]

Nonetheless, a clear distinction between science and politics must be made. Such was Weber's main standpoint on matters methodological, and it may serve here as the fourth and final distinction in the discussion of the dilemma of political cooperation. Weber conducted his work at a time when the professors of imperial Germany mixed their academic labors and their political beliefs without restraint. For Weber, the professionalization of scholarship meant holding these distinctly different undertakings apart. His colleagues did not understand the dependence of politics on values. Radical politicians did not appreciate the necessity for Realpolitik. Weber demanded of politicians that they base their program on a scientific analysis of reality; he also realized, however, that science was ultimately insufficient for deciding the matter: "As Weber sees it, the antagonism between the ethic of conviction and the ethic of responsibility is fundamentally insoluble by scientific means; only an act of personal *choice* leads to the acceptance of one rather than of the other as a standard of concrete behaviour. On the other hand, there are strong indications that Weber, in discussing the alternative between the two ethical orientations in the field of politics, accords a special prominence to the ethic of responsibility." The reason for this preference lay in the political context in which he held his lecture. The fact that Weber gave the lecture at all, in fact, should probably be ascribed to his ingrained dislike of politicians committed to the ethic of conviction. That is, he hesitated long before accepting the invitation and decided to do so only upon learning that the students thought to pass on the invitation to an idealistic but highly unrealistic left-wing intellectual. Intellectual morality demanded a more responsible attitude than that of the daydreamer, who shirks his duty to confront the gap between the desirable and the possible. Knowledge and personal choice were the conditions of politics, not romantic dreaming or the flight from responsibility.[53]

To clarify further, Weber's ideal was a political leader who realizes cooperation is necessary in politics and who therefore—through a careful analysis of the external, societal consequences of different courses of action—takes moral responsibility for how far he may deviate from his inner convictions.

Arend Lijphart, the theoretician of consensus democracy, would not find it hard to agree. But Lijphart is at once more concrete and more disposed to smooth things over. He is more concrete as far as the costs of cooperation are concerned, as when he expressly considers the risk for corruption when politicians cooperate. At the same time, he tends to smooth things over to a greater degree, as when he uses the analysis of statistical aggregates to sweep problems under the rug—thus, his doubtful formulation that corruption seems to be less likely in consensus than in majoritarian democracies. At no point does he seriously consider the corrective furnished by majoritarian democracy—namely, its alternation of different parties in power.

The recurrent metaphor in this chapter has been that of "hands." The fear that power will be abused has issued in the demand that all powers not be accumulated in "the same hands." This means in turn that different power-holders must cooperate—that is, they must "reach out their hands" to each other. Then, if they wish to get anything done in politics, they must be willing to "dirty their hands." But the ethic of responsibility points out a limit, a limit that in Italy—promised land of proportionalism and power-sharing—was badly transgressed: as a result, demands were raised for "clean hands."

No electoral method seems to guarantee a politics free from corruption. Italy served as the critical case for this chapter because that country has been subjected during the past half-century to a pair of full-scale experiments. Against the background of Fascism's majoritarian rule and with the support of strong arguments from intellectual history, proportional representation was introduced following World War II—for the precise purpose of counteracting the abuse of power. The belief was that if all had a share in power and kept watch over each other, politics would become cleaner. The framers of the Italian constitution considered this the most promising method for minimizing the abuse of power. It proved to be the case, however, that corruption flourished. The return to majoritarian democracy in the 1990s scarcely resulted in any palpable improvement; the continued corruption under Berlusconi is widely noted. The abuse of power can thus be found in both majoritarian and proportional systems: it is found in countries where power is concentrated in the hands of the majority; it is also found in countries where power is widely dispersed.

Blaming collaborators is not acceptable. Politicians are never spared the necessity for making a choice, for which they then must be held accountable. They may never seek to evade responsibility. If power is shared and many are involved, concessions become unavoidable; where such a culture of compromise prevails, moreover, the politics of blame avoidance gains credence more easily. But the ethic of responsibility cannot be interpreted— not even in such a situation—as freeing the individual from responsibility. On the contrary, Weber was the first to insist that the individual is responsible. Power-sharing does not exclude accountability.

CHAPTER 6

Implementation May Well Be Immaculate

The Theory of Budget Maximization

Politicians tend to blame the bureaucracy. After all, they are dependent on it—both for the information they require to make decisions and for ensuring that these decisions are implemented. One might say that politicians are dependent on bureaucrats at both ends—both for "input" and for "output." The bureaucracy is always there, and it operates purposefully and for the long-term. Political representation changes frequently, as a result of parliamentary elections or other political reshufflings. Thus, politicians end up in the hands of the bureaucrats. It should not be surprising, then, that politicians should try—when accused of mismanagement and mistakes—to put the blame on the bureaucrats. The classic distinction between politics and administration—wherein politicians make the decisions and bureaucrats immaculately implement them—paints a naive and idyllic picture. It is actually the bureaucrats who are in command. It is their self-interest that drives development forward—toward an ever stronger standing for themselves and an ever larger budget for the bureaucracy. Such is the conventional wisdom on the interplay between politicians and bureaucrats. It is humorously summed up by Sir Humphrey Appleby, the permanent undersecretary in the popular British television comedy *Yes Minister:* "The Civil Service does not make profit or losses. *Ergo,* we measure success by the size of our staff and budget. By definition, a big department is more successful than a small one . . . [T]his simple proposition is the basis of our whole system."[1]

In the scholarly literature, William A. Niskanen has given to this viewpoint a formulation both striking and theoretically sophisticated. It was in *Bureaucracy and Representative Government* (1971) that he developed his theory of "the budget-maximizing bureaucrat." He wrote this book against the background of his own experiences as an administrator in the U.S. Department of Defense, where he had served with Robert McNamara during the Kennedy years. He had started out fresh in mind and full of high hopes; soon, however, he became disillusioned by the weakness of politicians vis-à-vis the bureaucracy. Niskanen's theoretical point of departure was Rational Choice, which portrays bureaucrats as rational actors intent on realizing their preferences. More precisely, the theoretical framework he used was the special variant of Rational Choice that came to be known as Public Choice, or the assumption that these preferences are of a certain nature—expressive of bureaucratic self-interest. In a series of stringent and often mathematical analyses, Niskanen tried to show that it is first and foremost bureaucratic self-interest—not the requisites of loyal implementation—that explains the scope and standing of the public administration.

Economists had developed a demand model to depict the behavior of consumers on the market and a supply model to depict that of profit-oriented firms. In the academic analysis of politics and administration, however, it was the demand model by itself that dominated; this had led, according to Niskanen, to the naive conclusion that citizens and their elected representatives received the public goods for which they asked. But this was not at all true. It was the case, rather, that citizens got what the authorities offered. If researchers were to understand this process, they would have to develop a supply model for politics, too. It was this pursuit that Niskanen undertook. The closest equivalent in the political sphere to the private firm in the market, in his view, was the bureaucracy. Niskanen called his object of analysis the "bureau," which he defined as an organization in which the staff cannot appropriate the difference between incomes and expenditures as personal income. Instead, bureaucrats must find other ways of increasing the income and other perquisites they derive from work.

The very conception of politics as an offer made by bureaucrats to the public and their elected representatives reflects the view that the bureaucracy holds the initiative in moving developments forward. The "sponsoring organization"—that is, citizens and their representatives—plays a remarkably passive role in Niskanen's model. The reason for this is that he considers politicians to be completely under the control of bureaucrats. Because the distinguishing feature of state administration is the absence of competition, the bureaucracy has a monopoly on information. Politicians serving on committees charged with budget analysis and oversight are not really in any position to question the estimates of the bureaucrats. It is from the latter that they obtain the knowledge that they have. In fact, the situation is worse than that, given that due to the sectorization and segmentation of politics, committees of this kind are dominated by the very politicians with the greatest interest in, and demand for, the activity in question. Agricultural agencies, for example, ask for money to support farming. Farmers with the same interest sit on the budget committee, and they accept all of the arguments presented by the agencies for increasing subsidies. There is no chance, in such a world of supply politics, that expenditures will be reduced.

Niskanen concentrates his attention on the head of each agency. He presumes that this person, the bureaucrat, will seek to maximize his utility. This follows from the methodological individualism inherent in Rational Choice. The model is thus based on the motives of individuals, and not—in contrast to much previous research, which was based on the concept of a loyal and immaculate bureaucracy—on organic theories of the state à la Confucius, Plato, Max Weber, or Woodrow Wilson. These theorists all portrayed the state administration as an idealized collective body serving the public interest, with no thought of favor for itself. It seems that Niskanen was particularly persuaded of the methodological superiority of Public Choice on this point. The task, in his view, was to go behind the public choices that are actually made and to identify the self-interested motives of individual actors. When submitting proposals, the bureaucrat may talk about the common good. But his real motives are to satisfy his own material wants, and this can be done only with a larger budget. With a bigger budget, he may get a higher salary, a bigger office, a nicer car, a larger travel allowance, and other benefits of various kinds. Budget maximization is an instinct found in every forward-looking bureaucrat.

Furthermore, an increase in the budget is often the solution to any internal problem within a bureaucracy. In a bureau with an expanding budget, persons can be transferred and functions can be altered with relative ease; when the budget is static or shrinking, such moves occasion greater stress.

In a competitive industry, it is sufficient that a single firm be a profit maximizer for all the others to adopt the same strategy. In a bureaucracy, it is the other way round:

> In contrast, in a bureaucratic environment, one person who serves his personal interests or a different perception of public interest is often sufficient

to prevent others from serving their perception of the public interest. It is *impossible* for any one bureaucrat to act in the public interest, because of the limits on his information and the conflicting interests of others, regardless of his personal motivations. This leads the most selfless bureaucrat to choose some feasible, lower-level goal . . . A bureaucrat who may not be personally motivated to maximize the budget of his bureau is usually driven by conditions both internal and external to the bureau to do just that.

It is the basic difference between allocating resources through a bureaucracy and allocating resources through a market that makes budget maximization possible for the bureaucrat. While a bureaucracy maximizes its budget, a market maximizes the difference between total utility and total cost. There is no place in a bureaucracy for marginal cost analysis; therefore, a politician charged with approving appropriations never knows the marginal gain yielded by an additional unit of resources. As a result, bureaucracies are always too large. In fact, Niskanen contends, they are about twice as large as they ought to be. And they always lead to a waste of resources.

What will happen to a civil servant who can show that the present activities of his bureau could be carried out within a considerably smaller budget? In a profit-oriented enterprise, he will be rewarded with a bonus, a promotion, and an opportunity to work on his idea. If he does not succeed, he will always be able to move on to a competitor with his freshly won knowledge. In a state bureaucracy, by contrast, he may possibly receive a mention—or perhaps be transferred without a raise. Above all, he will win the disapproval of his colleagues.

Niskanen concludes his book with a call for steps to be taken to check swelling bureaucracy. The grip that bureaucracy has on representative government must be broken, by introducing competition within the state apparatus and privatizing parts of its operations.[2]

Bureaucracy and Representative Government has become perhaps the most influential and most cited work on public administration. In an earlier work, I structured the extensive debate on this topic with the help of four small auxiliary verbs; the same approach may be useful here. The question is whether bureaucrats in fact "may," "can," "dare," or "want" to devote themselves to budget maximizing.[3]

When we ask whether bureaucrats *may* do so, we call into question the thesis of the passive government. Is it really the case that politicians give bureaucrats the opportunity to budget maximize without interference? This is the main criticism leveled at Niskanen's model in the scholarly discussion. If the idea is to view politics from the supply side, critics argue, it would be more telling to cast politicians in the role of the entrepreneurs of public service. It is the programs of the political parties, after all, that are offered to citizens during election campaigns, when politicians try to maximize their share of the vote. After that, the relationship between politicians and bureaucrats is marked by a review on the part of the former that their programs are implemented in the manner intended.

A number of empirical studies support this more traditional view of bureaucracy. In the United States, for example, Congress has tightened its grip on the budget. Between 1966 and 1976, the number of hearings increased by 74 percent in the House of Representatives and by 55 percent in the Senate. Committees that increased costs gradually lost power to budget committees with a mandate to control them. President Reagan's slaughter of the budget is a good example of the way in which politicians can assert themselves against bureaucrats. As for Niskanen's recommendation that competition between bureaucracies be introduced, this appears to be an ineffective remedy: analyses of American defense policy indicate that when two bureaucracies discover they have a conflict of interest, they prefer to enter into a secret agreement, rather than to weaken each other in front of the politicians. The studies in question show as well that the motives of politicians and of bureaucrats can be the opposite of what Niskanen presumed: a politician can seek to expand a program, even as a bureaucrat may suggest various cuts:

> Niskanen's model of the interactions between rational vote-maximizing politicians and rational budget-maximizing bureaucrats is flatly wrong. It is wrong in suggesting that information-manipulation on the supply side will necessarily go unchecked, and in supposing that the demand side will necessarily be dominated by politicians with unusually strong desires for the goods in question . . . Niskanen's model is also wrong in supposing that bureaucrats will necessarily compete if their interests are in conflict, and it is wrong in attributing the motivations it does to actors on both sides of the bargaining game. Consequently, and inevitably, Niskanen is wrong in his conclusion that bureaucratic goods and services are oversupplied (or overpriced) by something up to a factor of two.[4]

It is the politicians, other researchers repeat, who account for the supply side of politics; bureaucrats neither promote nor restrict these tendencies to any decisive degree. The limits are instead set by other politicians; and it is the competition between parties that determines what the voters are offered.[5] Take, for example, the Vietnam War, which is often cited as the most devastating example of bureaucratic budget maximization. (Niskanen himself touches on this idea in his book.) Declassified documents available after the war suggest that this notion is simply wrong. It was not at all the case that politicians caved in to the budgetary demands of the military. President Johnson's administration had foreseen—with surprising accuracy—the consequences of various measures for reinforcing the troops. The large military venture that was launched was entirely the result of the assessments of politicians. Thus, not even with regard to what may have been the greatest increase for any budgetary item in modern history is it possible to substantiate the thesis of budget maximization. The politicians were in fact able, with the instruments of control at their disposal, to hold the line.[6]

Study after study stresses, moreover, that it is "the legislature, not the bureaucracy, [that] is primarily to blame for the problems of big government"[7]; that it is the motives of politicians that are decisive for the size of the bureaucracy[8]; and that it is the politicians in the budgetary process who are actually in a position to control developments.[9] Finally, the belief that bureaucrats always or often get their way misses the restraining and decisive role played by politicians in determining allocations to public agencies.[10]

Turning now to the second of our questions, scholars doubt that bureaucrats *can* maximize their budget. Niskanen argued that bureaucrats have this capability, because they have a monopoly in most cases over information; politicians, therefore, have no one else to turn to for information. But critics object that, much as different firms in a market compete to sell the same goods, different agencies in a political budgetary process compete for the same money. When politicians weigh the proposals of different agencies against each other, with an eye to channeling money into projects that make for a maximal increase in citizen welfare, the competition faced by the various bureaucracies is severe—as severe, in fact, as that faced by different firms in a market.[11] "The notion of a bureau as a single and independent monopolist becomes rather strange, since it might be expected that the many bureaux are competing for as large as possible a part of the total budget of the ministry. In this way there arises a picture which is quite different from that of the bureau as a monopolist, as sketched by Niskanen."[12]

Nor is it even clear that bureaucracies would be able to maximize their budget if they found themselves in a monopoly position. A distinguishing feature of bureaucracies, after all, is that they carry heavy costs for "special resources," which makes them less flexible than firms on the open market. These special resources can include both manpower and capital. The notion that expertise is the hallmark of bureaucracy goes back at least as far as Weber. High-level civil servants usually enjoy a more secure position than do business executives, and their specialization narrows the range of alternative employment open to them. In addition, large-scale operations within the state administration—for example, postal and telephone services or the manufacture of military aircraft—must be run at full capacity; nothing is gained by running them at half-speed. If one examines the state administration in detail, one discovers that the room for maximizing or otherwise manipulating the budget is far less than what Niskanen seems to believe.[13]

Niskanen developed his model against the background of his American experiences. How well does it accord with European experience? Badly, says the research. The European bureaucrat faces institutional conditions that prevent him from engaging in budget-maximizing behavior, however much he might wish to: "Perhaps the most important limiting factor is the expertise and the status of the sponsors. In addition to some concerns about the legislature and its committees, the average administrator in Western Europe must first worry about the ministry of finance or its equivalent central agency."[14] A bureaucrat seeking to maximize his bureau's budget will meet with rigorous counterstrategies on the part of highly competent officials. When applied to seventeen European countries, the hypothesis of budget maximization fails to garner empirical support. Furthermore, the development over time of the salaries paid to responsible top bureaucrats speaks against the picture painted by Niskanen, as do other factors that might measure the degree to which their personal interests are served:

> It is impossible to deny that there has been substantial growth and development in the public sector during the postwar period. What is possible to deny, however, is that this growth has benefited the senior civil service more than other government workers. The most obvious beneficiaries appear to have been the clients of public programs, rather than the workers administering those programs . . . [The] power [of the bureaucracy] may be used to maximize service to clients rather than to maximize personal benefits . . . The public bureaucracy may by now have become too central a policy maker in contemporary governments to allow it to engage in the type of self-seeking implied in the Niskanen model. This is probably true in the United States; it is certainly true in Europe.[15]

Budget maximizing is a risky business. It involves breaking the most fundamental rule in the political game, which for bureaucrats is to achieve credibility in the eyes of their political sponsors. Without such credibility, after all, bureaucrats risk getting no money at all. Would bureaucrats *dare* to put this confidence in jeopardy? "Bureaucrats must keep their lies down to believable proportions or else it will be worth the while of budget reviewers to invest some resources and catch them at their lies."[16] Or to quote another skeptical observation: "Disbelief, notice, is a counter-strategy you can play against a liar even if you do not know the truth yourself. You know enough to discount *his* reports, at least. Budgetary review committees of the political masters of bureaucracies seem to follow just some such procedure." American congressmen have punished bureaucrats who have spent more money than was expected. As another example, local politicians in Norway have shown themselves willing to make drastic budget cuts if they believe the figures of the bureaucrats are inflated.[17]

Finally, we come to Niskanen's core assumption: do bureaucrats really *want* to maximize their budget? It is in his excessively hierarchical picture of administration in Western Europe, his critics contend, that Niskanen's judgement fails him. The motives of high- and low-level civil servants diverge. Low-level bureaucrats would gain the most from a maximized budget, inasmuch as it would mean greater career opportunities for them. Given that their influence in the budgetary process is slight, however, they are more inclined to seek advancement in some other fashion: for example, by "doing a good job" (the recurrent answer given by low-level civil servants eager for promotion). Top-level civil servants, for their part, have greater influence on the budget, but they see little personal gain to be had from maximizing budgets; on the contrary, they perceive increased risks. They are also more interested in such immaterial rewards as status and influence, and these are not correlated with the size of their agency's budget. For this reason, top-level bureaucrats are not particularly wedded to budget maximization.[18] Niskanen considers his view of human beings to be much more realistic than the idealized image held out in administrative research in the Weberian tradition, wherein bureaucrats are portrayed as just as devoted to the public interest as the officers of Prussia were loyal to the Kaiser. Yet he himself is guilty of Weberian idealization, inasmuch as he describes bureaucracies as strictly hierarchical, with all power in the hands of supposedly budget-maximizing top-level civil servants.

Quite another reason for not wanting to maximize the budget is love of comfort. Attempts in this direction do not just incur political risks. Many bureaucrats also hesitate in the face of the uncertain gains, the considerable efforts, and the increased worries entailed by a larger staff. The choice for the bureaucrat is not self-evident: "Should he strive for a larger budget which will increase his salary and his psychic income, or should he increase his ease of administration and his leisure through a smaller budget?"[19] A variant of the comfort argument is that the head bureaucrat might fear a loss of control. If an office grows quickly and its tasks and structure change, new pressures are put on a chief officer who wishes to maintain his leadership.[20] Adherents of the hypothesis of budget maximization are highly critical of public administration in its present form, but they seem to have forgotten the traditional critique of bureaucracy—which sees it not as ambitious and expansionist, but as lethargic and lacking in initiative.

So what do top civil servants with budgetary responsibility want to do with their agencies? What are the secret dreams of the "Mandarins in Western Democracies," to quote the title of a famous study? If in-depth interviews with the heads of bureaus are to be believed, their dream is certainly not to run big welfare bureaucracies with enormous budgets for the routine disbursement of benefits to citizens. It is rather to work in a small, well-functioning agency at the center of the decision-making process, with close access to the prince's ear. Influence and position are the foremost goals of top bureaucrats, and to gain them they must be loyal to their political sponsors. An immaculate implementation need not presume, therefore, either idealism or self-effacing servility. Self-interest by itself is quite enough to ensure that bureaucrats will strive to implement government decisions in the intended manner.[21]

Notwithstanding these criticisms, however, *Bureaucracy and Representative Government* remains the central book within political science on the relationship between decision makers and administrators. This is not, in fact, a paradox. The important books in social science are those that provoke debate and stimulate efforts at falsification; insignificant works, by contrast, are never called into question, because no one cares enough about them to try. The scholars André Blais and Stéphane Dion make the following point: "Great ideas stimulate great debates. The debate on the Niskanen model is a rich one, as objections have been raised about each of its major arguments. Great ideas are not necessarily true, however, and it is imperative to confront Niskanen's ideas with hard data in order to assess their usefulness."[22]

What results have been yielded, then, by the confrontation with empirical data? Niskanen himself has stuck to his theory, although the debate on his book has not left him wholly unaffected. In a reassessment twenty years after his book was published, he repeats—not without pride—his belief in the hypothesis of budget maximization: "The basic structure of the theory outlined in my 1971 book will continue to be the most useful approach to understanding the behavior of bureaus." But certain changes, he thinks, ought to be made, the most important of which is the following: what bureaucrats actually seek to maximize, Niskanen now argues, is "the discretionary budget," defined as the difference between the total budget and the minimum cost of producing the output expected by the authorities. Because neither the bureaucrats nor the politicians can utilize this discretionary budget as personal income, the surplus is used in a fashion favorable to them both, for example to pay for additional staff, capital, and other perquisites. This modification yields a slight change in how Niskanen formulates his conclusion, but his message is substantially the same: that the budget of a bureau is always too large, the output always too low, and the production of the output uniformly inefficient. Niskanen further concedes that a deeper analysis of the review process is needed, in order to ascertain the extent to which political review committees are able to control expenditures. In perfect keeping with his original model, however, Niskanen's focus is on the self-interest of those sitting on such committees. We should not imagine, he says, that such politicians serve any idealized common interest; they work, rather, on behalf of their own interests.[23]

It is hard to find, however, any empirical support for the idea that bureaucrats are in so great a measure the entrepreneurs of the political sphere—with an agenda of their own, on which the promotion of their own material interests comes first—that politicians would be justified in pinning the blame for policy failures on them. The expansion of the public sector is explained better by social, economic, and technical changes in society and by shifts in the political values held by citizens and their representatives. The main personal interest of top-level officials is to exercise influence. This means they must keep the confidence of their political sponsors, which in turn motivates them to stay loyal to the political decisions that have been made.

The Politics of Retrenchment

Despite three decades of far-reaching discussion and criticism, Niskanen's pathbreaking book remains the most oft-cited explanation for the extensive bureaucracy of our day. In research and instruction on politics and adminis-tration, the material self-interest of bureaucrats in maximizing budgets is still depicted as the irresistible driving force behind the growth of public bu-reaucracy. Notwithstanding this, however, retrenchment has taken place. Bureaucracies have been cut and public agencies privatized. We see here, in other words, yet another example of the gap between theory and empirical evidence. I have chosen to take the empirical data for this chapter from Great Britain, and to give the critical case here the following formulation: How did it happen that, in direct contravention of what this theory of public administration contends, Margaret Thatcher was able, as British prime min-ister during the 1980s, to regain control over the bureaucracy and to reduce the number of bureaucrats?

The course of development in postwar Britain makes this country a most likely case for testing Niskanen's theory. The public sector was growing, and the number of bureaucrats was constantly increasing. Domestic politics was marked by a consensus between the political parties. Under the cover of this agreement of opinion, the Civil Service resolutely and calmly advanced its position. Right-wing Conservatives were intensely dissatisfied with this state of affairs; the country, they said with a sigh, seemed to need a bigger state apparatus to administer prosperity than Churchill had needed to win World War II.

Among the members of this right-wing was a young member of Parlia-ment, Margaret Thatcher. Under the influence of Sir Keith Joseph and his Center for Political Studies, Thatcher had become a confirmed adherent of Public Choice theory. (Joseph was to become her political mentor, and it was to him that she later dedicated her memoirs.) The Conservative gov-ernment was happy to enlist the services of this energetic woman, who by the time of her appointment had already studied at Oxford, worked as a chemist, and served as a solicitor. Her experiences during these early years in government were to leave an indelible mark on her ideas about public bureaucracy. She was made junior minister for pensions at the beginning of the 1960s and minister of education when the Tories returned to power in 1970. In the latter position, she gave priority, true as always to her ideology, to schoolbooks over "welfare spending" and so abolished free milk at school. This earned her the sobriquet "Maggie Thatcher, milk snatcher." The repeated difficulties Prime Minister Edward Heath met with in trying to gain the confidence of the voters led to an acute leadership crisis in the party; when he had lost three out of four elections, he was prevailed upon to make way for Thatcher, who became Conservative leader in 1975. Four years later, Thatcher became Britain's first female prime minister. Her program called for putting an end to "the nanny state," by restoring a sound market economy, taming the trade unions, supporting the family, strengthening the armed forces, upholding respect for law and order—and taking control over the Civil Service.[24]

Conservative prime ministers prior to Thatcher had also had plans to reduce the bureaucracy. Edward Heath, her predecessor, had started out strongly in this area. He did not manage, however, to follow through on his plans; indeed, he ended up making a U-turn. There were many who believed the new prime minister would be forced to do the same; they had not understood, however, that she was of a tougher fiber. Or, as she herself put it; "the lady's not for turning."[25] She "struck the Whitehall with the force of a tornado,"[26] with an eye to "put[ting] politics back in command."[27] The blows of her government "continued to rain down on the Civil Service; and far from petering out, the quest for efficiency eventually came to be translated into something akin to a grand strategy."[28] Sir Keith Joseph declared Niskanen's book required reading for civil servants,[29] and Thatcher herself urged all and sundry to study the literature on Public Choice,[30] so that they might understand the innermost nature of bureaucracy and the driving forces behind it. In this way, it would be possible to shift the system's center of gravity away from irresponsible bureaucracy and toward accountable democratic politics.

Thatcher's "grand strategy" for changing the bureaucracy aimed at three things: cutting the number of bureaucrats, deprivileging the civil service, and changing bureaucratic organization. Just days after taking power in May 1979, Thatcher's government introduced a hiring freeze in the Civil Service, and one year later she presented her program for reducing bureaucracy to Parliament:

> In the past Governments have progressively increased the number of tasks that the Civil Service is asked to do without paying sufficient attention to the need for economy and efficiency. Consequently, staff numbers have grown over the years. The present Government are committed both to a reduction in tasks and to better management . . . All Ministers in charge of departments will now work out detailed plans for concentrating on essential functions and making operations simpler and more efficient in their departments. When this Government took office the size of the Civil Service was 732,000.

As a result of the steps that we have already taken it is now 705,000. We intend to bring the number down to about 630,000 over the next four years.[31]

This program was carried out with impressive determination and accuracy. By 1987, when she was elected premier for the third time, Thatcher had succeeded in reducing the number of civil servants to its lowest level since 1945.[32] As can be seen in Figure 6.1, the number of civil servants rose between 1961 and 1979 from about 670,000 to a bit over 730,000. Then the reductions began. By 1984, Thatcher had fulfilled and even surpassed her plan: the number was now below 630,000. At the time of her resignation in 1990, the figure had fallen to 562,000.

Another part of Thatcher's strategy, as mentioned, was to deprivilege the Civil Service. Bureaucrats, in her view, occupied a position of undue privilege and influence. This was expressed most clearly in the system used for adjusting wages and other benefits: the so-called Priestley pay system, which had been in use since 1953. Under the previous system of Keynesianism, inflation, and public-sector growth, the salaries of civil servants had been automatically raised. But under Thatcher's setup of monetarism, price stability, and retrenchment, the Priestley system did not fit. Thatcher

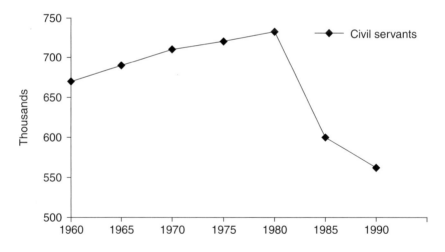

Figure 6.1. Number of civil servants, 1961–1990. *Data Source:* Brian W. Hogwood, *Trends in British Public Policy: Do Governments Make Any Difference?* (Buckingham, UK: Open University Press, 1992), 135. Published with permission of the author.

was more concerned with the plight of taxpayers than with the privileges of bureaucrats, and she refused to allow further increases. The bureaucracy then decided it had had enough, and a Civil Service strike broke out. This gave Thatcher the opportunity to show that she was serious about another of her fundamental policies: beating the unions. After a strike lasting 21 weeks, the unions had to admit defeat.

Third, Thatcher wanted to change the way the Civil Service was organized. One of the things she had noticed as a junior minister was that bureaucrats changed their proposals when one minister was replaced by another. When she wondered why, she was told that responsible bureaucrats knew that the new minister would never have accepted the proposals, and so refrained from presenting them to him; in other words, the bureaucrats decided what policies should be pursued. Thatcher realized that ministers were dependent on the input of bureaucrats, in just the way Niskanen had warned. The bureaucrats manipulated the politicians. The young minister was deeply shocked, and she decided that, come the day she had the power, there would be a change: "I decided then and there that when I was in charge of a department I would insist on an absolutely frank assessment of all the options from any civil servants who would report to me." The foremost requirement in the relationship between the government and civil servants was that the "civil servants owe ministers honest, accurate advice based on facts."[33]

Events during the strike strengthened her further in this conviction. To her dismay, Lord Soames, the minister responsible for the Civil Service Department, called for a compromise with the unions. She therefore dismissed him and abolished the Civil Service Department to boot. In the new organization that replaced it, every bureaucrat was made directly subordinate to a minister, and at the same time, the position of the prime minister was strengthened. One of Thatcher's advisors made this point: "I've never known a business organization with two headquarters at opposite ends of the street."[34] Ministers would strive for greater efficiency and see to it that the taxpayers got their money's worth. The politics of retrenchment was particularly successful in the Ministry of Environment, where Michael Heseltine introduced the Financial Management Initiative, a system for information and decentralization that enabled the minister to see in detail "who does what, why and what does it cost." However, one problem with such a system is that if individual bureaucrats are held personally responsible to a higher degree, then they must also be granted greater power to make decisions. Needless to say, such a result scarcely fit with the prime minister's grand strategy of strengthening politicians and weakening bureaucrats. Nor was this approach implemented with the same consistency in other ministries as in the Ministry of Environment. Most ministers took a stronger interest in political questions than in how their ministries were organized: there were not, unfortunately "that many Mr. Heseltines around." In addition, Thatcher recruited Sir Derek Rayner, from Marks & Spencer (which "everyone used to describe as [Thatcher's] favorite company"),[35] to serve as her economic advisor. Private business was held out as an example for public administration to follow.

The bureaucracy was reduced, deprivileged, and reorganized. On a descriptive level, scholars are able to unite behind this picture of the changes. On the other hand, the question of whether Margaret Thatcher succeeded in giving Britain a better bureaucracy is the subject of considerable debate. In a study of "The Thatcher Government, the Financial Management Initiative and the New Civil Service," Geoffrey Fry distinguishes among three viewpoints on this issue. The first interpretation of the changes, which likely comes close to that of Thatcher herself, is that the result was in fact the one sought: a "new" and more efficient Civil Service with a new spirit. The second assessment, embraced not least by the crushed trade unions, is that the changes led to catastrophe and were pushed through for reasons of blind ideology and without any thought for the disastrous consequences. Finally, there is the view taken by the ultra-Right, with *The Economist* at its head, which compares Thatcher's policies not with previous conditions but with the ideal of the minimal state; for them, the changes wrought by Thatcher were little more than ripples on the surface, and the Civil Service remains badly outsized.[36]

Behind these varied assessments, however, a consistent picture emerges: something happened in Britain during the 1980s. Margaret Thatcher demonstrated that politicians can, in fact, take command over a bureaucracy. She had a deeply rooted suspicion of bureaucracy as a phenomenon, a suspicion deepened through her study of Public Choice literature à la Niskanen. It is not surprising, therefore, that her favorite television-program was precisely *Yes Minister,* from which she took inspiration for a series of incessant measures aimed at liberating politicians and ministers from the bureaucracy's humiliating claws. One author goes so far as to claim that, "[t]hough Margaret Thatcher liked, respected and trusted individual civil servants, and was by all accounts a kindly and concerned employer, she hated the Civil Service . . . She considered public-sector employment a necessary evil and was determined to reduce its burden on the state."[37]

It should be stressed, however, that Thatcher's crusade against bureaucracy formed just a part of her program for political change. A sound economy was one central goal; the politics of retrenchment was a way to reach it. It was through private business, not bureaucracy or trade unions, that it would be possible to generate wealth. The forces of production must be stimulated, inflation must be abolished, and the market economy must be favored. In these efforts, Thatcher was strikingly successful: "Britain is a very different society in the late 1980s from a decade earlier. It may not be a 'kinder gentler nation', to transfer President [George H. W.] Bush's campaign refrain. In many respects Britain is a more divided, less secure and harsher society. But it is economically more competitive."[38]

In Thatcher's hierarchy of values, however, there were still higher goals than those bearing on the economy. In her memoirs, she cites the famous statement of John Maynard Keynes that economics is too important to be left to the economists.[39] Prosperity was important for how it could serve something else—something that, for lack of a better word, we may call Thatcher's patriotism. She wished to make her country great again. Britain, she thought, had declined. Strikes, inflation, and a spirit of the dole had made her country into a second-rate nation. Yet the place had potential. Britain could become a leading country once again, if the values she believed herself to share with the conscientious middle class and the aspiring working class were once again put front and center: family, hard work, thrift, property, and career (including for those not part of the establishment). She explained, "I want to see one nation, as you go back to Victorian times, but I want everyone to have their own personal property stake . . . I want them to have their own savings which retain their value, so they can pass things on to their children, so you get again a people, everyone strong and independent of government."[40]

The confrontation between theory and empirical evidence in this chapter casts a retrospective light on Niskanen's theory of the budget-maximizing bureaucrat. What may possibly have been true when his book was first written became palpably untrue subsequently. As we have seen, his work may have actually materially contributed to the changes that then took place; after all, Thatcher used it as an argument for changing the course along which society was developing. The events of the 1980s make his work look more like an epitaph for an epoch than a general theory. Up to the mid-1970s, most took for granted that the welfare state, Keynesianism, and public bureaucracy were here to stay. But then governments of the Right came to power in a number of countries and started carrying out their program of rolling back the state. *Thatcher, Reagan, Mulroney: In Search of a New Bureaucracy* is the significative title of a book that analyzes this shift.[41] If politicians had indeed ever lost control, they certainly regained it in the 1980s. They, not the bureaucrats, bear the responsibility.

Accountability and Bureaucracy

It is far from self-evident, however, that bureaucrats ought wholly to subordinate themselves to politicians in the way that Margaret Thatcher wished. Such an arrangement, which we may call the *model of obedience,* goes back to Weber's theory of "office hierarchy," wherein the duty of bureaucrats is to implement the decisions of politicians loyally, even if they run contrary to their own views: "The honour of the civil servant is vested in his ability to execute conscientiously the order of the superior authority, exactly as if the order agreed with his own conviction . . . The honour of the political leader[,] . . . however, lies precisely in an exclusive personal responsibility for what he does, a responsibility he cannot and must not reject or transfer." Obedience of this kind does not exclude thinking for oneself. At times, for example, the responsible minister has laid down only general guidelines, thus allowing a certain room for maneuver in their execution. The task of the bureaucrat in such a case is to give—in the spirit of the minister—specific form to the policy in question. He is to fill out the policy as he believes his minister would have wished and to disregard his own preferences altogether. The bureaucracy must be a reliable tool in the hands of politicians. No independent views on the part of bureaucrats can be allowed to distort policy.[42]

Weber thus justified his model by reference to the basic concept behind this study: that it is the politicians who are accountable for the policy conducted. Politicians must be able to trust the bureaucracy to implement their decisions in an immaculate manner. If the democratic chain is to function, bureaucrats must be placed under politicians, in a clear relationship of obedience (see Figure 6.2)

Those wishing to find a modern champion for this model can turn to an article by Neil Summerton published shortly after Thatcher came to power, under the title of "A Mandarin's Duty." Summerton starts out by noting

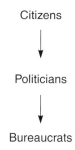

Citizens

Politicians

Bureaucrats

Figure 6.2. The model of obedience.

that the old criticism of top civil servants abusing their position had returned with renewed strength under the new government. This could be
interpreted "as reflecting the proper determination of new ministers to assert their political authority over their departments." There was little to object to in these plans. The criticism, as mentioned, was an old one; the doctrine laid down "that, in the absence of any limiting statute, order,
regulation, instruction or convention, the civil servant's duty, is to give conscientious and undivided service to the ministers of the Queen's Government for the time being."

A first aspect of the duty to serve the ministers involves furnishing the
government with the best possible defense for its policies and actions. A
second component is "the requirement of obedience in the execution of the
minister's instructions, in the implementation of policy." Or, as a permanent secretary states, "A department must really and deeply get to know
how its minister works and sustain him in every way it can"; there was a
need for "total subordination and a rather consistent attempt to consider
what the minister really needs." A third element is "the obligation to seek to
strengthen the Government's position by competent presentation of matters
of decision."

It was in connection with this third task, perhaps, that top civil servants
had acquired excessive influence. When bureaucrats engage in "picking and
choosing"—that is, when they gather materials on a question—there is a
risk that they will press their own departmental philosophy on the ministers. But the ministers, Summerton concludes, have very substantial
powers over their bureaucratic subordinates; he stresses emphatically "the
extent of ministers' power to require obedience from civil servants":
"[T]here are relatively few absolute limitations on the civil servant's duty to

his departmental ministers." Ministers can not, to be sure, ask of their subordinates that they commit criminal acts. Aside from that, however, bureaucrats must do as their ministers command. There is little reason to think that a bureaucrat is free "to define the public interest as being anything different from what politically responsible ministers tell him it is."[43]

The contrary view of the relationship between politicians and bureaucrats may be called the *model of discretion*. It is common in the political science literature. According to this model, bureaucrats should be loyal not just to their superiors but also to the law and to democratic principles. They must also stay loyal to their own conscience and expertise. Because these two norms can come into conflict, there is room for bureaucratic discretion (see Figure 6.3).

Arguments for the model of discretion often begin with a reference to the extreme conditions of Nazi Germany. Hitler's executioners sought to escape responsibility by pinning the blame on their political superiors: "We made no personal decisions. We were just following orders." Therefore, in order to understand Nazism, we need not assume any monstrous qualities on the part of the German people; they simply had a mistaken model of administration. So simple is the "the banality of evil" identified by Hannah Arendt. But the individual can never escape personal responsibility. Blind obedience is not a democratic value.[44]

In the research on administration, the question of the personal responsibility of bureaucrats is a theme rich in variation. Sometimes one value is stressed, sometimes another. Certain scholars stake out a middle position: bureaucrats, they say, should be loyal to their political superiors but should

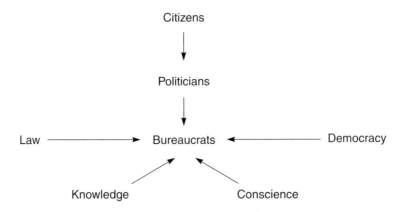

Figure 6.3. The model of discretion.

not obey their orders unreservedly. But on one thing all are agreed: bureaucrats bear personal responsibility for their decisions. Bureaucrats cannot be automatons carrying out the will of politicians; rather, they must reflect, deliberate, and assess. They must keep a critical eye on the tasks they are charged with performing.

Britain is often portrayed as a country with servile bureaucrats—notwithstanding the domestic critique, reviewed above, which avers the opposite. In a broadside at the British Civil Service for behaving, far more than its Continental counterparts, in accordance with the model of obedience, F. F. Ridley cites with approval the words of Sir Thomas More: "I am the King's good servant, but I am God's servant first." An official of the state should be loyal, most certainly—but not to just anything a politician might dream up: "[O]bedience is one thing, commitment to a set of politicians and their programme is quite another." It is to "the interest of the state," not "the policies of the state," that bureaucrats must be loyal: "The civil service should not, as a whole, be told that its only loyalty is to the ministers of the day. It should be a service of the state, dedicated to impartial administration based on its professional expertise, non-partisan concepts of the national interest and a much stronger anchor in administrative law."[45]

The U.S. Constitution, by contrast, lays down that each public employee must place high moral principle and the country before loyalty to any individual person, party, or agency. Experienced administrators all learn, as one attempt at interpreting this constitutional tradition points out, that conflicts of loyalty arise easily with rules of this kind. The larger and more complex the bureaucracy, moreover, the greater is the need for delegation (and thus for bureaucratic discretion). Conflicts of loyalty increase accordingly. When such arise, the good bureaucrat ought always to remember that he "is not required to sign documents within his sphere of responsibility which he does not approve." As an ultimate measure, finally, a bureaucrat should resign rather than accept an invalid interpretation of the law. "[A]ll administrators, elected officials, appointed political executives, and professional administrators alike are bound by the law of the land, and where there is discretion in interpreting and applying it, they are obliged to use their power in good faith in the public interest."[46]

"The public interest" is a recurrent term among advocates of the model of discretion. The task of bureaucrats is to use their relative independence vis-à-vis politicians to promote the common good. When different values are thought to need upholding in this way, as in Figure 6.3, the model can easily be divided up into several. "Administrative rationalism" may be be said to require that the value of knowledge be guarded—that is, bureaucrats must, by utilizing their expert knowledge, see to it that policies are implemented more effectively than they would have been had the ideas of the minister been followed in every detail. Promoting democracy thus means defending "administrative platonism" (a most striking use of language, it must be said, inasmuch as Plato was democracy's foremost critic). But the expression becomes intelligible if we take the view that bureaucrats, like Plato's guardians, are charged with safeguarding the prevailing form of government (whether meritocratic or democratic) against politicians and voters who cannot themselves define "the public interest." Following one's conscience means giving particular weight—when the interests of different groups must be weighed against each other—to the needs of weaker groups. Politicians are often incapable of doing this.[47]

Many champions of the model of discretion, in other words, see the bureaucracy as a source of moral power: "[P]ublic administration is not a kind of technology but a form of moral endeavor" (thus something different from what advocates of "administrative rationalism" have in mind). "The Honorable Bureaucrats . . . must never allow themselves to be a party to the compromising of the regime values, whether through partisan decisions, economic considerations, presumed administrative efficiencies, or professional neutrality. They must be active proponents of the regime values."[48]

Another author reminds us, however, that many different persons are involved in each decision, recalling the problem of many hands encountered in Chapter 5. Who, then, is be held responsible? The model of obedience points unequivocally to the relevant minister, but this is an antiquated notion: it does not correspond to the portrait of politics that emerges from modern studies of the making of public policy. "Instead of respecting a clear distinction between politics and administration, bureaucrats exercise discretionary authority either delegated to them, or simply assumed by them." But in that case they are responsible, too. Yet bureaucrats do not always acknowledge this; instead, they have a tendency to make excuses—for example, "if I don't do it someone else will." In the end, however, such an attitude means that no one is responsible. Responsibility must instead be understood as attaching to persons, not to offices.[49]

The established view here—that top civil servants enjoy discretionary power in the process of implementation and so bear personal responsibility for the content of the decisions made—is perhaps best expressed in a book with the descriptive title *The Responsible Administrator*. In this work, Terry L. Cooper subjects the fundamental predicament faced by the bureaucrat—whether to obey his minister or his convictions—to a thorough analysis. Most of the time such conflicts do not arise, and so the hierarchical structure works well. When an official finds, however, that a given decision contradicts his convictions, it is his duty to speak out:

> Responsible public administrators generally should acknowledge their accountability to the hierarchical structure of the organization. When functioning properly the hierarchy is . . . the structure of responsibility; it is the means for managing different levels of responsibility for the mission of the organization and the appropriate delegation of authority. However, being accountable to superiors does not necessarily mean simply following orders that are illegitimate. Administrators are also obligated to question, resist, and challenge orders that are inconsistent with the mission of the organization, established professional codes, the values of the political community, or their own conscience.[50]

It is striking, however, that key words and concepts in the model of discretion remain undefined. For what is really meant by "the interest of the state," "the public interest," "regime values," or "the mission of the organization"? If bureaucrats reserve the right to interpret such concepts as they will, is there not a great risk that they will impose their personal political values on politicians? Will not such discretion make more difficult any attempt at an immaculate implementation of the politicians' intentions?

It was this question that stood at the center in the now-classic debate between Carl Friedrich and Herman Finer in the early 1940s. With the serious political climate of this era as their backdrop, they debated the manner in which power was being exercised in the totalitarian states. Friedrich took the prevailing view: Weber's hierarchical model—with its categorical distinction between politics and administration—could no longer be sustained. He warned against the Fascist idea of a "will of the state" requiring unconditional obedience. When called upon to implement unacceptable decisions, a bureaucrat must listen to "his inner check." He is personally responsible, moreover, for any policies he helps to implement.

Finer, who claimed that his objections were "extremely elementary," insisted that the question was still the following: "Are the servants of the public to decide their own course, or is their course of action to be decided by a body outside themselves?" For him the answer was self-evident. Bureaucrats "are not to decide their own course; they are to be responsible to elected representatives of the public, and these are to determine the course of action of the public servants to the most minute degree that is technically feasible." Finer rejected Friedrich's reliance on the "inner check" as a guarantee against unethical decisions: it was an unreliable method, and furthermore, it was connected, *pace* Friedrich, with precisely the dictatorships and the slave morality prevailing there. In a democracy, accountability is not a moral but an institutional question: the constitution lays down that X is accountable to Y. The charge of bureaucrats in a democracy is not to work for the public good in the sense of what the public needs, but rather in the sense of what the public wants (as expressed by the public itself). Finer found it worrisome that Friedrich "feels that there is need of some elasticity in the power of the official, some discretion, some space for the 'inner check.'" Quite the contrary, it was necessary to reinforce the power of politicians to control the administration (this conclusion somewhat took on, however, the diffuse character of a pious hope): "Conceding the growing power of officials we may discover the remedy in the improvement of the quality of political parties and elections."[51]

So we cannot be certain that if we apply the model of discretion, the process of implementation will always be immaculate. There is a risk that bureaucrats will use their power to distort the intentions of politicians. The model of obedience and the majoritarian form of democracy associated with it lay a better ground for accountability. In this model, it is indisputable who has the responsibility and who is to blame, if anything goes wrong.

The British case analyzed here shows that Niskanen's theory must be reconsidered. Even in a country that conformed closely to the picture painted by Niskanen, politicians were ultimately able to bend developments in a different direction. Margaret Thatcher demonstrated that choice was possible. She was able to expand the room for political maneuvering and control by simply taking the leading explanation for the expansion of bureaucracy and turning it upside down to instead use as a guide for retrenchment. It was also the politics that her voters had asked for—in vain for many years, until Thatcher demonstrated that she could take back responsibility. It is, in the words of Finer, "extremely elementary" that politicians in a democracy be held accountable to voters. Neither as scapegoats nor as symbols of power, then, should bureaucrats come between citizens and politicians.

CHAPTER **7**

Consequences May Well Be as Intended

Unintended Consequences

Great advances in knowledge often appear obvious in retrospect. What had earlier seemed improbable or impossible—or had simply not crossed anyone's mind—suddenly becomes part of our mental world. "Yes, of course it can be done that way!" exclaims the man confronted with the solution to the Gordian knot for the first time. The unexpected becomes the routine.

This applies in an eminent degree to an observation made by Robert Merton in an article from the mid-1930s. Human actions, he declared, often do not lead to the intended results. Merton's original phrase was "unanticipated consequences," but "unintended consequences" has become the common term in the literature.[1] It is not hard to understand what is meant by this expression. In Merton's own words, the expression is "self-explanatory": it refers to an action that has consequences different from those expected. Formulated thus, it is a familiar concept in the long history of ideas. Indeed, Merton indicated that he had found inspiration in the message of medieval theology about the undesired consequences following from the inscrutable will of God. As a basis for the systematic analysis of human action, however, Merton's article was revolutionary.

To begin with, Merton made a series of observations and distinctions. Unforeseen consequences, for example, are not necessarily undesirable consequences. The result, perhaps, is not what one expected, but it may be welcome nonetheless.

In addition, Merton's focus was on "purposive action": the actor is a rational and calculating individual. Otherwise, Merton would have used the term "behavior" to describe the individual's action. Instead, this rational individual makes a conscious "choice between various alternatives."

Being rational does not mean one always gets what one wants. Even a person clearly conscious of his preferences, who informs himself thoroughly and calculates carefully—even such a person may fail to reach his goal: "[R]ationality and irrationality are not to be identified with the success and failure of action, respectively. For in a situation where the number of *possible* actions for attaining a given end is severely limited, one acts rationally by selecting the means which, on the basis of the available evidence, has the greatest probability of attaining this goal and yet the goal may actually *not* be attained."

Merton warned that individuals could fall into two methodological traps. The first has to do with the problem of causal imputation. To what degree are given consequences attributable to a certain action? To what extent, for example, is economic prosperity due to the measures taken by a certain government? The second trap concerns rationalization. If something good happens, there will be many who try to take the credit for it ex post facto. What has happened, they will claim, is exactly what they had intended.

The most obvious barrier to the correct anticipation of consequences is lack of knowledge. Merton argued strongly for a more intensive study of human nature, in order that we might better grasp the consequences of our actions. He distinguished between error and lack of knowledge; the former, he explained, involves various kinds of faulty thinking—for example, the all-too-ready assumption that actions that have led in the past to a desired outcome will continue to do so. He further warned of "the imperious immediacy of interest," whereby an actor's concern with the immediate consequences he foresees excludes any consideration of other or long-term consequences. If this concern has to do with "basic values," moreover, an individual may be programmatically set on carrying out his plans—whatever the consequences. The Protestant ethic analyzed by Weber was, for Merton, a good example of this phenomenon: an active asceticism led paradoxically to its own decline, as modest consumption and intense productive activity resulted in the accumulation of possessions and wealth.

Finally, Merton pointed to what we would now call self-fulfilling prophecies. As an example, he cited Marx's prognoses, which inspired the labor movement to adopt policies that undermined the predicted exploitation of the workers and thus prevented the collapse of the capitalist system.

The impact of Merton's article has been enormous. Indeed, identifying the unintended consequences of political action has become so common that social scientists now seem more interested in studying unintended consequences than in studying intended ones. It has become standard practice in political analysis to compare intentions and outcomes and to show that the results of various political measures are not at all what decision makers had in mind. The identification of "perverse effects" and "policy failures" has come to be a basic weapon in the methodological arsenal of political scientists. It is used both in purely theoretical studies and in widely varied practical applications—from economic policy to the organization of the fight against narcotics.[2]

In the wake of the master, highly ramified trees of classification have been worked out for the unintended consequences of social actions.[3] It is not my intention here to complicate the conceptual framework further by presenting yet another schema; it is easy for any social scientist to trace further connections between an action, the motives behind it, and effects and side effects of various kinds. I elect here to keep the question simpler, by focusing strictly on Merton's original conception—and mine—of politics as rational action. Moreover, I limit the analysis of unintended consequences to cases where the result qualifies as surprising in relation to what the acting subject had expected (and not in relation to more objective conditions that may serve to constrain freedom of action, such as are often incorporated into more general classification schemas in evaluation research). Thus, deficient information on the part of decision makers can be an explanation for why unintended consequences arise; however, a country's objective financial situation cannot be (although deficient information on the part of decision makers about the country's economy can be).

Without any pretense of originality, and on the basis of a rationalist perspective, I shall seek accordingly to explain unintended consequences as resulting from the effect of misperceptions, changed conditions, and new circumstances on the calculations of decision makers (see Figure 7.1).

One of the more spectacular examples in our time of how unintended consequences can arise from *misperceptions* on the part of decision makers is

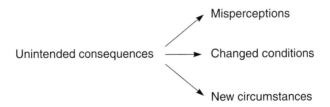

Figure 7.1. Causes of unintended consequences.

the role of Gorbachev in the fall of Communism. When the new Soviet leader started talking about renewal in the form of *glasnost* and *perestroika*, he did not expect the changes to take place against the Soviet system. He failed to appreciate how unpopular and illegitimate the regime was, and he underestimated the power of nationalism in the various Soviet republics. The fall of Communism was an unintended consequence on a grand scale.[4]

In the same way, the other superpower in the world, the United States, underestimated the power of nationalism in Southeast Asia. American participation in the Vietnam War had been based on the so-called domino theory—which claimed that if South Vietnam were to fall to Communism, a series of other countries would fall as well. Yet, that is not what happened. Vietnam did indeed become Communist, but the rest of Southeast Asia became the center of a flourishing capitalism.[5]

In addition, sometimes the initial conditions—those that prevailed when the original calculations and decisions were made—undergo change, so that the results prove to be different than intended. A curious example of *changed conditions* may be seen in the attempt to create a European army at the beginning of the 1950s. Against the background of the Cold War, the Adenauer government decided to work for rearmament, the reintroduction of conscription, and the integration of German forces with those of the West. The German Social Democrats sharply criticized this policy. They opposed rearmament and integration with the West, which they feared would make the division of Germany permanent. The struggle raged on for two years. It did not just take place in the Bundestag; it also escalated into the German Constitutional Court. It even gave rise, at the initiative of the government, to an intervention on the part of the president. The political maneuvering and juridical quibbling proved to be, however, a waste of effort. To Adenauer's surprise, the French National Assembly refused in the end to back the treaty for a European army. Unforeseen changes in the conditions facing West German decision makers led to the thwarting of such plans.[6]

It need not always be the conditions that undergo change; it can also be the actual decision maker. He or she carries out another policy than the one that was promised. It can be debated, of course, whether this is really a question of "changed conditions." Is it not, in such a case, a question of new preferences instead, such that the consequences that ensue are not necessarily unintended—seen in relation, that is, to these new preferences? This need not always be the case, however. It need not be a question of a change in values; it may instead be that the exercise of power yields new insights.

After all, taking power is one thing; exercising it is another. In the election campaign of 1981, for example, the French Socialists promised a new and less highbrow policy in the area of culture; upon assuming power, however, they started carrying out a policy as monumental as that of any earlier regime. (Indeed, it may even be they ended up exceeding their predecessors—in precisely the area for which they had criticized them.) A comparable change took place in Sweden in 1976, when the bourgeois parties took power after forty-four years of Social Democratic rule. They had campaigned on a free-market program; upon assuming office, however, they undertook even larger expenditures in the area of industrial and unemployment policy than had the Social Democrats. Both the French Socialists and the Swedish Non-Socialists sought recognition as fit parties of government—and that meant, in accordance with the political culture of each country, creating monuments and full employment, respectively. "When in power, do as powers do."[7]

Finally, plans can come to naught because *new circumstances* appear. Here, in contrast to the previous case, it is not a change in established conditions that upsets calculations, but rather something new altogether. Natural disasters are a good example. AIDS was an unforeseen epidemic that has struck tens of millions and made orphans of as many. Every year, half a million HIV-positive children are born, and the majority do not survive to their fifth birthday. In Zimbabwe, 1,500 people die of AIDS each day. In thirty-five of the worst-struck countries of Africa, the average life expectancy has sunk to forty-six years, and it continues to fall. In 1998, Hurricane Mitch brought mass death and material devastation to the people of Central America: 20,000 people died and 3 million were made homeless. A third of the plantations and farms in Honduras and Nicaragua were laid to waste. In Guatemala and southern Mexico, too, cloudbursts and landslides brought about great destruction. This does not mean, of course, that politicians do not also have a responsibility to prepare for disasters—even if there are disasters that no one can be reasonably expected to foresee.

The close connection between the theory of unintended consequences and the politics of blame avoidance is easy to see. "This is not what we had in mind," say the politicians, when they sees that the results are unhappy. In many cases, that is doubtless true. The inability to foresee the consequences of different courses of action is probably a better explanation for bad decisions than is the idea that politicians possess the conscious will not to live up to their promises.[8] The question, however, is whether well-meaning ineptitude is an acceptable excuse. The idea of politics as rational action implies a moral duty on the part of politicians to truly exert themselves to acquire knowledge of the probable effects and side effects of a certain decision. Or, as the Weberian paradigm discussed in Chapter 5 would have it, responsible politics means making informed choices between various alternatives.[9] In the third section of this chapter, we shall as usual go a little deeper into the nature of this constraint for the actors. How should a responsible politician act in order to better foresee the likely consequences of different alternatives?

The Gent System

A counterexample to the theory of unintended consequences would logically involve presenting a case in which the policy conducted actually led to the expected result. Such a study easily risks becoming trivial: "it ended up that way because those who decided wanted it that way." But it is not just a desire to avoid banalities that recommends a different approach. If scholars would like to identify situations in which intentions will likely go awry, they should search for cases in which politicians are not just pushing for their own viewpoint on a particular issue, but pursuing an ulterior objective as well. Politicians do not just wish to see their viewpoint on the immediate issue prevail. Politics is also about seeking to strategically strengthen one's own power position. Such a double goal is, quite naturally, especially difficult to reach. Such intentions are especially hard to fulfill. If politicians can succeed in such more challenging undertakings, the theory of unintended consequences may not be so devastating for the assumption of politics as rational action. Are there any good examples of a politician who has successfully used an issue in this way—not only to realize his short-term preference but also to strengthen his long-term standing?

One example—as remarkable as it is contested—may be seen in President Reagan's defense policy and its importance for the end of the Cold War. Reagan's champions have argued that it was the former that caused the latter. The need to strengthen U.S. defense was the justification adduced for the rearmament started under Reagan. But the true motive, the claim here goes, was to draw the Soviet Union into an arms race that would break that country economically and ultimately politically as well.

Reagan was a pronounced anti-Communist; he famously referred to the Soviet Union as "the evil empire." It was not difficult at the beginning of the

1980s to perceive the latter country as pursuing highly aggressive goals on the world stage as well as having an extremely strong military—perhaps stronger, in fact, than that of the United States.

The balance of terror, however, was something that Reagan repudiated—for moral reasons—as a tool of foreign policy. It was as if, he said, two persons were each aiming a loaded pistol at the other's head. Instead, he launched the Strategic Defense Initiative (SDI, known popularly as Star Wars). The United States would surround itself with a shield against the nuclear weapons of adversaries. But was it really possible to build such a shield? The experts were doubtful. It was extraordinarily difficult, technically speaking, to achieve the precision needed to shoot down missiles, and it was also hugely expensive. The president persevered, however, and technical efforts were intensified. And how did things really stand on the economic side of the equation? It could be considered an advantage, after all, if a new arms race were to lead to the economic impoverishment of the Soviet Union. Indeed, is that not precisely what happened? "By engaging Moscow in a prohibitively expensive arms race, and by staging, in 1984, a fake 'disinformation' test of the SDI system to fool the Soviets, the United States forced the Soviet Union into a competition, which exhausted their economic capacity and compelled them to jettison their objective of increasing their influence throughout the globe."[10] In this interpretation, rearmament in itself was not the motive for President Reagan's policy. The long-term goal, which he pursued with impressive foresight, was to bring about the fall of the Soviet Union: "The Soviet Union collapsed under the weight of its efforts to keep up."[11]

The administration was split on how to frame this policy more precisely. It was not the case that there was a division just between political rearmers and technical and economic skeptics. There were also two different groupings among the political advisors: the soft-liners led by Secretary of State Shultz, who certainly championed a strong defense but who also urged a dialogue with the Russians; and the hard-liners, with Secretary of Defense Weinberger at their head, who advised against early contacts with the Soviet Union. Weinberger placed great emphasis on the need to "negotiate from strength." Negotiations ought not to be undertaken too early, before the United States had achieved a better negotiating position through military superiority. Otherwise, the United States would be forced to make excessive concessions. It is difficult to place Reagan squarely in any of these camps. But one thing is clear: at no point did he let up on SDI. The idea was his personal pet project, in which he persisted in the face of all objections. And, it might be added, it is a project that President George W. Bush then took up again, at the beginning of the new century.

Those who question this account of the causes for the Soviet Union's fall have often cited the time factor as their first objection. When the purpose is to explain something, after all, the causes adduced for that something must precede it in time. And in fact, the United States started negotiating with the Soviets at an early stage, and a turning point had already been reached before Gorbachev came to power. Nor did the United States persist in an unyielding attitude all the way up until the Soviets collapsed.[12] The question, however, is how tenable this objection really is. In political terms, a rapprochement undeniably took place. But given that work on the costly SDI project continued, the president's hidden agenda may well have continued to be the long-term economic outstripping of the Soviet Union—a strategy all the more consummate in that the coup de grâce was administered in an atmosphere of friendliness and negotiation.

The great risks attending such a policy have also been cited as an objection. But this is more an objection to the substance of the president's policy than to the extravagant interpretation put forth to keep secret his other motives. The risks associated with nuclear weapons were indeed great, and President Reagan was in the highest degree aware of them. Certain experiences early in his presidency, in fact, had made him fully realize what a dangerous game the threat of nuclear weapons represented. For example, after North Atlantic Treaty Organization military exercises in the autumn of 1983, it had come to the president's attention that the Soviets had seriously believed that the United States and its allies were preparing an attack on the Soviet Union. The president was deeply affected by the realization that one of the superpowers might start a nuclear war because of misunderstanding. The shooting down of a Korean airliner that the Russians suspected of being an American spy plane, with 269 dead as a consequence, showed how easily disastrous military mistakes could be made. The president was also affected, as indeed American opinion was generally, by "The Day After," a film dramatizing the effects of a nuclear war.[13]

Rearmament and nuclear weapons literally involve playing with death—for all humanity. SDI, therefore, can be easily thought of as irresponsible. Far from providing the United States with a shield against attack, a spiraling arms race between the superpowers could lead to reduced security in both countries.[14] But was that not what was so unacceptable about the balance of terror and had prompted Reagan to start thinking along different lines? Pre-cisely because a war could begin by mistake, it was critical to erect a shield against the nuclear missiles of the enemy. At any rate, this is one defense that can be made for the portrayal of Reagan as a long-term strategist.

Another objection is that although Reagan was certainly highly anti-Communist in ideological terms, he shifted position constantly in his choice of tactical methods. He had no master plan; rather, he worked intuitively and spontaneously. In the debate between hard-liners and soft-liners, he leaned at times to the one side, at times to the other. He was influenced ex-tremely easily: "Perhaps in part because of his aversion to confrontation and his general tentativeness on issues where his ideological impulses were con-flicted or inapplicable, Reagan was allegedly vulnerable to being persuaded by the last adviser to have spoken with him alone before he made a major decision."[15]

Or put differently, the picture of a man driven by a bold, thought-out, unshakeable, and long-term plan for the destruction of the Soviet Union is something that does not fit with Reagan's personality. Reagan "was not a Machiavellian or even a Kissingerian figure seeking to manipulate the in-ternational environment through his pronouncements."[16]

No, when Reagan's colleagues and defenders credit him with having van-quished world Communism and ending the Cold War, they "fall victim to the propensity of exaggerating their own effect on the other's behavior . . . [T]heir simplistic interpretations are based more on speculation and ide-ology than on concrete evidence." The primary reasons for the fall of the Soviet Union were domestic in character: the economic crisis; the change in leadership, with Gorbachev as the successor to three old leaders (Brezhnev, Andropov, Chernenko) who had rapidly succeeded each other; and the misjudgments that Gorbachev subsequently made.[17]

But the question is whether this criticism is not just as ideological (albeit in the opposite way) and speculative (with conclusions based, for example, on impressions of Reagan's personality) as the thesis that Reagan was a long-term strategist. If one prefers a safe conclusion, it could simply be said that the Cold War ended in a way that well accorded with Reagan's anti-Communist values and that the heavier defense burden in the Soviet Union likely contributed at the margins to the country's collapse. But given that positive evidence is lacking for the proposition that Reagan in fact reasoned in the sophisticated manner that his champions claim, I am forced sorrow-fully to conclude that the case of SDI cannot serve as a good counterexample to the thesis of unintended consequences. Nevertheless, the right-wing interpretation of Reagan's Star Wars project furnishes an excellent illustration of the logic of the argument that strategic considerations can be decisive for the position that a politician takes, and that the consequences hereof may well be as intended.[18]

We must therefore search for a better example, for another long-term plan with the most essential characteristic that it actually has been implemented by a politician somewhere. This is something we can know only with empirical evidence. The search takes us to an altogether different political reality—namely, the Swedish Social Democracy and unemployment insurance policy.

The breakthrough of industrialism raised the question of whether the pain of unemployment could be moderated through unemployment insurance. Two different systems emerged to address this question. Certain countries introduced an obligatory state system. In others, a voluntary system emerged (although public financing was central here, too): this was known as the Gent System, after the Belgian city where the system was first introduced at the turn of the nineteenth century. In general, the state system was advocated by Social Democratic parties, and the voluntary system was favored by bourgeois parties—a pattern well in line with the former's proclivity toward state intervention and the latter's fear of state power and faith in individual responsibility. In Sweden, however, the opposite pattern prevailed. The Social Democrats there took the view early on that the state ought to subsidize the voluntary funds. It took quite awhile before Sweden got its system of unemployment insurance. Rather, the method for dealing with unemployment was the "work line": instead of insurance, the unemployed would be given jobs on public works. In the view of the Social Democrats and the Liberals, however, these public-works jobs were inadequate. The two parties therefore urged that provisions for the unemployed be improved. The only problem was assembling, under the parliamentary conditions then prevailing, the requisite majority for one particular proposal. Various compromises between the two systems were volleyed back and forth between the Social Democrats and Liberals, without success. Not even when the Social Democrats formed a government of their own were they able to present a bill to parliament, as the Conservative leader had noted sarcastically.[19] Why did the Swedish Social Democrats oppose an obligatory system of state unemployment insurance, which was regarded as the natural goal for socialists elsewhere? This will be our critical case in this chapter.

The long-time inability of the Social Democrats to solve the unemployment insurance issue was a manifestation of a more fundamental ideological dilemma faced by the Social Democrats in the 1920s. They were caught in a contradiction between "the long and the short view." According to the long-term Marxist view, capitalism was proceeding to its fated ruin. The more that capitalists squeezed wages, the more meager was the purchasing power of the workers, and the greater the consequent difficulty encountered by companies in selling their wares. This in turn would lead to higher unemployment and to yet lower purchasing power, and so on and on until the entire system collapsed in a massive crisis—at which point the workers would take power and socialize the means of production. In the short run, however, the task of Social Democracy was to alleviate the conditions of the workers, through social policy, for example, and through measures for fighting unemployment. According to the long view, in other words, there was nothing to be done but to "wait with arms folded for the revolution." According to the short view, however, the task was to intervene with reforms. However, if the government pumped up purchasing power, it would be undermining the preconditions for the fulfillment of the Marxian prognosis. The more successful the reforms are in the short-term, the more effectively do they work against the long-term victory of socialism. Keynesianism, which gained an early champion in Ernst Wigforss, economic spokesman for the Social Democrats, offered a way out of this bind. It proposed a method for strengthening the role of the state in the economy now—without nationalization and without any crisis for capitalism. Such was the Social Democratic program for expansion of the welfare state. With this new economic policy, the Social Democrats won the election of 1932. The unemployment insurance issue was a part of this program.[20]

In a brochure from 1926 entitled *Arbetslöshetsförsäkringen* (Unemployment Insurance), Gustav Möller—the party spokesman on these issues and also the influential party secretary and self-evident candidate for minister of health and social affairs—discussed the two alternatives in question: obligatory insurance and voluntary insurance. Undeniably, Möller conceded, the former had certain "advantages [which are] not to be despised." First and foremost, an obligatory system would ensure that virtually everyone threatened by unemployment was protected. There were many groups in

Sweden, after all, who could not themselves be expected to take the initiative for voluntary insurance: small farmers, older workers, the young, the less able-bodied, and certain groups of unskilled laborers. Möller also liked the fact that under an obligatory system, it would be possible to collect fees from employers. In addition, the voluntary system provoked "a highly emotional resistance" in some quarters, because it involved giving public subsidies to funds administered by the trade unions. Did not a voluntary system therefore involve, in fact, state support of the trade-union movement that was supposed to administer the insurance? Möller pretended that the question had to do with a purported misuse of public monies in connection with industrial disputes and responded with feigned indignation: "It is a matter of course that unemployment funds and strike funds are not to be mixed." But was it not the case all the same—as the bourgeois parties contended— that the granting of public subsidies to unemployment funds administered by the unions entailed state support for the trade-union movement? If so, Möller replied scholastically, one could as well say that such subsidies involved providing state support to employers like "tailors and shoemakers, among whom the member of the unemployment fund customarily makes his purchases, since his capacity to increase his purchases of various kinds also increases if his premiums to the unemployment fund are reduced."

It is easy, when reading Möller, to get the impression that he found the arguments for an obligatory system to be persuasive: it is "the most rational solution," he wrote. In a couple of abrupt sentences, however, he rejected such a system all the same. The costs would be too high, he opined, and the administration too heavy and expensive.[21] A Conservative could not have said it better.[22]

Möller's justification for the party line was similar in quality to one he had made in the 1920s, when, under the burden of the Social Democrats' ideological dilemma, he had been forced to defend an unemployment policy that was different from what he actually preferred. However, as the Swedish political scientist Bo Rothstein has shown, Möller had another reason for preferring the Gent system.[23] The two fundamental questions in the administration of unemployment insurance are to determine which part of the nonworking population is entitled to support and what qualifies as an "appropriate job" to which an unemployed person can be referred. First, the portion of the population that cannot be reasonably said to stand at the disposal of the labor market must be identified. Second, it bears noting that an unemployed person is not without a job "in general"; rather, he lacks an "appropriate job"—that is, a job for which he is trained or otherwise suitable. It lies in the interest of both society and the individual that he not be referred to such employment as may destroy his skills within his ordinary profession. Both of these delineations involve delicate questions of judgment, and the person who makes them wields considerable power. Gustav Möller wished to ensure that this power lay in the hands of the trade unions. And the power of the unions, in this context and at this time, was the same as the power of Social Democracy. Möller expressed himself here in a rather unvarnished fashion. That the Gent system "drives people into the trade unions" was not something one needed to "sweep under the rug."[24] Unemployment benefits should not be paid out "independently of the workers' own interest in the formation of unemployment funds." It was right and proper that the state not be neutral here—that it limit its support to "workers who show, by their membership in [a union-administered] insurance fund, their concern for themselves and their relatives."[25]

One year after the electoral victory in 1932, the Social Democrats reached an agreement with the Farmers' League and some of the Liberals, thus solving, among other things, the question of unemployment insurance at last. The Social Democrats were able to push through the principles of the Gent System, in return for which they made a number of concessions: levels of compensation would be low, and there would be public control over the unemployment funds.

The reason for the Swedish Social Democrats to oppose a state system and favor a voluntary system, then, was strategic: the long-term consequences of such a policy would be to strengthen the position of the unions and the party. This strategy was to prove exceptionally successful. Unemployment insurance did indeed drive people into the trade unions. The unionization rate in Sweden became the highest the world; collaboration between "the two branches of the labor movement"—trade unions and the party—became very intimate; and starting in the early 1930s, the Swedish Social Democrats were to rule without interruption for forty-four years.

The association between the Gent system and the strength of the unions constitutes an international pattern. As can be seen in Table 7.1, countries that apply the Gent system have a substantially higher unionization rate than do countries that do not. Rothstein demonstrates, moreover, that this conclusion holds even when two other variables often used in this research are taken into account: (1) the size of the labor force and (2) the extent of participation by labor parties in government since 1919. The differences

Table 7.1. Rate of unionization and type of unemployment
insurance.

Country	Unionization rate (percent)	Gent system
Sweden	86	Yes
Denmark	83	Yes
Finland	80	Yes
Iceland	74	Yes
Belgium	74	Yes
Ireland	68	No
Norway	58	No
Austria	57	No
Australia	51	No
Great Britain	43	No
Canada	38	No
Italy	36	No
Switzerland	34	No
West Germany	31	No
The Netherlands	29	No
Japan	28	No
United States	18	No
France	15	No

Source: Bo Rothstein, *Den korporativa staten* [The corporate state]
(Stockholm: Norstedts, 1992), 313. Published with permission of the author.

among Nordic countries here are interesting to note. These countries, so similar to each other in social, cultural, and historical respects, diverge when it comes to their rate of unionization: Norway is substantially less unionized, and it is also the only Nordic country with an obligatory system of unemployment insurance.

As Rothstein concedes, however, the direction of causality cannot be necessarily inferred from the statistical analysis: "It could as well be that a labour movement which was relatively strong from the beginning introduced the Gent system (in order to increase its strength further), rather than vice-versa. The question is what came first: administrative corporatism or labour-movement strength."[26] Rothstein seeks the answer in a reconstruction of the strategic calculations of Gustav Möller. He is able to show, in fact, that the actions of the Social Democratic party secretary were an instance of utterly purposive social action. It was not just an important policy decision that the Swedish Parliament made in 1934. It was also a "conscious and successful design of political institutions" that took place.[27] The consequences arising from the introduction of a Gent system in Sweden proved to be exactly what the actor intended.

Accountability and Expertise

To put the point simply, sometimes politicians get what they want; sometimes they do not. No other conclusion can be upheld as a general statement. It does indeed happen, as we saw in the case of the Swedish Social Democrats and their plans for unemployment insurance, that matters proceed as planned. That things usually go wrong, on the other hand, has become something of a political scientist's prejudice, favored by those who find the cynical entertaining. It is against them that I champion the thesis summarized in the title of this chapter. In addition, a more positive view of the possibilities of politics yields a stricter moral demand on political leaders that they take responsibility for their decisions. In the spirit of Merton and Weber, I would call attention to the task of the politicians to acquire for themselves the best possible knowledge as a basis for making a decision, before proceeding. Politics is not just a question of willing and choosing. Leaders also have a duty to think through alternative solutions to the problems they face, and to analyze—free of preconceptions—the consequences of different courses of action.

As for where such expertise might be available, the university is one of the first places that springs to mind. In this respect, there is a marked likeness between the state university and the state administration, and it is no accident that Max Weber is the foremost ideologue both of the duty of the state administration to obey the politicians and of a state university to stay independent of them. Entire libraries have been written on the problem of academic freedom, but to summarize the question in as few words as possible, the following may be said.[28] While the state administration takes its charge from the government, even a state university is responsible for its own program. In making economic appropriations, politicians determine the areas in which the research of a state university is conducted, but the choice of theory, method, and publication form is a scholarly privilege.

In practice, however, there is a constant tug-of-war on how to apply this principle. Politicians are often tempted to meddle in the question of what qualifies as good research or even in decisions about what kind of research may be undertaken in the universities they finance. Nor is it unusual for politicians to sit on the research councils responsible for allocating monies. Aside from the feeling of power that draws politicians to such assignments—not a small matter in a time when the role of universities in the development of society has become so important—it would appear that the conflict turns on the question of which form of organization actually is best suited to achieving this goal. An overwhelming majority among scholars also want research to lead to an improvement in the human condition; only an extreme minority take the view that research is not to be of service.[29] According to the classic view deriving from Weber, research that is free is also research of the greatest service to society. Just as in the market economy, the freedom of individuals to pursue their own plans is thought also to work to the maximal benefit of the system as a whole, whereas by contrast, politically directed research runs the risk of identifying the wrong problem, the wrong theory, and the wrong method. Research monies, the claim goes, have been wasted in great quantities because funding, for political reasons, has been funneled in a direction that is not intellectually fruitful. According to the opposite standpoint, it is precisely free research and the self-governing university that serve to delay progress, by ensuring that a proper basis is not provided for the decisions that stand on the political agenda. For this reason, the old type of organization—with free-standing universities and independent faculties—should be scrapped in favor of politically governed organs.[30]

So may the debate on research policy be summarized. What guidance, then, does this give a politician who is trying to stake out a position on a political issue—like defense policy and its implications for the projected enemy, or unemployment policy and its consequences for the recruitment of members to his party? My answer is that this debate is of little help to a politician seeking guidance on a concrete question. The debate on research policy concerns the outer, bureaucratic form through which research is organized. Much less has been written on the inner, intellectual relationship between knowledge and action in connection with particular questions. One scholar who has taken up this question in a most interesting way is Alexander George, in a brief book with the admonishing title *Bridging the Gap*.

The "gap" to which George refers is between politicians and academic scholars, within the area of foreign policy. With their differing qualifications and interests, these two important groups often end up dealing with the same problems—without, however, granting to the other the benefit of their own experience. With better communication, this gap could be bridged, although never eliminated, and the efforts of both groups would be enhanced. George is keen to emphasize the mutual benefits here. It is not just that politicians would be surer in their aim if they made more use of the findings of scholars; it is also that researchers on foreign policy would produce higher quality work if they concerned themselves more closely with the problems faced by politicians.

There are three things, according to George, that makers of foreign policy can learn from researchers: (1) the conceptualization of strategies, that is, "a conceptual framework for each of the many different strategies and instruments available to them for attempting to influence other states"; (2) general or generic knowledge "of each strategy, based on study of past experience that identifies the uses and limitations of each strategy and the conditions on which its effective employment depends"; and (3) actor-specific behavioral models for "a sophisticated, insightful understanding of each of the state-actors with whom they interact." However, politician opposition to the use of such concepts is considerable. George has found that "the eyes of the practitioners often glaze over at the first mention of the word 'theory' in conversation."

Academia and policymaking constitute, in fact, two sharply different cultures—each with its own distinct way of thinking. Even so, the prospects for bridging the gap ought to be good, inasmuch as those who make foreign policy have often been exposed in the course of their education to the academic view of the world; moreover, substantial exchange between politicians and scholars takes place through expert commissions and seminars. Nevertheless, the prejudices held by each group about the other are considerable. Politicians tend to think, for example, that researchers do not understand how policy is actually made, that they overintellectualize policymaking, that they work on too high a level of abstraction, and that they write mainly for each other. In addition, the effort to put foreign policy on a scientific basis is misguided. The quantitative studies commonly undertaken are furthermore often of little help—as when they claim, for example, to be able to account for 75 percent of the variance in the outcome of a particular phenomenon, but without telling, of course, whether an actual case falls into that group or is instead found among the 25 percent not accounted for. Studies of this kind also frequently neglect domestic political and decision-making variables. Academics, furthermore, are chiefly interested in raising the general level of knowledge, whereas politicians are more interested in knowledge that increases their ability to influence and control events. Politicians also often find psychological studies to be unusable, because they are carried out under carefully controlled laboratory conditions of dubious applicability to real-world situations. George concludes that politicians take the view that it is not possible to generalize from one historical crisis to another. Indeed, such an effort can be downright dangerous, "for it can lead us to believe we have an understanding of events and a control over their flow which we do not have."

In the same way, academics have their objections to the policymaking world. Policymakers, in their view, are aconceptual and atheoretical. They proceed too narrowly on the basis of the ruling paradigm and pay scant attention to academic criticisms of this paradigm. They also have small chance of replenishing or updating their knowledge (which is another side of the same thing). They fail to appreciate that intuitive judgment does not suffice to conduct a foreign policy capable of achieving its objectives. They seek answers to questions that are much too sweeping and unspecified. ("If appeasement, then World War III," for example, is the wrong way to reason. One should rather ask, "Under what conditions is appeasement counterproductive and serves to increase the likelihood of war?") Policymakers tend to rely carelessly on—and often to misuse—a single historical precedent or analogy. They are unconscious of their subjective values. They take positions, finally, more on the basis of ideological and tactical judgments than on the basis of objective analysis.

These differences are reinforced by divergent socialization experiences. Politicians work in groups and make decisions collectively. When such cooperation breaks down, the policy process is then driven by the dynamics of bureaucratic politics. Academia, by contrast, is less conducive to participation in group work. Scholars "seek the truth" individually; they do not play in a group game. "It is not surprising that academics who enter government often find that with the individualistic professional style into which they have been socialized they encounter difficulties in the world of policymaking."

To bridge the gap between the two cultures, George presents what he considers to be a more realistic conception of the role of knowledge in poli-

cymaking. Academics should endeavor to conduct more policy-relevant research. Knowledge, he writes—doubtless with his academic colleagues in
mind—is not all. Political decision making involves trade-offs. On the one
hand, there is a need for high-quality decisions, and these in turn are facilitated if a widespread consensus is sought. On the other hand, time and
other policymaking resources are limited and so must be managed pru-
dently. Little is gained, Weber taught us, by a unique understanding of the
truth if one enjoys no support in the critical decision-making body. If one
spends a great deal of time trying to make a policy decision of superior
quality, the right moment for the decision may pass by. Scholars must understand that politicians have a great many more issues to consider than
just the merits of the case.

The larger part of George's book is devoted to a case study, entitled "The
Inadequate Knowledge Base for U.S. Policy toward Iraq, 1988–91." The
course of events George describes is much an unhappy one. A U.S. victory
over the enemy did indeed take place; however, the responsible policymakers did not really know how to conclude the war, and they failed to
achieve their coveted goal of removing Saddam Hussein. It would take us
too far afield to examine in detail George's scathing criticism of this policy.
Suffice it to say that he distinguishes six different strategies employed by the
United States, of which five failed and one had a mixed outcome. The war
taught us much about what not to do when making use of such instruments
as the resocialization of outlaw states and rogue leaders, appeasement, reas-
surance, war termination, deterrence, and coercive diplomacy.

But how then should a politician act, in order to improve his chances of
reaching his goals? For one thing, he must take a more realistic attitude
toward the value he can derive from research (just as the researcher must
take a more realistic view of the political process). Thus, George's major
point—to which he returns constantly—is that research is more useful for
diagnosis than for prescription. Nor can research ever replace politics:
"[K]nowledge . . . can be only an input to, not a substitute for, the policy
analysis of a specific problem." Other elements besides knowledge affect, as
mentioned, the decision of what action to undertake; before the decision is
made, however, as much knowledge should be gathered as possible. The attribute in this exhortation is important: of the objections that academics
have to politicians, paradigmatic one-sidedness would seem to be the most
serious. The challenge for all people is to be conscious of their prejudices
and to master them, so that they can see reality with as open eyes as pos-

sible. In George's specialty of foreign policy, above all else it is the academically dominant neorealist school, with its ideological conceptions like "national interest," that has encouraged policymakers to perceive the world selectively. Gathering information is, of course, important in itself, and the weak intelligence available on Iraq during the 1988–91 period certainly contributed to the failure of the policy. More important yet, however, is the fact that the information was placed within a mistaken conceptual framework. Policymakers must not be deterred by the academic predilection for parsimony and a high level of abstraction (something that George urges scholars to tone down, in fact). "A rich theory—which I define as one that encompasses a relatively large number of the variables that can influence the outcome of a policy—is often more useful in policymaking than a simpler theory of narrow scope." If they are to get a firmer grip on the consequences of their decisions, politicians must be prepared constantly to reconsider their general theoretical assumptions, which often serve to mislead them. Scholars, for their part, can assist policymakers in this respect by meeting them halfway. "[T]op policymakers often operate with inadequate conceptual and generic knowledge of [the] strategies they employ . . . The development of better conceptual generic knowledge of strategies is likely to proceed more expeditiously if undertaken by academic scholars who are interested in developing policy-relevant knowledge."[31]

The argument of this chapter can thus be summarized in the following way; Purposive political action sometimes leads to unintended consequences—but not as regularly as the books on methodology often imply. Some actors succeed in formulating policies that lead in fact to the realization of their long-term goals. Ronald Reagan may have been such a politician; Gustav Möller certainly was. To test the theory, I have chosen cases in which it was obvious that the politicians' basic motivation was of a strategic kind. I have done this in order to give the best possible odds to the theory in question. After all, the chance that intentions will go awry is especially high if, in addition to their immediate policy goals, politicians are attempting to advance their strategic ambitions. In fact, our counterexample shows that it is possible for a politician to succeed also in this more difficult and far-reaching undertaking. However, these ambitions are seldom shared by a broader public. Even if Möller was surprisingly outspoken, it is in the nature of things that strategies normally are kept secret.

When unintended consequences arise, the question is how much politicians can be held accountable. That they cannot be when wholly new circumstances appear—for example, epidemic catastrophes such as AIDS and natural disasters such as Hurricane Mitch—would seem to be something on which most can agree. Changed conditions, too, can absolve politicians of responsibility. By contrast, it is less clear that politicians can escape blame with the plea that they misunderstood the situation and the context. A more energetic and unbiased search for information, together with a willingness to engage available expertise—such as that found in the academy— can provide politicians with a better basis for making decisions. Rational politicians must raise their sights above the routines into which they are drawn, and which prevent them from seeing any alternative. The goal should be that a counterfactual, choice-seeking policy analysis precedes any decision about what action to undertake. Unintended consequences often arise because a situation is affected by factors overlooked by the conventional wisdom. A more theoretical and broad-minded analysis can help to disclose such factors. Voters have a right to demand that politicians be knowledgeable and well-informed—and not just about details, but also about attitudes and expectations among different groups both at home and abroad. We do not accept the excuse that the mistakes of politicians were a matter of oversight—not in cases in which expertise was available and could have been consulted.

CHAPTER **8**

Action Can Be Meaningful
Even if Irrational

The Logic of Rational Action: The Roots

In this chapter, I shall break with the main thrust of this book and discuss a situation in which the idea of politics as rational action does *not* fit. Up until now, I have analyzed a number of cases in which political leaders, thanks to their imagination and ingenuity as well as their political will, have been able to find a way to intervene in the course of events and distinguish a choice in regard to prevailing trends and patterns. Their actions have made a difference. Here I will deal with the opposite situation, in which the leader does *not* want to procure such freedom to choose. He will rather bind himself to the expected development, which is said to be predetermined and even synonymous with Fate or History.

First, however, I should say a few words about the roots of the assumption of politics as rational action, and then, as usual, I will follow with a counterexample of the leader who says he has no choice.

Rational choice theory, in the words of Kaare Strøm, is "the most ambitious research program in political science" today.[1] In this tradition, rationality is understood as choosing the alternative that, after comparison, stands out as the one that leads to the greatest possible satisfaction of one's preferences. There is no intrinsic value associated with any of the alternatives. Consequences are decisive. The alternative that results in the highest possible utility for the actor is the one that should be chosen. The fruitfulness of this approach has been brilliantly demonstrated over the last half-century by such scholars as Arrow, Axelrod, Barry, Buchanan, Davidson, Downs, Elster, Hardin, Ostrom, Rapoport, Riker, Sen, and many others.[2] Yet nothing under the sun is new. Behind these theorists, we glimpse their predecessors: for example, behind Arrow we espy the shadow of Condorcet;

160

behind Buchanan, that of Hobbes. And the origin of the rationalist theory can be traced even further back in time. Hobbes, for example, was anticipated in much by Epicurus, who led the revolt during antiquity against Platonic idealism. In the search for the right form of government, Epicurus argued, it is better to fasten on the desires of individual persons, rather than to engage in endless speculation about the nature of the just state. The strongest human desire is to achieve security and peace of mind. It is on this we ought to fasten and then search for such means as might accomplish this end. Politics, to use the expression later made famous by Hobbes, is naught but "a war of all against all." This must be avoided at all costs. The pleasure of the individual ought to form the basis for political theory. And the happy message of Epicurus to mankind was that individuals who act rationally do in fact have certain opportunities to achieve such ends.[3]

This individualist doctrine of pleasure was then criticized by the church father Augustine, who set forth a historicist philosophy in its stead. According to Augustine, history proceeded along its fated course, irrespective of the hopes of men, and it would issue in the victory of the Kingdom of God. The right form of government could be ascertained by deciphering the irrevocable will of God. The actor-focused doctrine of individualists like Epicurus, Machiavelli, and Hobbes therefore came across as a blasphemy. The church's condemnation of the Florentine master did not reflect so much the unscrupulous "prince morality" he championed as the idea that Machiavelli put forth that man could be his own master. Man was said to be capable—through his *virtú*, his capacity both to adapt and to exert influence—of shaping his world according to his own inclinations and preferences, and without regard to the word of God. Machiavelli insisted "that the achievement of great things is never the outcome merely of good Fortune; it is always the product of Fortune combined with the indispensable quality of *virtú*, the quality that enables us to endure our misfortunes with equanimity and at the same time attracts the goddess's favourable attentions."[4] It may be an exaggeration, Isaiah Berlin writes, to say that Machiavelli explicitly defined politics as a pluralism of values "between which conscious choices must be made. But this follows from the contrasts he draws between the conduct he admires and that which he condemns." Different men pursue different ends. "To make it possible for them to do so, governments are needed, for there is no hidden hand which brings all these human activities into natural harmony." Man must himself identify his goals and then "choose rationally between them."[5]

Hobbes drew far-reaching conclusions from the individualistic doctrine. How does the world look if all attend only to their self-interest? The answer was that men act as wolves toward each other. To protect the individual from being destroyed in the war of all against all (or in the civil war that formed the political backdrop to Hobbes's philosophy), the state was established—the mighty, absolutist state. Rational choice, in other words, was no easy task for Hobbes: it was to choose between perishing in anarchy and war or suffering oppression by Leviathan, the fire-breathing crocodile symbolizing the state. But because Hobbes, like Epicurus, preferred security to liberty, the choice he made was for Leviathan. The paradox of Hobbes, then, is that although he based his reasoning strictly in the preferences of individual citizens, he logically proceeded, step by step, to a defense for despotism. Citizens find themselves in an iterated Prisoner's Dilemma, which ultimately prompts them to accept Leviathan in order to uphold the common good.[6]

The philosophers of the Enlightenment—with original thinkers like Condorcet, Borda, and Rousseau—developed this rationalist approach further and even had the intellectual strength to point out the weaknesses in the theory they espoused. They elucidated the practical problems of democratic decision making with a keenness that would first be exceeded 200 years later.[7] The late eighteenth century—the 27 years from the publication of *Du Contrat Social* to the outbreak of the French Revolution—stands out as a golden age of political science.

Nineteenth-century utilitarianism was rational choice theory empirically applied. The opponent was again idealism, and the conservative and historicist speculation—revived after the bloodbath of revolution—was that the fate of the world was something above and beyond individuals and immune to their preferences and actions. Utilitarianism made for a practical and present-oriented politics, and it laid the basis for social-policy reform. The very name of the doctrine makes clear that it is the utility or happiness of citizens that forms the basis for political calculation and action. It is among the paradoxes of utilitarianism that in order to maximize the utility of society, it calls for sacrificing the utility of an individual. It was not for another 150 years that philosophers would settle accounts with this principle on a broad front. In the rehabilitated theory of rights associated with John Rawls, the instrumental view of people embodied in utilitarianism is rejected. Yet it is indicative of the status of rational choice theory in our time that even a rights theorist like Rawls uses rationalist concepts and game theory to drive home his arguments.[8]

The Logic of Appropriateness: Götterdämmerung

Sometimes, however, people do not act with the consequences in mind. The calculation of utilities is not what they think politics is all about. Politics is instead supposed to follow certain routines, roles, standard-operating procedures, or norms of practical or ideological character; these norms prescribe, with varying degrees of forcefulness, what behavior is appropriate in different situations. The institutions are decisive, as March and Olsen emphasize, and by "institutions" they mean these norms and rules of the game, broadly understood. Against the *logic of rational action*, these two authors launch their *logic of appropriateness.* According to their garbage-can model, everything in politics is a big mess; yet, to keep chance from prevailing altogether, there are certain rules of thumb that politicians can follow in situations that they recognize.[9]

Rationality should be distinguished from meaningfulness. Contradictory beliefs and desires can be understood as meaningful, even if they are irrational.[10] Instead of carefully comparing, like his consequentialist counterpart, the outcomes resulting from the pursuit of different strategies, the deontologist determinedly pursues the purpose he has set out for himself.

As counterexample to the utility-based rationalist theory of politics, I have chosen the most extreme expression of deontology in the political thought of our time; namely, National Socialism. Hitler was determined, to the very bitter end, to follow his course regardless of the consequences. He was convinced that Germany had given him a historic role and that there was no alternative. The sharp question in this section may be formulated as follows: Why did Hitler not flee from Berlin in the spring of 1945? Were he to stay, after all, he would most certainly die. What induced him to sacrifice his life in this way?

In the spring of 1945, it was obvious to everyone in the German leadership that the Nazis would lose the war. The Allies had invaded Germany, Berlin was surrounded, and the rounds fired by the Red Army could be heard in Hitler's bunker. Hitler's closest collaborators pleaded with him to leave the capital. As late as his birthday, 20 April, when a large conference was held in the bunker, an escape route was still open to the south:

The great question before the conference concerned the imminent threat to the geographical unity of the Reich. In a few days, perhaps hours, the last land route to the south would have been cut. Would Hitler, or would he not, move his headquarters to the south, whither all the service headquarters and ministries had gone or were going? His advisers were unanimous that the Russian ring around the city would ultimately close; that once caught in it, there would be no escape; that the only alternative was to withdraw to the south, to Obersalzberg; and that such a withdrawal must be made now, while the road remained open, or perhaps never. Goering and Keitel, Himmler and Bormann, Goebbels, Krebs, and Burgdorf all entreated Hitler to leave the doomed city; but Hitler would neither agree nor disagree. The most he would do was to implement the decision reached ten days earlier against such a situation as had now arisen. Then it had been decided that if the Allied armies should cut the Reich in half, two separate commands should be set up in the two disconnected areas. In the north, Grand Admiral Doenitz, in the south Field-Marshal Kesselring should command all the German forces, unless Hitler himself chose to move his headquarters to one or other of the two theatres. Now Hitler decided to confer upon Doenitz full military powers in the north; but in regard to the south he still made no appointment.[11]

After the conference, "the visitors left the Bunker, and a long convoy of lorries and airplanes led the general exodus from Berlin to Obersalzberg." Among those to leave were the high commanders of the Luftwaffe. They left with relief: "In Obersalzberg at least they would be free from the endless insults, the impossible orders, the violent recriminations with which Hitler had recently received their every failure. 'One or two Luftwaffe officers should be shot!' he would shout at some self-exculpating general; 'then we would have a change!' 'The entire Luftwaffe staff should be hanged!' he would scream down the telephone at the trembling General Koller, and bang the receiver on the hook."[12]

Hitler chose to remain in his bunker and wait for the end.[13] When he heard the next day that a desperate counterattack he had ordered was never carried out, he flew into a rage. It was all over; the Third Reich was a failure. His generals, his army—the entire German people, in fact—had let him down. He would die along with Germany. And he would never leave Berlin.

The flight of his collaborators from Berlin took the form of a veritable migration. Two of his oldest and closest comrades, Himmler and Goering, also left the capital, the latter in a lorry caravan with all the booty he had accumulated at his fabulous *Carinhall*. Renewed appeals to the *Führer* to leave as well were in vain. General Jodl protested Hitler's decision to stay and declared him derelict of duty as supreme commander: at this catastrophic time, after all, he had not taken command of the defense. Gauleiter Wegener, whom Doenitz had put in charge of civil affairs in the north, telephoned the bunker and asked whether Hitler might not sanction a surrender in the west, in order to reinforce the eastern front and thus avoid a double surrender. "He was crying for the moon. Hitler did not want to avoid devastation; devastation was just what he wanted—the more the better—to illuminate his Viking funeral."[14]

The end was near, and Hitler made his last preparations. He acceded to Eva Braun's desire to marry him. Following Nazi ritual, they swore they both were of Aryan descent and that neither bore any hereditary diseases that might constitute a hindrance to their marriage. In his last will and testament, Hitler explained his decision to remain in Berlin:

> After a six-years' war, which in spite of all setbacks will one day go down in history as the most glorious and heroic manifestation of a people's will to live, I cannot forsake the city which is the capital of this state. Since our forces are too small to withstand any longer the enemy's attack on this place, and since our own resistance will be gradually worn down by an army of blind automata, I wish to share the fate that millions of others have accepted and to remain here in the city. Further, I will not fall into the hands of an enemy who requires a new spectacle, exhibited by the Jews, to divert his hysterical masses. I have therefore decided to remain in Berlin, and there to choose death voluntarily at the moment when I believe that the residence of the Fuehrer and Chancellor can no longer be held.[15]

At four o'clock in the morning on 29 April, Hitler signed his last will and testament. A series of farewell ceremonies then took place. After lunch the next day, Hitler and Eva Braun (who now proudly called herself Frau Hitler) took their leave of more collaborators, among them Bormann, Burgdorf, and Goebbels; Frau Goebbels stayed the whole day in her room, unnerved by the approaching death of her children. After shaking hands with them, Hitler and Eva Braun withdrew to their suite. A single shot was heard. Hitler was found lying in his own blood on the sofa. He had shot himself through the mouth. Eva Braun was on the sofa too, likewise dead. A revolver lay at her side, but she had not used it. She had swallowed poison. It was half-past three.

Hitler's decision to stay in Berlin is comprehensible in the light of National Socialist ideology, which gave him no choice. Germany's greatness or its ruin—these were the only alternatives. There was no third option. Hitler had stuck to this line with great consistency ever since writing *Mein Kampf:* "The right to possess soil can become a duty if without extension of its soil a great nation seems doomed to destruction. And most especially when not some little nigger nation or other is involved, but the Germanic mother of life, which has given the present-day world its cultural picture. Germany will either be a world power or there will be no Germany."[16] Germany could never submit to the will of another state. Those who urged capitulation in order to avoid the very worst destruction pleaded in vain. The destruction in question was the Götterdämmerung foreseen in National Socialist ideology. "The voice that issued from the doomed city of Berlin in the winter of 1944 and the spring of 1945 was the authentic voice of Nazism, purged of all its accessory appeals, its noonday concessions, and welcoming once more the consequences of its original formula, World Power or Ruin."[17]

National Socialist ideology broke with the main thrust of Western political thought over the last 250 years. Instead of focusing on the preferences of citizens, it took its inspiration from an idealist and historicist vision of a future Thousand-Year Reich—tacitly understood as a future Greater Germany. Instead of trying to push through its will by outmaneuvering its opponents, National Socialism set out to annihilate its opponents (including in a physical sense). Its solution was dictatorship and one-party rule. Instead of compromising, being practical, and trying to get as much as possible, National Socialism demanded all or nothing. Thus, the heroic defeat, the idea of sacrifice, is considered almost as glorious as victory. Reason must make way for will; calculation is replaced by raw force. "The beauty of unreflected action" was an oft-repeated phrase, designed to disparage the sickly tactics of democracy.

It took a long time before the idealist reaction to the worship of reason degenerated into this ideology of violence. The roots of Nazism are found in the Sturm und Drang tradition of the French revolutionary period and its protest "against the abstractions of the Enlightenment." To Romanticism was added racialism, mysticism, and a passion for the world as portrayed in

Richard Wagner's operas.[18] "German thinking, at its best and also at its worst, represented a reaction against the bourgeois materialism of the nineteenth century; and, since the great Romantic movement had originated mostly in Germany, also a reaction against the cold and increasingly lifeless rationalism of the eighteenth. Neo-idealism was the great German contribution in the intellectual history of Europe, ranging from philosophy to physics." But Romanticism, then, was perverted step by step. "These ideas served [the Germans] well for a long time. In the end, however, German idealism degenerated into a kind of unrestrained and fanatical spiritualism, represented by Hitler. He thought that the power of that spirit was sufficient unto itself to defy most of the world, including the material power of his enemies."[19]

The Romanticists "wanted to enjoy and behold the world as a whole, not as portrayed and dissected by simplistic rationalism. Only intuition could serve as the vehicle for attaining this goal, the visualizing of the 'world picture.'" They fled from reality into an emotional and mystical ideology. Germans came "to repudiate a European heritage which was still alive elsewhere: that of the rationalism of the Enlightenment and the social radicalism of the French Revolution." With Nazism, "the crisis of German ideology" was a fact. The world view of the Nazis was beyond such values as rationalism and utility. "This irrational world view was itself objectified in the form of a new religion with its own mysticism and its own liturgical rites . . . [A]bove all, [the Nazis] exalted a Nietzschean love for action."[20]

On the one hand, then, irrationalism signifies the embrace of values other than those cherished in the Enlightenment tradition: intuition, mysticism, will, and action. On the other hand, irrationalism can also mean confusion, intellectual disorder, and a lack of systematic reasoning. Indeed, these things were also characteristic of National Socialism. Even as the spirit was regarded as dominant over the material world, thought was seen as subordinate to action. Almost any idea could therefore be utilized, as long as it served the immediate purpose. As one author puts it, "one could rightfully speak of Nazi ideology as a catch-all, a conglomeration, a hodgepodge of ideas." It displayed an "uncommitted fanaticism, without content, believing only in its own irresistible momentum." The Nazis based their actions on ideological rather than on rational considerations. The classic example of this can be seen in their policies at the end of World War II. The defeat of Germany had long been a foregone conclusion, yet the Nazis increased the deportation of Jews to the death camps: "[M]ilitary considerations should have argued against such shipments of the Jews. This clearly shows that the drive for it did not stem from rational motives, but came out of deranged ideological attitudes."[21]

Such was the legacy of ideas that the Nazis were able to exploit after German defeat in World War I. They offered the defeated nation an explanation and a promise. Bourgeois democracy was an offense against the laws of history; the Treaty of Versailles was an infamy demanding vengeance; the Jews were the cause of all evil. Germany was the land of the future, but it could regain its greatness only if it came under the rule of a great leader—one who could discern the fated path of the German people.

In remarkable detail, in fact, Hitler described what would happen if these grandiose schemes for world domination fell short of their fruit. The only alternatives, as mentioned, were "World Power or Ruin." In this tradition of thought, he found inspiration in Wagner's operas for his notions of a magnificent ruin, in which all of Germany would go up in flames with him. In a book published in 1939, Hermann Rauschning—once a highly placed Nazi in Hitler's immediate circle, then a disillusioned defector—told of a conversation he had had with the *Führer* seven years before. The topic was a disturbing one: it had to do with the possibility of a future gas and bacteriological war. The author described vividly how he was sitting together with Hitler on the veranda of Wachenfeld House, in Obersalzberg. Hitler's magnificent Alsatian sheepdog lay at his feet. "The mountains of the opposite side of the valley glowed above a pleasant meadow. It was a magical August morning of the austere, autumnal clarity which is so refreshing in the Bavarian highlands." Communicative at first, Hitler fell suddenly into a dry silence. He then declared that he would seize power shortly and lead Germany to a new destiny. In a new war, the dishonor of Versailles would never be repeated. " 'We shall not capitulate—no, never', Hitler exclaimed. 'We may be destroyed, but if we are, we shall drag a world with us—a world in flames.' He hummed a characteristic *motif* from the *Götterdämmerung*."[22] The experiences of World War I made capitulation impossible. Hitler's overarching goal was "delivering Germany from defeat": "There is no doubt that Hitler made this principle, false even then [during the First World War], his own: No voluntary retreat under any circumstances. Later he transferred this tactical principle to strategy and therewith among other things sealed the fate of the Sixth Army in Stalingrad."[23]

Hitler was as immovable as he was extreme. Once set on a course of action, he showed a "tendency to carry it to a full finish—to fashion 'a new war a hundred times more dreadful and cruel that will complete what the old one started.' "[24]

Part of the reason for Hitler's determination to let Germany go to rack and ruin with him was his reaction to the Yalta agreement on unconditional surrender. This decision was not only widely acclaimed in the United States, Great Britain, and the Soviet Union. "It also delighted Goebbels, for it gave him an opportunity to resurrect the bogey of unconditional surrender. The decision of Roosevelt, Churchill and Stalin at Yalta to dismember Germany and force her to pay crushing reparations, he argued, proved that Germany must fight with renewed vigor—or be obliterated." Hitler was satisfied with this "propaganda windfall."[25]

Germany had let him down. It had fallen short of his expectations. He thus rebuked Albert Speer for protesting his order to continue—even at this late stage—to destroy bridges, dykes, and factories and thus to undermine further the German people's chances of sustaining themselves. Hitler replied with an implacable consistency. He pointed out his deadly foe as the one who would now, through the right of the stronger, gain dominion over the world: "He summoned his quondam architect moments after reading his memorandum and said icily: 'If the war is lost, the people will be lost also. It is not necessary to worry about what the German people will need for elemental survival. On the contrary, it is best for us to destroy even these things. For the nation has proved to be the weaker, and the future belongs to the stronger Eastern nation [the Soviet Union]. In any case only those who are inferior will remain after this struggle, for the good have already been killed.' "[26]

When a social scientist chooses to explain a phenomenon with a certain theory rather than another, the principle is that the model should be adequate. Purely theoretically, of course, one could apply a rationalist approach to an irrational phenomenon and then conclude that such a model does not explain anything. A more efficient way of proceeding, however, would be to formulate a model—from the beginning—that fastens on the elements one intuitively senses are important. Hitler's decision to stay in Berlin is not a suitable candidate for rational choice analysis. Trying to reconstruct his understanding of the options in terms of rank-ordered preferences—such that he chose "victory-ruin-capitulation," whereas most people would reverse the second and third preferences and choose "victory-capitulation-ruin"—would be a parody of consequentialism. Hitler did not weigh the probable consequences of different courses of action. The "logic of appropriateness" is better suited to explaining his decision. For him, the greatness of Germany was an intrinsic value. It was not to be weighed or compared or rank-ordered; it was not to be judged by its consequences. "All or nothing" best sums up his attitude. Now that he had lost the war, he refused to accept the humiliation of being captured and put on display "like an ape in a cage at the London Zoo." History had chosen him to play out his role to the end. The National Socialist view of the world could be upheld only if the defeat took the form imagined—a violent, glorious finale.

The circumstances were imperative. For Hitler, there was no choice.

Accountability and History

According to democratic theory, as we have seen, there is no accountability if there is no choice. But for Hitler, paradoxically enough, there was an accountability of sorts—not to the voters but to History. Hitler's sense of responsibility was in fact extremely strong. To be sure, Hitler rejected parliamentary democracy; in a metaphysical sense, however, there is no doubt that the führer saw the will of the people as his guiding light.

To understand the deeper meaning of this principle, let us turn to Hitler's most important work, *Mein Kampf* (1925). He wrote therein that he had already come to hate Parliament during his youth in Vienna, because, in his view, in this "representative body . . . the Germans were always misrepresented rather than represented." But after having visited Parliament many times and having studied its political chaos and the incompetence and low morality of its members, he came to the realization that the fault lay in parliamentary democracy: "My innermost position was no longer against the misshapen form which this idea assumed in Austria; no, by now I could no longer accept the parliament as such. Up till then I had seen the misfortune of the Austrian parliament in the absence of a German majority; now I saw that its ruination lay in the whole nature and essence of the institution as such." It was the members' lack of responsibility that made him angry:

> What gave me most food for thought was the obvious absence of any responsibility in a single person. The parliament arrives at some decision whose consequences may be ever so ruinous—nobody bears any responsibility for this, no one can be taken to account. For can it be called an acceptance of responsibility if, after an unparalleled catastrophe, the guilty government resigns? Or if the coalition changes, or even if parliament itself is dissolved? Can a fluctuating majority of people ever be made responsible

in any case? Isn't the very idea of responsibility bound up with the individual? But can an individual directing a government be made practically responsible for actions whose preparation and execution must be set exclusively to the account of the will and inclination of a multitude of men? . . . Is the incapacity of a leader shown by the fact that he does not succeed in winning for a certain idea the majority of a mob thrown together by more or less savory accidents?

Two principles emerge from this quotation. As we saw in Chapter 1, "responsibility" is something different from and richer than "accountability." As Hitler saw it, democratic accountability was nothing but a flight from responsibility: the government resigns, the coalition changes, and parliament may even be dissolved. The führer had an obligation, in Hitler's view, to keep power also during times of adversity, in order to carry out his program—or to go down trying. In addition, this unshakable responsibility had to be personal. Responsibility could not be shared by many, nor could the person possessing it be held answerable to a collective (or a "momentary mob," in Hitler's words). The führer stands alone before a higher power with a responsibility he cannot foreswear.

Hitler's ideal was a personally responsible leader chosen by the people. Such an arrangement embodied "the truly Germanic democracy." The duty of the leader was to "assume all responsibility for his actions and omissions. In it there is no majority vote on individual questions, but only the decision of an individual who must answer with his fortune and his life for his choice." "[The] principle [of] absolute responsibility" should be associated with "[the principle of] absolute authority."[27]

For Hitler, too, then, the people were the only source of legitimate power. (The deposed imperial Right, by contrast, opposed universal suffrage in principle.) National Socialism took on the role of a mass movement within a democracy and claimed popular legitimacy even after it had abolished all the outward features of formal democracy. But bourgeois democracy was not true democracy. This bourgeois democracy was led by scheming talkers incapable of political action—and in a fateful moment, when Germany was suffering mass unemployment and economic crisis. In *Mein Kampf*, Hitler was altogether clear about the fact that, in the twentieth century, there was only one basis on which to build power—and that was the people. For the prosperity and greatness of the people, therefore, he set forth an action program, which he was to carry out with an appalling consistency up to the bitter end. Although the Socialists, with their international solidarity, were "traitors and enemies of the German people," they understood far better than "anxious monarchists and supporters of the Kaiser" that power would fall to those able to awaken the sleeping masses and to win their support.

Along with street violence and provocations, propaganda became the most important weapon in the political struggle. *Mein Kampf* can thus be regarded in large part as a (highly unscrupulous) manual on rhetoric. The task of the leader was to cultivate, through propaganda and indoctrination, the best side of the people. The concept of the people, as used in *Mein Kampf,* comprised three distinct classes:

> One constituted the very best and noblest of mankind, another the very worst—the criminals—and in between was the major third group or class, which was neither brilliant, heroic, nor criminal . . . Strong leadership was required to suppress that [criminal] element and to guide the middle majority. Under those circumstances democracy [in the bourgeois sense] could not function; there were no geniuses among elected officials. Only one true leader emerges in a millennium *(alle heilige Zeiten)* and true German democracy required the election of a *Fuehrer* who was totally responsible for the nation.[28]

The Nazi doctrine of the state was dictatorship. General elections did not disclose the true will of the people. Parties other than the Nazis had no function to fill and would therefore be forbidden. And, indeed, this is what happened after the Nazis took power: the National Socialist Party declared itself the "bearer of the German idea of the state, and indissolubly bound up with the state." The mere attempt to form another party or to spread (whether in speech or writing) such particulars as may aim to undermine "the German people's sense of community"—that is, the interests of the National Socialist Party—was made subject to harsh punishment. It was the führer who divined the will of the people; revealingly enough, the title of führer was originally a term for the party leader and was then transferred to the head of state.

Hitler himself, however, rejected the designation "dictator." In the aforementioned discussions with Rauschning, Hitler said that those who described him as a dictator had mixed up the concepts of "leadership" and "dictatorship." "[Hitler] would never make a decision according to his own arbitrary views. No individual could carry the great responsibility involved in such status. I [Rauschning] was under a complete misapprehension as to the meaning of 'leadership,' and made the current mistake of confounding leadership with dictatorship. 'The fact that we do not vote and carry out our policy by majority decisions does not mean that we evade all control, whether it comes from the mass of the party or from factors outside the party.'"[29] The legitimacy of his decisions, Hitler explained to Rauschning, lay in the interplay with the National Socialist Party. The will of the people was best interpreted by this means. "Hitler, the creator of a new form of democracy—that was the true *motif* of his speech. The democracy that had degenerated into parliamentarism would be rescued by National Socialism."[30]

On the basis of his historicist doctrine, Hitler foresaw the victory of the stronger, whereupon the leader's task would be to guide his people to victory. "Politics is nothing more than the struggle of a people for its existence . . . [I]t is an iron principle . . . [T]he weaker one falls so that the strong one gains life." Three values determined a people's fate: blood- or race value, value of personality, and sense of struggle *(Kampfsinn)*. These values, embodied in the "Aryan race," were threatened by the three vices of democracy, pacifism, and internationalism—all of them the work of "Jewish Marxism."[31]

From this analysis of Hitler's political outlook emerges the picture of a leader who sought to take the concept of responsibility with literally bloody seriousness and to lead the German people in a fateful struggle with other nations. The people, in this respect, were more than the members of parliament, more even than the citizens then living. It was, rather, "the eternal people" *("das ewige Volk")*. This view embraced not just citizens then alive, but also generations gone by and yet to come. The latter could not make their voices heard, of course, but the führer could divine their message. The people thus became, in Hitler's speeches and writings, a metaphysical concept. The living people may have been tired, divided, incapable of action, and seduced by their parliamentary representatives. But the eternal people had power and vigor—or, more strictly, they had the potential of such traits. What was needed was a leader who could bring this to life—a leader who felt a personal responsibility to guide the people along their fated path and who furthermore was prepared to suffer the consequences should he fail in this mission.

At the party congress of 1933, Hitler said the following:

"When we repudiate the parliamentary-democratic system, we also resolutely champion the right of the people to determine its own life. For we

do not recognise the parliamentary system as a true expression of the popular will, which logically can only be a will to the people's self-preservation;
in this system we see, rather, a misrepresentation . . . of the popular will.
The people's will to survive appears most clearly in its best citizens . . . [The
popular will is] the people's own law of life, which in the form of the
people's will to self-preservation and further development becomes reality
in the leader, thereby actively gaining the power to shape history."[32]

The leader, the ideology, and the party become one: "The leader is the party
and the party is the leader," said Hitler in 1935. "Just as I feel myself merely
a part of the party, the party feels itself merely a part of me."[33] The cult of
the leader, together with the metaphysical interpretation of the fate of the
eternal people, became a norm of action for contemporary politics—a way
of justifying the Nazi exercise of power.[34]

In a ruthlessly one-sided manner, the Nazis used two of the West's foremost political thinkers in their attempts at legitimization. Rousseau's theory
of the general will (a favorite concept of despots from Napoleon to Lenin)
was used to ignore, in the name of people, the will of the people as it was
actually expressed. The "true popular will" was something different from
the electoral results produced under the irresponsible system of parliamentary democracy. What the people really wanted was something different—
something only the führer understood. But Rousseau's passion for the sovereignty of the citizen—as opposed to the private person—is conspicuous by
its absence in Hitler's speeches. National Socialism stood for the opposite of
the basic democratic idea.

The other thinker was Macchiavelli, whose analysis of means and ends—
often interpreted to imply that any means are permitted as long as the end
is a good one—cascaded within National Socialism into a worship of violence. Opposition parties were forbidden, opponents were physically anni-
hilated, and executions and threats thereof became legion. Of Macchiavelli's
recipe for good government—the channeling of social tensions through
competing groups or parties—not a trace was left. The National Socialist
Party was instead given a monopoly, and the führer was made the sole legitimate interpreter of the will of the eternal people.

The view one takes of accountability and responsibility thus becomes the
dividing line in our time between democracy and nondemocracy. The distinguishing feature of democracy is that leaders are held accountable to
voters, as the will of the latter finds expression in free, general, and regular

elections. Every manipulation of this process—whether it entails broadening the demos to include persons other than citizens entitled to vote, or subordinating the expressed will of the people to the judgment of the leader—is a step in an undemocratic direction. Responsibility in the Nazi sense, by contrast, does not mean voters are able to hold their leader to account. Because of the metaphysical concept of the "das *ewige* Volk," the leader is not accountable to the voters; on the contrary, he cannot be removed, for his responsibility, which is as absolute as his power, is to achieve the grandiose goal that he calls the fate of his people. In the same way that Hitler's immovability is antipodal to the conception of utility maximization and consequentialist ethics, his concept of responsibility is the very opposite of the notion of accountability as a democratic value.

CHAPTER **9**

Conclusion:
The Necessity for Choice

Choice Is Possible

The message of the empirical findings in this book can be summarized simply: choice is possible. If politicians take the time to analyze, without preconceptions, the conditions with which they are faced, they may be able to distinguish alternatives. The course of development is seldom predetermined. More often than not, it is the politicians who have the ultimate power over it, and it is they who are responsible.

In political science, there is an entire genre devoted to the question of how politicians can free themselves from blinkers and gain a clearer understanding of their options. It goes by the name of *policy analysis.* This method is based, like this book, on the assumption of politics as rational action. Politicians should identify goals and apply means to achieve them. In the same way that Secretary of State Marshall and his colleagues could be likened to physicians treating a patient when they analyzed the Communist threat to Europe following the advance of the Red Army, policy analysts stress the fruitfulness of making a "diagnosis" and considering an "intervention"—with an eye to preventing the illness from taking a dangerous course and imparting to it a more desirable direction. The politician who seeks to evade responsibility, whilst pleading that nothing can be done about the situation, resembles the physician who sits with arms folded, trying neither to help the patient nor to alleviate his pain.

More exactly, four different steps within policy analysis can be distinguished. Scholars refer to them by various names, but I shall call them *policies, possibilities, procedures,* and *prohibitions.* The empirical results of this study are summarized below in connection with these steps.

When, to begin with, politicians must formulate such *policies* as ensure

176

that choices are truly available, it is crucial that they free themselves from prevailing prejudices and conventions. The advice runs:

Be Brave!

Through open-ended brainstorming, politicians can try to shake off their accustomed modes of thought: "Much of the intellectual fun of policy analysis arises in trying to come up with creative alternatives. Be brave! You can always weed out your failures when you begin your systematic comparison of alternatives. Indeed, you may not be able to identify your failures until you begin your comparative evaluation."[1]

Henry Kissinger has elegantly demonstrated this ability. The subtitle of this chapter is borrowed from his 1960 book, *The Necessity for Choice.* In it, Kissinger criticized American foreign policy for not facing up to new challenges. In the years immediately following World War II, according to Kissinger, the United States had carried out major acts of statesmanship; for example, the Marshall Plan, NATO, and the decision to enter the Korean War. Since then, however, U.S. foreign policy had simply followed established routine: "Creativity, innovation, sacrifice pale before tactical considerations of dealing with day-to-day concerns. A powerful incentive exists for deferring difficult choices. It is not surprising, then, that our policies have lacked vitality and that public discussion has focused on symptoms, not causes. But it is equally clear that such attitudes doom us to sterility in a revolutionary period." The United States could not afford another decline like that. The margin vis-á-vis other great powers had narrowed dangerously. Some room for maneuver yet remained, however. America confronted, "directly and urgently[,] the necessity for choice."[2]

It fell to politicians to draw up policies capable of restoring the initiative in world politics to the United States. The responsibility was theirs. Like Alexander George later,[3] Kissinger took the view that academics could help. They could help make available a policy analysis that was clearer and more distinct as well as freer from preconceptions. Alternatives truly existed; one but needed the capacity to see them. *History is not predetermined,* Kissinger might have said. Politicians could not, of course, disregard concrete circumstances of various kinds when formulating their policies (indeed, Kissinger had made this very point in his doctoral thesis). But they were not powerless before history:

What then is the role of statesmanship? A scholarship of social determinism has reduced the statesman to a lever on a machine called "history," to the agent of a fate which he may dimly discern but which he accomplishes regardless of his will. And this belief in the pervasiveness of circumstance and the impotence of the individual extends to the notion of policy-making . . . It cannot be denied, of course, that policy does not occur in a void, that the statesman is confronted with material he must treat as given. Not only geography and the availability of resources trace the limits of statesmanship, but also the character of the people and the nature of its historical experience. But to say that policy does not create its own substance is not the same as saying that the substance is self-implementing . . . The test of a statesman, then, is his ability to recognize the real relationship of forces and to make this knowledge serve his ends.[4]

When taking the first step and formulating policies, then, politicians should question routine and let their fantasy go. It is worth recalling, however, that routine is not always an expression for thoughtlessness. The ruthless propagandist, after all, presents his chosen course as something that cannot or may not be altered. The rhetorical trick involved is a simple one: he presents his preference as something unavoidable. Other and more powerful actors—even history itself—are said to have made the choice for us. The voluntarist makes paradoxical use of a determinist rhetoric. The propagandist says that there is no alternative to the course he himself has laid out. And indeed it does not appear, at least superficially, that it is he who is directing things. It is his will that is being secretly disguised as the meaning of history. Therefore; *action can be meaningful even if irrational.* Only thus, for example, can we understand Hitler's desire to submit to the will of history. Submission, after all, was not otherwise his political style, to put it mildly—not, that is, until Götterdämmerung was a fact, and he had literally fallen into the hole he had dug for himself. But the need to submit to a supposed fate was only apparent, for Hitler was playing with a stacked deck. Democracy rests on the ability of citizens to express their political desires by choosing among different options. By contrast, the theory of directional history is based on the secret proviso that there is no alternative, and we must submit to fate (because it means moving in a direction the propagandist prefers).

Once policies have been identified and formulated, the next step is to analyze the *possibilities* for getting them accepted. The necessity of taking possibilities into account is what separates politics from academia. In politics, if you are alone, it does not matter whether you are right. The task in politics is to make possible worlds real, with the support of others. Politics is the art of the possible. Politicians must expend a great deal of time and effort convincing others that the policy they recommend is the best. They must also show great flexibility, inasmuch as they often must adjust their proposed policy to the preferences of others; that way, they can get at least some of what they want, when not all good things can be had at once. Yet, such adjustments involve great danger. Selling the policy to others risks blurring the entire process. Given that agreements often are reached behind closed doors, there is a risk that you are forgotten all together. Policy analysis therefore offers a second bit of advice:

Be Visible!

In negotiating with other politicians—or administrators, who are often the counterparts that policy analysts take an interest in—one runs the risk of going astray. The argument "for opening up and making more visible" the process of accountability in public agencies is therefore highly relevant also to the problem of accountability in a representative democracy, especially one characterized by power-sharing.[5]

Cooperation and compromise mean that, to a degree, politicians must diverge from the mandate they got from the voters; accordingly, the ethic of responsibility becomes even more imperative as consensus democracy in our time seems to take the place of majoritarian democracy. The European Union is the foremost example of consensus democracy and of the great challenge that follows from this for politicians both to cooperate for the common good and to be honest and open vis-à-vis the voters who have given them their confidence. It cannot be said that the representatives of the EU have succeeded in this double mission. Through Jean Monnet's distinctive combination of passion and pragmatism, the peace project could be pushed forward step by step without the destination becoming the object of any fundamental decision; the consecutive successes in themselves became an argument for continued integration. After centuries of bloody conflict, Europeans experienced something singular: that *nation-states need not go to war.* But how are they to go further, now that peace has been secured? European leaders have felt a responsibility for peace—even when their peoples did not understand their own best interests. But paternalism cannot be the long-term solution in a democracy, for this form of government presumes accountability. The idea of strengthening the democratic legitimacy of the EU by conducting a successful economic policy means, in principle, proceeding further along the path of responsibility blazed by Monnet. The democratic deficit can, however, be overcome only if the leaders of the Union are made more visible to the voters, and if the ability of the latter to hold the former accountable is strengthened.

This second piece of advice, too, is intentionally disregarded at times. Just as politicians can misuse the philosophy of history, with an eye to presenting their own preferences as the dictate of fate, they can consciously obstruct transparency by cooperation in order to avoid being blamed for mistakes. But *power-sharing does not exclude responsibility.* The Italian case leaves no room for doubt on that score. For reasons that can be readily understood, in view of the Fascist background, the Italians made an effort to counteract the concentration of power in a single party. Power was dispersed into many hands. As a result, however, Italian politics became enmeshed in a fine web of cooperation, cronyism, and corruption, and every form of democratic control was undermined. At last it became too much for the people of Italy. The doors to the closed rooms were flung open, and the establishment was tossed out on its ear. The advice on visibility, therefore, is categorical. Power-sharing had not promoted the goal of a clean government. The smoke-filled rooms with secret agreements explain much of what today is known as "the democratic deficit" and "the confidence gap."

The third step involves taking a position on what *procedures* are to be followed. In principle, there are only two systems for implementing decisions: markets and bureaucracies. A prominent feature of both is that they easily take command over politics. Those who approach either can easily end up being swallowed, like Jonah in the belly of the whale. The next piece of advice proffered by policy analysis is therefore that politicians be very clear in how they formulate their message. In a democracy, it can never be forgotten that the last word goes to the politicians and in the end, via the process of accountability, to the voters (whom the politicians, after all, are appointed to serve). As one policy analyst writes, with more than a touch of ethnocentric pride: "It is only in the US and the UK that for the most part liberty and freedom have been continually protected for generations of uninterrupted political development. The reason for this is accountability."[6] The recommendation runs:

Be Explicit!

As we have seen, a favorite sport among politicians who seek to evade blame is to be fuzzy about their goals and to plead that their policies must be qualified with regard to what seems necessary from an economic or administrative point of view. How can they, as politicians, assert their will against the market in a globalized world? The answer is that politicians can also co-operate across national borders, with an eye to asserting the primacy of pol-itics. *Globalization has not wiped out the freedom to choose.* Many would deny the existence of such freedom of choice. During the 1980s, the world wit-nessed the rise of a new current: neoliberalism, which sought the greatest possible transfer of power from the political sphere to the market. But such measures cannot be unconditional. If the political intentions behind it are not achieved, a delegation—to a market as surely as to a bureaucracy—can always be revoked, in the spirit of Hayek. Neoliberals have not always ob-served this principle. Many have made the mistake of not formulating with sufficient explicitness the goals that the market is to serve; as a result, they have been disinclined to take measures when such goals are not reached. To quote a critical remark:

> In short, it has been an attempt to get the state to wither away. This is not the way to protect liberty. The wisdom of America's Founding Fathers was clear upon this point: only if men were angels could we do away with gov-ernment. The Americans and their English cousins did not prescribe mar-kets to govern people, but layers of administration and legislators account-able to each other and to the people, imbued with the practice and wisdom of centuries . . . It is not through accident that liberty has flourished best in those countries where separation of powers and the accountability of gov-ernment have been most insisted upon.[7]

Blaming bureaucrats has been almost as popular as blaming the global market. But here, too, the requirement of explicitness applies. Politicians can never be too explicit on the question of what goals the bureaucracy must work toward, and they can never hesitate to revoke a delegation if the goals behind it are not fulfilled. If politicians act in this fashion, they can in-deed induce the administration to carry out their intentions. *Implementation may well be immaculate.* In an analysis of the breakthrough of so-called sys-tems analysis in American defense policy, Ida R. Hoos furnishes an eloquent exposé of how policy analysis can force politicians to think in terms of clear alternatives and how it can bring decisions up to the level of elected officials rather than remaining hidden within daily routines at a low level:

> The catechism was simple but strong. The system would force the military to identify and justify its objectives; indicate various alternatives for achieving them; compute the cost and effectiveness of every alternative; and provide

greater certainty as to scope, objectives, technical characteristics, management arrangements, and probable costs through research and development (R&D) programming in instances where unknowns or new technology were involved. An otherwise critical observer of bureaucracy praised the procedure on the ground that, by avoiding "concealed, parochial and *de facto* decisions in the lower echelons, and misdirected control by arbitrary budget ceilings," it "boils out real policy choices and exposes them to top-level decision" and thus "gives military expertise and judgment sharper focus and greater pertinence." "By phasing the level of commitment from low-budget, widely diversified preliminary and program definition studies, the government can contain the blind tendencies of a runaway technology fueled by service rivalries and by the Contract State. It can retain flexibility and choice at every point of the process at lowest possible cost."[8]

Is there also perhaps a conscious wish to refrain from following this advice—a desire not to be so explicit on the question of the goals to be achieved by markets or bureaucracies? It is exactly this that Martin and Schumann accused politicians of doing vis-à-vis markets and that Niskanen accused them of doing vis-à-vis bureaucracies. According to Martin and Schumann, for example, the deregulation of currency and capital markets at the end of the 1970s was an instance in which politicians first freely abdicated power and then stood helpless before developments over which they had lost control. The authors could not discover any will on the part of politicians to recover the initiative—not even when citizens started experiencing a decisive deterioration in the environment. In the same way, Niskanen accused politicians of passivity vis-à-vis the bureaucracy, which in his view has taken command over which collective goods are offered to citizens. Against this weakness of will, however, there are politicians who have sought to restore the primacy of politics. The secretary-general of the UN, as we saw, took the initiative for an internationally coordinated environmental policy for counteracting the negative effects of globalization. Margaret Thatcher urged her colleagues to read and interpret Niskanen as a warning, and to take measures against exactly those bureaucratic strategies that Niskanen had so thoroughly demonstrated.

This does not mean, of course, that just anything can be done in politics. Voluntarism is an untenable and extreme position. It is important to see what *prohibitions* there are on the capacity of politicians to control events. There are, of course, limits to what can be done: "[P]olicy-making takes place in the context of the constraints of economic, social, geographical, historical and cultural limits."[9] Thus, the last piece of advice provided by policy analysis is that politicians not lose their head—that they understand the "freedom within constraints," the context in which they operate. There are no guarantees that politicians will get everything they desire. The fourth bit of advice therefore runs:

Consider the Consequences!

If a politician ignores the constraints that actually exist on what can be done in a given case, there is a risk that something will happen other than what he hopes. Ever since Robert Merton's observation several decades ago, we have known that political decisions sometimes have unintended consequences—a rather trivial truth nowadays, but a revolutionary new insight when first it was formulated. Considering the consequences means acting interactively in one's decision making: the rational politician moves back and forth between intentions and outcomes in his mind, and he adjusts his policy if the result proves different from what he intended. There are various techniques for such consequence analysis. One such method, monitoring, entails looking back at what has happened before:

> Monitoring provides policy-relevant knowledge about the consequences of previously adopted policies, thus assisting policymakers in the policy implementation phase. Many agencies regularly monitor the outcomes and impacts of policies by means of various policy indicators in areas of health, education, housing, welfare, crime, and science and technology. Monitoring helps to assess degrees of compliance, discover unintended consequences of policies and programs, identify implementational obstacles and constraints, and locate sources of responsibility for departures from policies.[10]

Another technique, evaluation, involves reformulating one's policies in light of actual outcomes: "Evaluation yields policy-relevant knowledge about discrepancies between expected and actual policy performance, thus assisting policymakers in the policy assessment phase of the policy-making process. Monitoring not only results in conclusions about the extent to which problems have been alleviated; it also may contribute to the clarification and critique of values driving a policy, aid in the adjustment or reformulation of policies, and establish a basis for restructuring problems."[11]

The frequent warnings about how decisions can lead to unintended results prompt me to remind the reader that, notwithstanding everything, matters may in fact transpire as intended—if, that is, the actor in question considers the likely results in a cool and analytical way. Then he can get what he wants. *Consequences may well be as intended.* It may be difficult to prove that the Cold War ended because Reagan purposefully engaged the Soviet Union in an arms race that would lead to its collapse. On the other hand, it is easy to show that the Swedish Social Democrats intentionally chose an unemployment insurance policy that drove workers into the trade-union movement, and thereby into the party. Successful political action is in much a question of strategic thinking, and the achievement of such long-range goals is by no means excluded.

But this advice, too, can be ignored—in the most conscious way. The most grotesque example, perhaps, is how the centuries-old dream of equality led instead to slaughter and oppression, after both the French and Russian revolutions. The revolutions sowed the wind but reaped the storm. The destruction of the old regime became a goal in itself for the new oppressors.

So choice is indeed often possible—if political leaders manage to carry out a serious policy analysis of the prospects for intervening in the course of events. But the voice of scholars does not always reach the ear of decision makers; policy analysts accordingly worry about "the analyst's lack of power base; thus the experience of experts in the policy process tends to be of being weak vis-à-vis political and bureaucratic interests."[12] And even if the message gets through, it is not clear that politicians will want to consider alternative solutions. Alternative thinking may be regarded as something negative. It can upset efforts to reach agreement, for example. Thus, democracy is not thought to refer to the ability of the people to choose between different options; on the contrary, it is taken to mean that as many citizens as possible should be united behind a common policy. This is supposed to make popular government effective and forceful. Being sensible—that is, able to compromise and work together—is a way to reach results, and democracy is being redefined as consensus. I conclude this book, accordingly, with a warning against this striving for consensus solutions. The reason for this warning is that the new consensus doctrine does not place the same stress as the old one on the opportunity to choose, or on the ability of citizens to hold their representatives accountable for the policies they pursue.

Choice Is Necessary

In this section, I will shift the perspective from the politicians to the citizens. In Chapter 1, I developed two arguments. "The first argument" was that

| DEMOCRACY | procedure | choice | accountability |
| REPUBLICANISM | result | consensus | deliberation |

Figure 9.1. Two concepts of popular government.

politicians do have a choice. How this is possible was discussed in the previous section. "The second argument" implied that these choices were visible to a broader public and could be understood and evaluated by them. Is that also the case? This is more doubtful. Still, it is essential that the citizens are given the opportunity. For in a democracy, the choice of the people is necessary.

However, as has been discussed in this book, a new doctrine of "republicanism" has emerged, with the emphasis on result, consensus, and deliberation instead of old-fashioned procedural values, such as procedure, choice, and accountability (Figure 9.1).

The important thing is said to be that the policy carried out be for the people's best. The result, in form of economic prosperity, is what counts; consensus is stressed and the deliberation of elites is regarded as a guarantee for the quality of decisions.

Let us begin our discussion of the role of the citizens by taking a closer look at these three pairs of concepts.

Resist the Shift from Procedure to Result!

The new republicanism involves policies for the people rather than by the people, often implemented by an enlightened elite. Indeed, some observers place economic result, as seen in earlier chapters, on a level with democratic procedure. This is true, for example, in the discussion of the creation of the European Union as a way to gain legitimacy. Fritz Scharpf, for whom accountability means "input-oriented legitimization," refers to successful economic policy as "output-oriented legitimization."[13] In other words, also from a democratic point of view, what politicians do is supposed to be as important as how they do it. Giandomenico Majone maintains that democratic legitimacy is best achieved through governance by independent experts, as their competence is the best guarantee for promoting prosperity.[14]

The welfare of the people is certainly not irrelevant for the health of democracy. Many democracies have been destroyed because they have not delivered what the people demanded. But, on the other hand, antidemocratic or even totalitarian regimes have also produced prosperity. The better competence of the elites to offer what was good for the people was indeed

Edmund Burke's argument against popular government. The capacity of the Nazi state to obliterate unemployment and stimulate economic growth was Hitler's cause against the Weimar Republic. Prosperity in itself is consequently no proof of democracy.

Resist the Shift from Choice to Consensus!

Another important change is the tendency to replace choice by consensus. In the history of popular government, there has always been a tension between consensus and disagreement. Democratic politics can be described as a process of trying to find out whether people can agree on a certain policy. Is it possible to find consensus? However, in comparison, the right to speak one's mind is also a fundamental value in this process. According to Schumpeter, democracy is defined as a form of government in which elites acquire the right to decide by competing for the people's votes.[15] In this normative discourse, it is basically what politics does to people that counts. Consensus may be nice, and results are certainly essential. But neither is found exclusively in democracies. The right to choose, on the other hand, is. It turns subjects into citizens and stimulates personal growth. This vision of democracy is the normative component of my reasoning. In the words of John Stuart Mill, it is only by gaining the opportunity to choose among different alternatives that the people of a country become masters of their own house, and so are transformed into full citizens. In Isaiah Berlin's interpretation of Mill,

> man differs from animals primarily neither as the possessor of reason, nor as an inventor of tools and methods, but as a being capable of choice, one who is most himself in choosing and not being chosen for; the rider and not the horse; the seeker of ends, and not merely of means, ends that he pursues, each in his own fashion: with the corollary that the more various these fashions, the richer the lives of men become; the larger the field of interplay between individuals, the greater the opportunities of the new and unexpected; the more numerous the possibilities for altering his own character in some fresh or unexplored direction; the more paths open before each individual, and the wider will be his freedom of action and thought.[16]

As I see it, the moral basis of democracy lies in this procedure of choice aimed at holding the politicians accountable. By participation in government, individual citizens, Aristotle and Mill taught, are enabled to develop their civic spirit.

Resist the Shift from Accountability to Deliberation!

In the new republicanism, accountability is replaced by deliberation. In the constitutional design of the European Union, this shift of values brings matters to a head. When leading theorists like Scharpf and Majone emphasize the importance of result and prosperity, they are anxious to underline the necessity of argumentation. Experts should furnish good reasons for why the long-term consequences of their decisions can be expected to be good, and they should seek to justify their policies through giving reasons.[17] As Erik Oddvar Eriksen and John Erik Fossum conclude in their anthology on European cooperation, proposed policies must comply with the normative requirement of arguing: "integration through deliberation."[18] And Amy Gutman and Dennis Thompson define democracy as a system in which "each is accountable to all. Citizens and officials try to justify their decisions to all those who are bound by them and some of those who are affected by them. This is the reason-giving process of deliberative democracy."[19]

In the new doctrine, ordinary citizens have a very passive role. The conservative anti-democrats of the nineteenth century have reason to rejoice in their heaven. A system in which elites communicate with each other in an enlightened spirit, and without needing to worry about what the people think, is now called democratic:

> The EU has developed an elaborate system of deliberation at *elite* level . . .
> The Union is likewise characterized by often respectable levels of inter-elite accountability. As yet, however, the public is scarcely involved at all. At the risk of some frivolity, we might characterize it as democracy without the people; or, if this sounds too self-contradictory, a system that is based on a plurality of elites, each with its own uneven and unsystematic linkage to public opinion. The public lacks opportunities to substitute one set of rulers by another, or at least to carrry out a comprehensive "spring-clean" of the Union's political leadership. Behind this lies an absence of choice and competition; elites do not have to compete for power in the Union's political system in a manner that requires them to anticipate the needs and values of the public.[20]

How remarkable: a democracy without the people! My point is that deliberation by the elites can be no substitute for the power of the people to choose and hold the politicians accountable.

Resist Apathy, Frustration, and Distrust!

As far as my "second argument" is concerned, the analysis is rather discouraging. Whereas politicians do seem to have a choice, the citizens are obviously far away from the influence that democratic theory entrusted them with. My message, then, would be to resist the underinvolvement of citizens as well as the new consensus- and elite-oriented doctrine of republicanism.

The change of democratic theory to the doctrine of new republicanism has been a slow process over a long time. If one could single out a decisive moment for this shift, it would be the fall of Berlin Wall in 1989. With its far-reaching consequences for world politics, this event also had a great impact on our vision of democracy.

An old tale reported by Arnold Toynbee nicely illustrates what happened then. The story concerns the technique used by English fishermen to haul back the herring they had caught in the Atlantic. The fish were put in large coves. The fishermen found, however, that many of the fish died in the time between being caught and being sold at the English ports—notwithstanding the ample feed they had been given. They died of laziness, easy living, lack of exercise. But the fisherman devised a solution. They set dogfish—a kind of small shark—loose among the herring in the holds. The dogfish chased the herring and devoured some of them. The great majority of the herring survived, however, and became vigorous and healthy—through their efforts to survive. Now they had something to live for, to be frightened of.

In the same way, world Communism helped Western democracies—through the threat, danger, and rivalry it provided—to maintain their vitality. Now that the Russian shark is dead, there is a declining interest in democratic procedures, and the question of economic result and prosperity dominates. What for Toynbee was a theoretical point to illustrate the value of procedure appears today as an accurate historical event.

The threat to democracy in the post-Communist world is a milder one. Juan Linz has taught us to distinguish between totalitarian and authoritarian regimes: the latter is characterized by a certain degree of pluralism for various groups, apathy among citizens, and a feeling that there is no point in trying to make an effort because the elites decide whatever they want

anyway. Authoritarianism is something different from the exclusive, elabo-
rated ideology of totalitarianism in absolute control of society.[21] It is this
problem of new authoritarianism that I see for democracy today.

One indicator of this tendency toward apathy and new authoritarianism
is the drop in voter turnout. It is not a dramatic one, but in contrast to expectations, turnout has not continued to rise but has fallen by about 7 percent in the Western world over the last twenty years. Twenty-two countries
(Australia, Austria, Belgium, Britain, Canada, Denmark, Finland, France,
Germany, Iceland, Ireland, Israel, Italy, Japan, Luxembourg, Malta, the
Netherlands, New Zealand, Norway, Sweden, Switzerland, and the United
States) have held elections continuously since within one electoral cycle
(generally four years) of the end of World War II, 356 elections in all. This
development is charted in Figure 9.2.[22]

Another expression for the feeling of political uneasiness among ordinary
people is that more and more citizens vote against the incumbent government. Sitting governments tend to lose votes. In a comparative study of 385

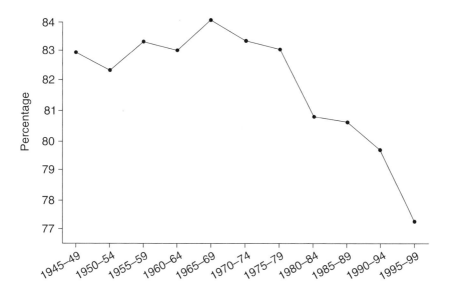

Figure 9.2. Average turnout in five-year periods for twenty-two countries,
1945–1999. *Source:* Mark N. Franklin, *Voter Turnout and the Dynamics of Electoral
Competition in Established Democracies since 1945* (Cambridge: Cambridge University Press, 2004), 120. Published according to Cambridge University Press
policy.

governments, the average loss for incumbent governments is a bit over 2.5 percent. The differences between countries are great, however. Spanish governments lose the most badly. Voters in Germany and Denmark show a greater patience with the sitting government.[23]

Figure 9.3 portrays this development over time. As can be seen, the tendency to lose votes has increased greatly over recent decades. During the 1940s, governments largely succeeded in maintaining their position; during the 1990s, they lost on average more than 6 percent of the vote.

Yet this does not always have an effect on which government is subsequently formed. Table 9.1 and Figure 9.4 indicate which governments have taken office after elections. If the loss is a large one (over 5 percent), a change in government usually results; only 15 percent of governments with losses of this magnitude have been able to cling to power. Smaller losses, however, are more common, and in such cases the effect is less dramatic. In

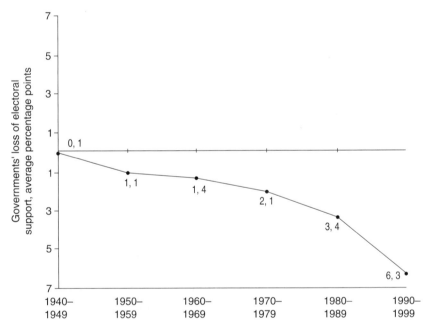

Figure 9.3. Average electoral losses for Western governments, 1945–1999. *Source:* Olof Petersson, Sören Holmberg, Leif Lewin, and Hanne Marthe Narud, *Demokrati utan ansvar: Demokratirådets rapport 2002* [Democracy without accountability: Report from the Council of Democracy 2002] (Stockholm: SNS, 2002), 39. Published with permission of SNS Förlag.

Table 9.1. Correlations between loss in vote for ruling parties and subsequent formation of governments in seventeen West European countries, 1945–1999.

	Change in composition of government after election				
Electoral outcome for ruling party	No change	Some change	Only new parties	Total percentage	Number of elections
Loss of more than 5 percent	15	25	60	100	63
Loss of 1–5 percent	27	36	23	100	65
Gain or unchanged	58	39	17	100	91

Source: Olof Petersson, Sören Holmberg, Leif Lewin, and Hanne Marthe Narud, *Demokrati utan ansvar: Demokratirådets rapport 2002* [Democracy without accountability: Report from the Council of Democracy 2002] (Stockholm: SNS, 2002). Published with permission of SNS Förlag.

27 percent of cases in which the loss is between 1 and 5 percent, the government stays in power. And when the ruling party either gains votes or retains the same proportion, it stays in power in 58 percent of cases.

There is a variety of theories as to who should form a government. The majority principle says simply that the party with a majority ought to do so. The plurality principle prescribes that the party with the most seats in parliament forms the government. The election-wind principle says that the parties that advanced at the election should form the government. According to this last principle, then, ruling parties that won the election should remain in power, and ruling parties that lost should leave the government: thus, the scores in Figure 9.4 should be 100 and 0 percent, respectively. But the real figures, as we see, are 77 and 62 percent. What the voters say does not seem to be very important (unless they make the point very loudly). Governments remain in power all the same. Whether a party wins or loses an election makes a difference of only 15 percentage points to the probability of its remaining in government. Indeed, a multiparty system can function so perversely that there are actually examples in which the probability of a losing party staying in government is greater than the likelihood of a winning party doing so.[24] The dealings between party leaders following the election are more decisive than the judgment of voters on election day. It might be said—to paraphrase Stein Rokkan's famous aphorism—that votes count but negotiations decide.

In our time, then, people vote less, and those who vote have less influ-

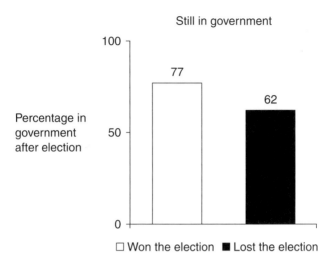

Figure 9.4. Encounters between voters and ruling parties in Western Europe, 1945–1999. *Source:* Olof Peterson, Sören Holmberg, Leif Lewin, and Hanne Marthe Narud, *Demokrati utan ansvar: Demokratirådets rapport 2002* [Democracy without accountability: Report from the Council of Democracy 2002] (Stockholm: SNS, 2002), 48. Published with permission of SNS Förlag.

ence over the formation of government. Against this background, it is not to be wondered at that researchers at the turn of the millennium reported rising dissatisfaction among citizens with the way in which politics is conducted. As Christopher J. Anderson and Christine A. Guillory put it, "In fact, after the much-heralded victory of liberal democracy around the globe in 1989–90, satisfaction with democracy and intermediary political institutions declined considerably in West European democracies."[25] What happened to us, then, at a time when we otherwise enjoyed a better standard of living, a better life, than ever before? "What's Troubling the Trilateral Countries?" is the revealing question raised in one of the many reports about modern citizens' distrust in politics. In study after study, political scientists have shown that voters in America, Europe, and Japan have lost confidence in government. And the decline is dramatic. Only a minority of voters nowadays think that politicians can be trusted, that the government is doing a good job, or that leaders look first and foremost to the good of the country rather than to the advantage of their party.[26]

One possible explanation for the distrust, of course, is that policies have in fact become worse—that citizens have less reason than before to feel confidence in political institutions. After the expansion of the welfare state—with the state as the "giver of all good things"—a change has taken place in recent years, with a retrenchment of the public sector and an increased reliance on the market. While state intervention was earlier justified by reference to market failures, the talk now is of government failures that necessitate a return to the market. In reality, however, the picture is a more divided one than such sweeping formulations imply, and it is hard to find corroboration for the idea that the new conditions faced by the welfare state provide a complete explanation for the distrust of politicians. After all, the crisis of confidence is greatest both in leading welfare states, such as Sweden, and in countries where the social provision is relatively limited, like the United States.

Another explanation sometimes proffered zeros in on the mass media, with their predilection for reporting on scandals and political corruption. But even if some television watching doubtless leads to distrust and political apathy, the afore-mentioned studies in fact show that the overall effect of exposure to the mass media is a higher level of information among citizens, together with an increase in civic mobilization and an enhanced support for the political system.

It should not be forgotten, in any case, that the ideal citizen of democratic theory is supposed to keep a distance from leaders. It is presumed that citizens will test the arguments presented in a critical spirit and form their own ideas on social questions. The increase in civic competence seen in Western democracies over recent decades necessarily involves a greater distance from political parties as compared with earlier times, when class voting was more common, party loyalty was larger, and voters were less well-oriented on the issues. But critical reflection is one thing. In the long run, we can not live with leaders that we distrust.

Distrust in politicians does not mean, however, distrust in democracy—not yet at least. Researchers report that citizens' faith in the fundamental values of democracy is stronger than before. This is "the democratic paradox": even if the distrust in politicians is high, the support for the system these politicians represent is also very high.[27]

In this way, a vicious circle is created. Distrust in politicians makes citizens vote against the incumbent party. But often this has little consequence because losing parties can remain in power in consensus democracies. Such experiences increase the distrust in politics further.

The problem of democracy is a complicated issue, perhaps even more so today than before, and there is certainly no single solution. But if we should resist the tendencies toward apathy, frustration, and distrust, it seems to me that at least one value should be paid attention to. It is the key concept of this book: accountability. I agree with Anthony King when he says that if the voters want to "throw the rascals out," at least in majoritarian democracies they know whom the rascals are and whom they should throw out. Therefore, he modestly suggests, "it would be surprising if the high level of distrust in government . . . did not owe something to this quite awesome deficit of accountability."[28]

In the new republican view of popular government, the people as actors have been forgotten. In deliberative democracy, the elites are the principals, not the ordinary voters. Citizens should again have opportunities to hold the politicians accountable and be able to dismiss governments. More transparency, and less consensus formation by elite cartels behind closed doors, is needed in today's politics. It is the will of the citizens—expressed through politicians—that must leave its mark on society's development. It is not enough that elites be able to distinguish choices or deliberate on politics. Citizens must be able to do so as well. But they can not do that if the politicians do not offer them alternatives. In democracies, citizens' choice is necessary. Briefly put, in accordance with the above-cited interpretation of the great political philosopher John Stuart Mill, the capacity to make choices is what distinguishes the human being from the animal—or, we might also say, the citizen from the subject. The citizen is the rider, not the horse.

NOTES

BIBLIOGRAPHY

ACKNOWLEDGMENTS

INDEX

Notes

1. Introduction

1. R. Kent Weaver, "The Politics of Blame Avoidance," *Journal of Public Policy* 6 (1986): 371–398.
2. John Plamenatz, *Ideology* (London: Macmillan, 1970), 75–76.
3. *Longman Dictionary of Contemporary English,* 2nd ed. (Essex, UK: Longman House, 1987), s.v. "responsibility."
4. Philip Selznick, "Reflections on Responsibility: More Than Just Following Rules," *The Responsive Community* 10 (Spring 2000): 57.
5. Robert A. Dahl, *Democracy and Its Critics* (New Haven, Conn.: Yale University Press, 1989), 42–43.
6. Carl J. Friedrich, ed., *Responsibility* (New York: The Liberal Arts Press, 1960).
7. Karl R. Popper, "Popper on Democracy: The Open Society and Its Enemies Revisited," *Economist,* 23 April 1988.
8. Leif Lewin and Evert Vedung, eds., *Politics as Rational Action: Essays in Public Choice and Policy Analysis* (Dordrecht: D. Reidel, 1980). The so-called PARA-project (Politics as Rational Action) was a leading research program at the Department of Government in Uppsala, Sweden, during the 1980s.
9. William H. Riker and Peter C. Ordeshook, *An Introduction to Positive Political Theory* (Englewood Cliffs, N.J.: Prentice-Hall, 1973).
10. Donald Davidson, "Action, Reasons and Causes," *The Journal of Philosophy* 60 (1963): 685–700.
11. Jon Elster, *Sour Grapes: Studies in the Subversion of Rationality* (Cambridge: Cambridge University Press, 1983).
12. John Stuart Mill, *A System of Logic: Ratiocinative and Inductive* (Toronto: University of Toronto Press, [1843] 1967). The present-day conception is well summarized in Gary King, Robert O. Keohane, and Sidney Verba, *Designing Social Inquiry: Scientific Inference in Qualitative Research* (Princeton, N.J.: Princeton University Press, 1994). On special problems in the methodology of deviating cases used in this study, see David Collier and James Mahoney, "Insights and Pitfalls: Selection Bias in Qualitative Research," *World Politics* 49 (1996): 56–91.
13. Charles C. Ragin and Howard S. Becker, eds., *What Is a Case? Exploring the Foun-*

dations of Social Inquiry (Cambridge: Cambridge University Press, 1992); Harry Eckstein, "Case Study and Theory in Political Science," in *Handbook of Political Science,* ed. Fred I. Greenstein and Nelson W. Polsby, vol. 7, *Strategies of Inquiry* (Reading, Mass.: Addison-Wesley, 1975), 79–137.

14. Seymour Martin Lipset, Martin A. Trow, and James S. Coleman, *Union Democracy: The Internal Politics of the International Typographical Union* (Glencoe, Ill.: Free Press, 1956).

15. Karl R. Popper, *Conjectures and Refutations: The Growth of Scientific Knowledge* (London: Routledge & Kegan Paul, 1963).

16. Alexander L. George, "Case Studies and Theory Development: The Method of Structured, Focused Comparison," in *Diplomacy: New Approaches in History, Theory, and Policy,* ed. Paul Gordon Lauren (New York: Free Press, 1979), 43–68; Andrew Bennett and Alexander L. George, *Case Study and Theory Development* (Cambridge, Mass.: MIT Press, 1998).

17. Stanley Lieberson, "Small *N*s and Big Conclusions: An Examination of the Reasoning in Comparative Studies Based on a Small Number of Cases," in *What Is a Case? Exploring the Foundations of Social Inquiry,* ed. Charles C. Ragin and Howard S. Becker (Cambridge: Cambridge University Press, 1992), 105–118.

18. King, Keohane, and Verba, *Designing Social Inquiry,* 218.

19. Margaret Levi, "A Model, a Method, and a Map: Rational Choice in Comparative and Historical Analysis," in *Comparative Politics: Rationality, Culture, and Structure,* ed. Mark Irving Lichbach and Alan S. Zuckerman (Cambridge: Cambridge University Press, 1997), 23.

20. Edgar Kiser, "The Revival of Narrative in Historical Sociology: What Rational Choice Theory Can Contribute," *Politics and Society* 24 (1996): 261.

21. Robert Bates, Avner Greif, Margaret Levi, Jean-Laurent Rosenthal, and Barry R. Weingast, *Analytical Narratives* (Princeton, N.J.: Princeton University Press, 1998), 11.

2. History Is Not Predetermined

1. Francis Fukuyama, *The End of History and the Last Man* (New York: Free Press, 1992). Quotations in Chapter 2 are from xii, 51, 80, 125, 143, 207, 245, 300, 312, 313, 334, 338, and 339. The book is based on an article by Fukuyama titled "The End of History," originally published in *The National Interest,* no. 16 (1989): 3–18.

2. Some of the contributions to this far-reaching debate are collected in Timothy Burns, ed., *After History? Francis Fukuyama and His Critics* (London: Littlefield Adams, 1994).

3. Kristan Kumar, "The Revolution of 1989: Socialism, Capitalism, and Democracy," *Theory and Society* 21 (1992): 313.

4. Karl R. Popper, *The Open Society and Its Enemies I–II* (London: Routledge & Kegan Paul, 1945).

5. Karl R. Popper, *The Poverty of Historicism* (London: Routledge & Kegan Paul, 1957), 3.

6. For the impact of this fight on German idealism, historicism, and finally Nazism, see Chapter 8.

7. *Encyclopedia of Philosophy,* repr. ed. (New York: Mac Millan, 1972), s.v. "historicism."

8. *Dictionary of the History of Ideas* (New York: Scribner's, 1973), s.v. "historicism."

9. There is no entry for "historicism" in the *International Encyclopedia of the Social Sciences* (New York: Macmillan, 1968); however, historicism is treated in a number of articles therein, see Index. Quotation from vol. 9, p. 50.

10. Roland B. Levinson, *In Defense of Plato* (Cambridge, Mass.: Harvard University Press, 1953).

11. T. E. Mommsen, "St. Augustine and the Christian Idea of Progress," in *Medevial and Renaissance Studies,* ed. Eugene F. Rice Jr. (Ithaca, N.Y.: Cornell University Press, 1959), 265–298; Robert A. Markus, *Saecuklum: History and Society in the Theology of St Augustine* (Cambridge: Cambridge University Press, 1970).

12. Maurice Cornforth, *The Open Philosophy and the Open Society: A Reply to Sir Karl Popper's Refutations of Marxism* (London: Lawrence & Wishart, 1968).

13. Paul Johnson, "The End of History and the Last Man," *Commentary* 93 (March 1992): 51–53.

14. David Stove, "More Responses to Fukuyama," *The National Interest,* no. 17 (1989): 97–98.

15. Fred Halliday, "An Encounter with Fukuyama," *New Left Review* (May–June 1992): 95.

16. Richard Peet, "I. Reading Fukuyama: Politics at the End of History," *Political Geography* 12 (1993): 71.

17. Samuel P. Huntington, "No Exit: The Errors of Endism," *The National Interest,* no. 17 (1989): 10.

18. Timothy Fuller, "More Responses to Fukuyama," *The National Interest,* no. 17 (1989): 94.

19. John Grumley, "Fukuyama's Hegelianism—Historical Exhaustion or Philosophical Closure," *History of European Ideas* 21 (1995): 388.

20. Arthur Marwick, review of *The End of History and the Last Man,* by Francis Fukuyama, *History: The Journal of the Historical Association,* n.s., 79 (1994): 83.

21. Bruce Cumings, "The End of History or the Return of Liberal Crisis?" *Current History* 98 (1999): 16.

22. Huntington, "No Exit," 8, 10.

23. Stephen Holmes, "The Scowl of Minerva," *The New Republic,* 23 March 1992, 33.

24. Isaac Deutscher, *Stalin: A Political Biography* (London: Oxford University Press, 1967), 552.

25. William O. McCagg Jr., *Stalin Embattled, 1943–1948* (Detroit, Mich.: Wayne State University Press, 1978), 31–36.

26. Some important works on the Marshall Plan are George F. Kennan, *American*

Diplomacy, 1900–1950 (Chicago: University of Chicago Press, 1951); Harry Bayard Price, *The Marshall Plan and Its Meaning* (Ithaca, N.Y.: Cornell University Press, 1955); Robert H. Ferrell, *The American Secretaries of State and Their Diplomacy* (New York: Cooper Square, 1966); George F. Kennan, *Memoirs, 1925–1950* (London: Hutchinson, 1968); Hadley Arkes, *Bureaucracy, the Marshall Plan, and the National Interest* (Princeton, N.J.: Princeton University Press, 1972); John Gimbel, *The Origins of the Marshall Plan* (Stanford, Calif.: Stanford University Press, 1976); Leonard Mosley, *Marshall: Hero for Our Times* (New York: Hearst Books, 1982); Charles L. Mee Jr., *The Marshall Plan: The Launching of the Pax Americana* (New York: Simon & Schuster, 1984); Michael J. Hogan, *The Marshall Plan: America, Britain, and the Reconstruction of Western Europe, 1947–1952* (Cambridge: Cambridge University Press, 1987); Allen W. Dulles, *The Marshall Plan* (Providence, R.I.: Berg, 1993).

27. President Truman's address to Congress, 12 March 1947, in Mee, *Marshall Plan,* Appendix I.

28. Secretary of State Marshall's speech at Harvard University, 5 June 1947, in Mee, *Marshall Plan,* Appendix II.

29. Hogan, *Marshall Plan,* 36–38.

30. Price, *Marshall Plan,* 26–27, 85.

31. X [George F. Kennan], "The Sources of Soviet Conduct," *Foreign Affairs* 25 (July 1947): 567, 572–573, 575, 580, 582.

32. Leopold von Ranke, *Sämtliche Werke,* vols. 33–34, *Geschichten der romanischen und germanischen Völker von 1494 bis 1514* (History of the Romanic and Germanic peoples from 1494 to 1514) (Leipzig, [1824] 1874), vii. Such a viewpoint did not in itself exclude, however, the reconstruction of historical contexts.

33. Ernst Breisach, *Historiography: Ancient, Medieval and Modern* (Chicago: University of Chicago Press, 1983).

34. Georg G. Iggers, *The German Conception of History: The National Tradition of Historical Thought from Herder to the Present* (Middletown, Conn.: Wesleyan University Press, 1983).

35. Robert W. Fogel, "The New Economic History: Its Findings and Methods," *The Economic History Review* 19 (1966): 656.

36. Robert W. Fogel, *Railroads and American Economic Growth* (Baltimore: Johns Hopkins University Press, 1964).

37. David Hackett Fisher, *Historians' Fallacies: Toward a Logic of Historical Thought* (New York: Harper & Row, 1970), 19.

38. Niall Ferguson, ed., *Virtual History: Alternatives and Counterfactuals* (London: Papermac, [1997] 1998).

39. Philip E. Tetlock and Aaron Belkin, eds., *Counterfactual Thought Experiments in World Politics* (Princeton, N.J.: Princeton University Press, 1996).

3. Nation-States Need Not Go to War

1. Charles Tilly, *Coercion, Capital, and European States, AD 990–1990* (Cambridge: Basil Blackwell, 1990), 70–76.

2. Niccolò Machiavelli, *The Prince and the Discourses* (New York: Random House, [1513] 1950).

3. Thomas Hobbes, *Leviathan* (Harmondsworth, UK: Penguin, [1651] 1968).

4. Vladimir Iljitj Lenin, *Imperialism, the Highest Stage of Capitalism: A Popular Outline* (Beijing: Foreign Language Press, [1917] 1969).

5. Adolf Hitler, *Mein Kampf,* trans. Ralph Manheim (New York: Mariner Books, [1925] 1999); Benito Mussolini, *The Doctrine of Fascism* (Florence: Vallechi editore, 1938).

6. *Documents on the History of European Integration,* ed. Walter Lipgens, vol. 1, *Continental Plans for European Union, 1939–1945* (Berlin: Walter de Gruyter, 1985), 471–484.

7. William Diebold Jr., *The Schuman Plan: A Study in Economic Cooperation 1950–1959* (New York: Praeger, 1959); Roger Morgan, *West European Politics since 1945: The Shaping of the European Community* (London: Batsford, 1972); Alan S. Milward, *The Reconstruction of Western Europe, 1945–51* (London: Methuen, 1984); David W. P. Lewis, *The Road to Europe: History, Institutions and Prospects of European Integration, 1945–1993* (New York: Peter Lang, 1993); John Gillingham, *Coal, Steel, and the Rebirth of Europe, 1945–1955: The Germans and French from Ruhr Conflict to Economic Community* (Cambridge: Cambridge University Press, 1991); Douglas Brinkley and Clifford Hackett, eds., *Jean Monnet: The Path to European Unity* (London: Macmillan, 1991); Alan S. Milward, *The European Rescue of the Nation-State* (London: Routledge, 1993); Francois Duchêne, *Jean Monnet: The First Statesman of Interdependence* (New York: Norton, 1994); Philippe C. Schmitter, "If the Nation-State Were to Wither Away in Europe, What Might Replace It?" in *The Future of the Nation-State: Essays on Cultural Pluralism and Political Integration,* ed. Sverker Gustavsson and Leif Lewin (Stockholm: Nerenius & Santérus, 1996); Philip Thody, *An Historical Introduction to the European Union* (London: Routledge, 1997); Michael Newman, *Democracy, Sovereignty and the European Union* (London: Hurst, 1997); Andrew Moravcsik, *The Choice for Europe: Social Purpose and State Power from Messina to Maastricht* (Ithaca, N.Y.: Cornell University Press, 1998); David McKay, *Federalism and European Union: A Political Economy Perspective* (Oxford: Oxford University Press, 1999); Catherine Hoskyns and Michael Newman, eds., *Democratising the European Union: Issues for the 21st Century* (Manchester, UK: Manchester University Press, 2000).

8. Jean Monnet, *Memoirs* (London: Collins, [1976] 1978), 288–289, 293.

9. See Chapter 2.

10. The memorandum was printed twenty years later in *Le Monde,* 9 May 1970.

11. The Schuman Declaration may be read in David de Giustino, ed., *A Reader in European Integration* (London: Longman, 1996), 58–60.

12. Sverker Gustavsson, "Varför överstat utan demokrati?" [Why suprastate without democracy?], in *Europaperspektiv 1998: Årsbok för Europaforskning inom ekonomi, juridik och statskunskap* [European perspectives 1998: The annual review of European research within the fields of economics, law and political science], ed. Ulf Bernitz, Sverker Gustavsson, and Lars Oxelheim (Stockholm: Nerenius & Santérus Förlag, 1998), 92–99.

13. "EUF Executive Bureau: The Federalists and the Schuman Plan," in *Documents on the History of European Integration,* ed. Walter Lipgens and Wilfried Loth, vol. 4, *Transnational Organizations of Political Parties and Pressure Groups in the Struggle for European Union, 1945–1950* (Berlin: Walter de Gruyter, 1991), 91–93.

14. Altiero Spinelli, "Report on the Proposal for a European Assembly to Draft a Pact of Federal Union," in *Documents on the History of European Integration,* ed. Walter Lipgens and Wilfried Loth, vol. 4, *Transnational Organizations of Political Parties and Pressure Groups in the Struggle for European Union, 1945–1950* (Berlin: Walter de Gruyter, 1991), 94–97.

15. Ferrico Parri, "Panorama of 1950," in *Documents on the History of European Integration,* ed. Walter Lipgens and Wilfried Loth, vol. 3, *The Struggle for European Union by Political Parties and Pressure Groups in Western European Countries, 1945–1950* (Berlin: Walter de Gruyter, 1991), 256. Parri was chairman of the federalist group in the Italian Senate.

16. Philip Cerny, *The Politics of Grandeur* (Cambridge: Cambridge University Press, 1980); Jean Lacouture, *De Gaulle: The Ruler, 1945–1970* (London: Harvill, [1985, 1986] 1991). De Gaulle's press conference is reproduced in De Giustino, *Reader in European Integration,* 189–192.

17. de Giustino, *Reader in European Integration,* 247–250.

18. George Ross, *Jacques Delors and European Integration* (Cambridge: Polity Press, 1995), 47, 232–233.

19. Andrew Moravcsik, "Europe without Illusions: A Category Error," *Prospect* (July 2005).

20. Carl Schmitt, *Politische Theologie* (Berlin: Duncker & Humblot, [1922] 1993), 13–21.

21. Hans J. Morgenthau, *Politics among Nations: The Struggle for Power and Peace* (New York: Knopf, 1948). At the level of the world, the EU might be thought expressive of the idea of balance, and at the level of Europe, of the idea of integration.

22. Bruce Russett, *Grasping the Democratic Peace: Principles for a Post–Cold War World* (Princeton, N.J.: Princeton University Press, 1993).

23. Giandomenico Majone, *Regulating Europe* (London: Routledge, 1996), especially 284–300.

24. Fritz W. Scharpf, *Governing in Europe: Effective and Democratic?* (Oxford: Oxford University Press, 1999), 1, 187–204.

25. Moravcsik, "Europe without Illusions."

26. Ibid.

27. Christer Karlsson, *Democracy, Legitimacy and the European Union* (Uppsala: Acta Universitatis Upsaliensis, 2001); see especially 284–289.

4. Globalization Has Not Wiped Out the Freedom to Choose

1. Hans-Peter Martin and Harald Schumann, *The Global Trap: Globalization and the Assault on Democracy and Prosperity* (London: Zed Books, [1996] 1997). Quotations in Chapter 4 are from pp. 10, 29, 39, 60, 67, 114, 132, 165, and 227. The

book was first published in German in 1996 under the title *Die Globalisierungs-falle: Der Angriff auf Demokratie und Wohlstand* (Reinbek bei Hamburg: Rowolht Verlag GmbH, 1996). Hans-Peter Martin is an Austrian political journalist, educated in Austria and the United States, with a doctorate in law and political science from the University of Vienna. In 1986, he joined the German news magazine *Der Spiegel,* where he worked as a foreign correspondent in Latin America and elsewhere, later to become bureau chief in Vienna. Harald Schumann is a German journalist, who was educated in social science at Marburg and the Techninal University of Berlin. In 1986, he joined the staff of *Der Spiegel,* then moved to the German daily *Der Morgen,* before returning to *Der Spiegel* as deputy bureau chief of the Berlin office.

2. This is also the title of a book by Ian Clark that has attracted attention.

3. Important works in this debate include the following: Robert B. Reich, *The Work of Nations: Preparing Ourselves for 21st Century Capitalism* (New York: Knopf, 1991); Winfried Ruigrok and Rob van Tulder, *The Logic of International Restructuring* (London: Routledge, 1995); Martin Albrow, *The Global Age: State and Society beyond Modernity* (Oxford: Blackwell, 1996); Robert Boyer and Daniel Drache, eds., *States against Markets: The Limits of Globalization* (London: Routledge, 1996); Paul Hirst and Grahame Thompson, *Globalization in Question,* 2nd ed. (Cambridge: Polity Press, [1996] 1999); Kenichi Ohmae, *End of the Nation State* (London: HarperCollins, 1996); Saskia Sassen, *Losing Control? Sovereignty in an Age of Globalization* (New York: Columbia University Press, 1996); Susan Strange, *The Retreat of the State: The Diffusion of Power in the World Economy* (Cambridge: Cambridge University Press, 1996); Ian Clark, *Globalization and Fragmentation: International Relations in the Twentieth Century* (Oxford: Oxford University Press, 1997); Ian Clark, *Globalization and International Relations Theory* (Oxford: Oxford University Press, 1999); James N. Rosenau, *Along the Domestic-Foreign Frontier: Exploring Governance in a Turbulent World* (Cambridge: Cambridge University Press, 1997); David Held, Anthony McCrew, David Goldblatt, and Jonathan Perraton, *Global Transformations: Politics, Economics and Culture* (Cambridge: Polity Press, 1999); Ramesch Mishra, *Globalization and the Welfare State* (Cheltenham, UK: Edward Elgar, 1999). Held et al. divide globalization debaters into champions and critics; the latter in turn break down into skeptics and transformalists. Typical adherents of the first school are Reich and Ohmae, mentioned here; of the second, Ruigrok and van Tulder as well as Hirst and Thompson; of the third, Rosenau. The criterion of classification is not altogether clear, however; all are agreed, for example, that the economy has been internationalized. On the other hand, if the criterion is whether an author considers politicians to be powerless and accountability accordingly impossible (as Martin and Schumann do), then it is hard to find any serious representatives at all for the first school. In addition, I classify certain individual works differently than do Held et al.

4. Paul Krugman, *Pop Internationalism* (Cambridge, Mass.: The MIT Press, 1996).

5. Paul Bairoch, "Globalization Myths and Realities," in *States against Markets: The*

Limits of Globalization, ed. Robert Boyer and Daniel Drache (London: Routledge, 1996), 173.

6. Hirst and Thompson, *Globalization,* 19–61; quotation from p. 60.

7. Robert B. Zevin, "Are World Financial Markets More Open? If So, Why and with What Effects?" in *Financial Openness and National Autonomy: Opportunities and Constraints,* ed. Tariq Banuri and Juliet B. Schor (Oxford: Clarendon Press, 1992).

8. Fritz W. Scharpf and Vivien A. Schmidt, eds., *Welfare and Work in the Open Economy,* vols. 1–2 (Oxford: Oxford University Press, 2000); Mishra, *Globalization.*

9. Reich, *Work of Nations;* Kenichi Ohmae, *Triad Power: The Coming Shape of Global Competition* (New York: Free Press, 1985); Ohmae, *End of the Nation State.*

10. Ruigrok and van Tulder, *Logic of International Restructuring,* 168.

11. Hirst and Thompson, *Globalization,* 273, 270, 256–257.

12. Ruigrok and van Tulder, *Logic of International Restructuring,* 178–179.

13. Clark, *Globalization and International Relations Theory,* 44.

14. Albrow, *Global Age,* 2.

15. Sassen, *Losing Control.*

16. Albrow, *Global Age,* 3.

17. Rosenau, *Along the Domestic-Foreign Frontier.*

18. Daniel Bell, *The End of Ideology* (New York: Free Press, 1960).

19. Seymour Martin Lipset, *Political Man* (London: Mercury Books, 1963).

20. Adam Przeworski and Henry Teune, *The Logic of Comparative Social Inquiry* (New York: Wiley, 1970).

21. Francis Castles and Robert D. McKinley, "Does Politics Matter? An Analysis of the Public Welfare Commitment in Advanced Democratic States," *European Journal of Political Research* 7 (1979): 169–186.

22. Boutros Boutros-Ghali, "Global Leadership after the Cold War," *Foreign Affairs* 75 (March/April 1996): 86–98.

23. Martin and Schumann, *Global Trap,* 28, 184–186, 189, 213. In their characteristic way, they describe Boutros-Ghali as follows: "Like so many world celebrities, he looks much smaller and frailer in real life than he does on the television screen; permanent conflicts surrounding his global commitment have left behind visible traces. It is 22 July 1996. He has been on his feet since three in the morning, trying once more in vain to arouse the world community before all it can do is react to the consequences of the latest outbreak of fighting." (184–185).

24. World Commission on Environment and Development, *Our Common Future: The World Commission on Environment and Development* (Oxford: Oxford University Press, 1987), x, xi, 85–86, 90, 261, 309, 343.

25. United Nations Conference on Environment and Development, *Agenda 21: Earth Summit—The United Nations Programme of Action from Rio* (New York: United Nations Department of Public Information, 1993), chap. 1, sec. 1.1; Caroline Thomas, *The Environment in International Relations* (London: Royal Institute

of International Affairs, 1992); Adam Roberts and Benedict Kingsbury, eds., *United Nations, Divided World: The UN's Roles in International Relations* (Oxford: Clarendon Press, 1993).

26. United Nations General Assembly, 19th Special Session, *Programme for the Further Implementation of Agenda 21: Resolution adopted by the General Assembly,* A/RES/S-19/2, 1997 (New York: United Nations Department of Public Information, 1998); Derek Osborn and Tom Bigg, *Earth Summit II: Outcomes and Analysis* (London: Earthscan, 1998). The secretary-general's report, "Overall Progress Achieved Since the United Nations Conference on Environment and Development," is reproduced in Osborn and Bigg's work as Annex 3.

27. United Nations Environment Programme, *Global Environment Outlook (GEO-1)* (Nairobi: United Nations Environment Programme 1997), vii, 19, 131, 252.

28. Felix Dodds, ed., *The Way Forward: Beyond Agenda 21* (London: Earthscan, 1997); Tim O'Riordan and Heather Voisey, eds., *The Transition to Sustainability: The Politics of Agenda 21 in Europe* (London: Earthscan, 1998); William M. Lafferty and Katarina Eckerberg, eds., *From the Earth Summit to Local Agenda 21: Working towards Sustainable Development* (London: Earthscan, 1998); William M. Lafferty, ed., *Implementing LA21 in Europe: New Initiatives for Sustainable Communities* (Oslo: ProSus, 1999); Iftikhar Ahmed and Jacobus A. Doeleman, eds., *Beyond Rio: The Environmental Crisis and Sustainable Livelihoods in the Third World* (New York: International Labour Organization, 1995); Mikael Román, *The Implementation of International Regimes: The Case of the Amazon Cooperation Treaty* (Uppsala: Uppsala University, Department of Government, 1998); Mary MacDonald, *Agendas for Sustainability: Environment and Development into the Twenty-First Century* (London: Routledge, 1998).

29. United Nations, Economic and Social Council, Commission on Sustainable Development, *Implementing Agenda 21: Report of the Secretary-General,* 2001, E/CN.17/2002/PC.2/7, 4.

30. Ibid, 6.

31. Ibid.

32. United Nations, Economic and Social Council, Commission on Sustainable Development, *Review of Progress in Forests since the United Nations Conference on Environmental Development: Report of the Secretary-General,* 2001, E/CN.17/2001/PC/15.

33. United Nations, Economic and Social Council, Commission on Sustainable Development, *Oceans and Seas: Report of the Secretary-General,* 2001, E/CN.17/2001/PC/16.

34. United Nations, Economic and Social Council, Commission on Sustainable Development, *Water: A Key Resource for Sustainable Development: Report of the Secretary-General,* 2001, E/CN.17/2001/PC/17.

35. United Nations, Economic and Social Council, Commission on Sustainable Development, *Global Status of Biological Diversity: Report of the Secretary-General,* 2001, E/CN.17/2001/PC/18.

36. United Nations, Economic and Social Council, Commission on Sustainable De-

velopment, *Protection of the Atmosphere: Report of the Secretary-General,* 2001, E/CN.17/2001/PC/12.

37. United Nations, Economic and Social Council, Commission on Sustainable Development, *Agriculture, Land and Desertification: Report of the Secretary-General,* 2001, E/CN.17/2001/PC/13.

38. United Nations, Economic and Social Council, Commission on Sustainable Development, *Changing Consumption Patterns: Report of the Secretary-General,* 2001, E/CN.17/2001/PC/8, 4.

39. United Nations, Economic and Social Council, Commission on Sustainable Development, *Energy and Transport: Report of the Secretary-General,* 2001, E/CN.17/2001/PC/20.

40. United Nations, Economic and Social Council, Commission on Sustainable Development, *Finance and Trade: Report of the Secretary-General,* 2001, E/CN.17/2001/PC/10, 5.

41. William Lafferty and James Meadowcroft, eds., *Implementing Agenda 21: Strategies and Initiatives in High Consumption Societies* (Oxford: Oxford University Press, 2000), 347, 412, 420–421, 454.

42. Friedrich A. Hayek, *The Road to Serfdom* (London: Routledge & Kegan Paul, 1944).

43. J. Gray, *Liberalisms* (London: Routledge & Kegan Paul, 1989), 89.

44. Here I follow the interpretation offered by Mats Lundström, *Politikens moraliska rum: En studie i F. A. Hayeks politiska filosofi* [The moral space of politics: An analysis of the political philosophy of F. A. Hayek] (Uppsala: Almqvist & Wiksell, 1993); Mats Lundström, "Is Anti-Rationalism Rational? The Case of F. A. Hayek," *Scandinavian Political Studies* 15 (1992): 235–248. Lundström distinguishes between a "theoretical" and an "instrumental" level in Hayek's thought.

45. Chapter 7 is devoted to this concept.

46. Friedrich A. Hayek, *The Constitution of Liberty* (London: Routledge & Kegan Paul, 1976), 41.

47. Robert Nozick, *The Examined Life* (New York: Simon & Schuster, 1989), 286–287.

48. Clark, *Globalization and International Relations Theory,* 170.

49. Susan Strange, "Finance, Information and Power," *Review of International Studies* 16 (1990): 266.

5. Power-Sharing Does Not Exclude Accountability

1. Gunning Bedford of Delaware, Federal Convention of 1787.

2. James M. Buchanan and Gordon Tollock, *The Calculus of Consent: Logical Foundations of Constitutional Democracy* (Ann Arbor: University of Michigan Press, 1962), 17. From this point of departure, the authors develop their original and influential rejection of majority rule in favor of the politics of logrolling.

3. For a critical discussion of the public-choice school, see Leif Lewin, *Self-Interest and Public Interest in Western Politics* (Oxford: Oxford University Press, 1991).

4. Kenneth J. Arrow, *Social Choice and Individual Values,* 2nd ed. (New Haven, Conn.: Yale University Press, [1951] 1963).

5. Anthony Downs, *An Economic Theory of Democracy* (New York: Harper & Row, 1957).

6. William Riker, *Liberalism against Populism: A Confrontation between the Theory of Democracy and the Theory of Social Choice* (San Francisco: W. H. Freeman, 1982).

7. Buchanan and Tollock, *Calculus of Consent,* 24–25.

8. Robert A. Dahl, *A Preface to Democratic Theory* (Chicago: Phoenix Books, 1956), 4–33.

9. In his lecture as Johan Skytte Prizewinner in Uppsala on 4 October 1997, Lijphart gave a witty overview of how his terminology had changed (perhaps "accommodation" referred to "a study of Dutch housing policy"?): Arend Lijphart, "Consensus and Consensus Democracy: Cultural, Structural, Functional, and Rational-Choice Explanations," *Scandinavian Political Studies* 21 (1998): 99–108.

10. Arend Lijphart, *Patterns of Democracy: Government Forms and Performance in Thirty-Six Countries* (New Haven, Conn.: Yale University Press, 1999), 275.

11. For a range of views on determinants of and remedies for the abuse of power, see the following: James C. Scott, *Comparative Political Corruption* (Englewood Cliffs, N.J.: Prentice-Hall, 1972); Michael Clarke, ed., *Corruption, Causes, Consequences and Control* (London: Frances Pinter, 1983); Alison Jamieson, *Political Corruption in Western Europe* (London: Research Institute for the Study of Conflict and Terrorism, 1996).

12. Lijphart, *Patterns of Democracy,* 289.

13. Ibid., 1–2.

14. Ibid., 275. Lijphart's more important works also include the following: *The Politics of Accommodation: Pluralism and Democracy in the Netherlands* (Berkeley: University of California Press, 1968); *Democracy in Plural Societies: A Comparative Exploration* (New Haven, Conn.: Yale University Press, 1977); *Democracies: Patterns of Majoritarian and Consensus Government in Twenty-One Countries* (New Haven, Conn.: Yale University Press, 1984). See also Markus M. L. Crepaz, Thomas A. Koelble, and David Wilsford, eds., *Democracy and Institutions: The Life Work of Arend Lijphart* (Ann Arbor: University of Michigan Press, 2000).

15. Arend Lijphart, "Democracies: Forms, Performance, and Constitutional Engineering," *European Journal of Political Research* 25 (1994): 1–17; quotation from 12. The data he presents in support of this conclusion, however, are rather skimpy.

16. Leading review articles on Lijphart's theory include the following: Hans Daalder, "The Consociational Democracy Theme," review of *The Politics of Accommodation: Pluralism and Democracy in the Netherlands,* by Arend Lijphart, *World Politics* 26 (1974): 604–621; Brian Barry, "Political Accommodation and Consociational Democracy," review of *The Politics of Accommodation: Pluralism and Democracy in the Netherlands* and "Consociational Democracy," by Arend Lijphart, *British Journal of Political Science* 5 (1975): 477–505; G. Bingham Powell, review of *Democracy in Plural Societies,* by Arend Lijphart, The *American Political Science Review* 73 (1979): 295–297, quotation from 295.

17. G. Bingham Powell, "Political Responsiveness and Constitutional Design," in *Democracy and Institutions: The Life Work of Arend Lijphart,* ed. Markus M. L. Crepaz, Thomas A. Koelble, and David Wilsford (Ann Arbor: University of Michigan Press, 2000), 17–18.

18. Pippa Norris, "Choosing Electoral Systems: Proportional, Majoritarian and Mixed Systems," *International Political Science Review* 18 (1997): 310–311.

19. For a more comprehensive treatment of the history of democratic ideas, see Leif Lewin, *"Bråka inte!" Om vår tids demokratisyn* ["Don't be a trouble-maker!" The democratic theory of our time] (Stockholm: SNS, 2002).

20. Thomas Hare, *The Machinery of Representation* (London: W. Maxwell, 1857); Thomas Hare, *A Treatise on the Election of Representatives, Parliamentary and Municipal* (London: Longman, Brown, Green, Longmans & Roberts, 1859). On Hare's influence on Mill, see Jenifer Hart, *Proportional Representation: Critics of the British Electoral System 1820–1945* (Oxford: Clarendon Press, 1992), 24–55.

21. John Stuart Mill, "Recent Writers on Reform" [1859], in *Collected Works of John Stuart Mill,* ed. John Mercel Robson, vol. 19, *Essays on Politics and Society* (Toronto: University of Toronto Press, 1977), 365.

22. John Stuart Mill, "Considerations of Representative Government" [1861], in *Collected Works of John Stuart Mill,* ed. John Mercel Robson, vol. 19, *Essays on Politics and Society* (London: Routledge, 1977), 448–466; quotations from 455–456.

23. Arnold Heidenheimer, ed., *Political Corruption: Readings in Comparative Analysis* (New York: Holt, Rinehart & Winston, 1970), 362.

24. Carl J. Friedrich, *The Pathology of Politics: Violence, Betrayal, Corruption, Secrecy, and Propaganda* (New York: Harper & Row, 1972), 167. Friedrich bases his argument on data from a study on the power game in Chicago: Edward C. Banfield, *Political Influence* (Glencoe, Ill.: Free Press, 1961).

25. Mill, "Considerations of Representative Government," 412.

26. Vernon Bogdanor, *What Is Proportional Representation?* (Oxford: Martin Robertson, 1984), 147–157; quotation from 156; cf. Axel Hadenius, *Institutions and Democratic Citizenship* (Oxford: Oxford University Press, 2001), 45–48, 91–99.

27. Lani Guiner, *The Tyranny of the Majority: Fundamental Fairness in Representative Democracy* (New York: Free Press, 1994), 3, 6.

28. Robert Williams, *Political Corruption in Africa* (Aldershot, UK: Gower, 1987), 135.

29. J. David Greenstone, "Corruption and Self-Interest in Kampala and Nairobi," in *Political Corruption: Readings in Comparative Analysis,* ed. Arnold Heidenheimer (New York: Holt, Rinehart & Winston, 1970), 465–468.

30. Richard K. Matthews, ed., *Virtue, Corruption and Self-Interest: Values in the Eighteenth Century* (London: Associated University Press, 1994).

31. G. Bingham Powell, *Elections as Instruments of Democracy: Majoritarian and Proportional Visions* (New Haven, Conn.: Yale University Press, 2000), 254.

32. Hart, *Proportional Representation,* 99.

33. Martin Clark, *Modern Italy, 1871–1982* (London: Longman, 1984); David Hine, *Governing Italy: The Politics of Bargained Pluralism* (Oxford: Clarendon Press,

1993); Mario B. Mignone, *Italy Today: A Country in Transition* (New York: Peter Lang, 1995); Hilary Partridge, *Italian Politics Today* (Manchester, UK: Manchester University Press, 1998).

34. Denis Mack Smith, *Modern Italy: A Political History* (New Haven, Conn.: Yale University Press, 1997), 435.

35. Mack Smith, *Modern Italy,* 436.

36. In addition to earlier cited works by Clark, Hine, Mignone, and Partridge (see note 33), reference is here made to the following: Frederic Spotts and Theodor Wieser, *Italy: A Difficult Democracy* (Cambridge: Cambridge University Press, 1986); Paul Furlong, *Modern Italy: Representation and Reform* (London: Routledge, 1994); Giuseppe Chiarante, *Italia 1995: La Democrazia Difficile* [Italy 1995: The difficult democracy] (Rome: Edizioni Sisifo, 1995); Patrick McCarthy, *The Crisis of the Italian State: From the Origins of the Cold War to the Fall of Berlusconi and Beyond* (London: Macmillan, 1995); Michael von Tangen Page, *Prisons, Peace and Terrorism* (London: Macmillan, 1998); René Seindal, *Mafia, Money and Politics in Sicily, 1950–1997* (Copenhagen: Museum Tusculanum Press, 1998).

37. Donald Sassoon, *Contemporary Italy: Economy, Society and Politics since 1945*, 2nd ed. (London: Longman, [1986] 1997), 192.

38. Joseph LaPalombara, *Democracy, Italian Style* (New Haven, Conn.: Yale University Press, 1987), 158–159.

39. Giuseppe Di Palma, *Surviving without Governing: The Italian Parties in Parliament* (Berkeley: University of California Press, 1977), 223–224 (on Lijphart); quotation from 251.

40. Gianfranco Pasquino and Patrick McCarthy, eds., *The End of Post-War Politics in Italy: The Landmark 1992 Elections* (Boulder, Colo.: Westview Press, 1993); Carol Mershon and Gianfranco Pasquino, eds., *Italian Politics: Ending the First Republic* (Boulder, Colo.: Westview Press, 1995); Richard S. Katz and Piero Ignazi, eds., *Italian Politics: The Year of the Tycoon* (Boulder, Colo.: Westview Press, 1996); Stephen Gundle and Simon Parker, eds., *The New Italian Republic: From the Fall of the Berlin Wall to Berlusconi* (London: Routledge, 1996); Martin Bull and Martin Rhodes, eds., *Crisis and Transition in Italian Politics* (London: Frank Cass, 1997); Vittorio Bufacchi and Simon Burgess, *Italy since 1989: Events and Interpretations* (London: Macmillan, 1998); Stanton H. Burnett and Luca Mantovani, *The Italian Guillotine: Operation Clean Hands and the Overthrow of Italy's First Republic* (Lanham, Md.: Rowman & Littlefield, 1998); Sondra Z. Koff and Stephen P. Koff, *Italy: From the First to the Second Republic* (London: Routledge, 2000).

41. Indro Montanelli and Mario Cervi, *L'Italia di Berlusconi, 1993–1995* [Berlusconi's Italy, 1993–1995] (Milan: Rizzoli, 1995), 341. Translation from Italian by Karolina Larfors, research assistant. In original, the quotation reads "spietato, urlante, una vera iena."

42. Burnett and Mantovani, *Italian Guillotine,* 67.

43. Quoted in Burnett and Mantonvani, *Italian Guillotine,* 87.

44. Mark Gilbert, *The Italian Revolution: The End of Politics, Italian Style?* (Boulder, Colo.: Westview Press, 1995), 147.

45. Francesco Di Natale, *Appunti di storia della Prima Republica* [Notes on the history of the First Republic] (Perugia, Italy: Guerra Edizioni, 1994), 39. The person quoted by Di Natale was a certain Enzo Biagi.

46. Montanelli and Cervi, *L'Italia di Berlusconi*, 236–237. Translation from Italian by Karolina Larfors, research assistant. In original, the quotation reads "senza alcuna polemica, in punta di piedi, quale ultimo spirito di servizio, con la morte nel cuore e senza alcuna prospetti ova per il mio futuro."

47. Max Weber, "Politics as a Vocation," and "Science as Vocation," in *From Max Weber: Essays in Sociology*, ed. and trans. H. H. Gerth and C. Wright Mills (London: Routledge & Kegan Paul, [1919] 1948), 77–156; quotation from 127. The German words Weber used were "Gesinnungsethik" and "Verantwortungsethik." Several variants are used in English translations; the former word, for example, is sometimes rendered as "ethics of ultimate ends."

48. Donatella della Porta, "The System of Corrupt Exchange in Local Government," in *The New Italian Republic: From the Fall of the Berlin Wall to Berlusconi*, ed. Stephen Gundle and Simon Parker (London: Routledge, 1996), 221–222.

49. Nicholas Gane, "Max Weber on the Ethical Irrationality of Political Leadership," *Sociology: The Journal of the British Sociological Association* 31 (1997): 553–555.

50. Weber, "Politics as a Vocation," 127.

51. H. H. Bruun, *Science, Values and Politics in Max Weber's Methodology* (Copenhagen: Munksgaard, 1972), 240–290; quotations from 257, 260–262.

52. Stephen P. Turner and Regis A. Factor, *Max Weber and the Dispute over Reason and Value: A Study in Philosophy, Ethics, and Politics* (London: Routledge & Kegan Paul, 1984), 48.

53. Bruun, *Science, Values and Politics,* quotation from 267; on the circumstances surrounding Weber's lecture, see 271; Guenther Roth and Wolfgang Schluchter, *Max Weber's Vision of History: Ethics and Methods* (Berkeley: University of California Press, 1979), 65–116.

6. Implementation May Well Be Immaculate

1. Quoted by Andrew Dunsire in Jan-Erik Lane, ed., *Bureaucracy and Public Choice* (London: Sage, 1987), 112.

2. William A. Niskanen, *Bureaucracy and Representative Government* (Chicago: Aldine-Atherton, 1971), 39. In an article a few years later, entitled "Bureaucrats and Politicians," *Journal of Law and Economics* 18 (1975): 617–643, the author comments on the debate that his book provoked. He then expands his account of the motives of bureaucrats to include "slack resources"—a change that does not, however, affect his thesis in any vital respect.

3. Leif Lewin, *Self-Interest and Public Interest in Western Politics* (Oxford: Oxford University Press, 1991), 79–97.

4. Robert E. Goodin, "Rational Politicians and Rational Bureaucrats in Washington and Whitehall," *Public Administration* 60 (1982): 23–41; quotation from 38.

5. Albert Breton, *The Economic Theory of Representative Government* (London: Macmillan, 1974).

6. Albert Breton and Ronald Wintrobe, "The Equilibrium Size of a Budget-Maximizing Bureau: A Note on Niskanen's Theory of Bureaucracy," *Journal of Political Economy* 83 (1975): 195–208.

7. Gary J. Miller and Terry M. Moe, "Bureaucrats, Legislators, and the Size of Government," *The American Political Science Review* 77 (1983): 297–322.

8. Bruce L. Benson, "Why Are Congressional Committees Dominated by 'High-Demand' Legislators? A Comment on Niskanen's View of Bureaucrats and Politicians," *Southern Economic Journal* 48 (1981): 68–77.

9. Richard Rose, *Understanding Big Government: The Programme Approach* (London: Sage, 1984), 44.

10. Peter Self, *Political Theories of Modern Government* (London: George Allen & Unwin, 1985), 67–68.

11. Ibid., 67.

12. Gert T. de Bruin, "Economic Theory of Bureaucracy and Public Good Allocation," in *Bureaucracy and Public Choice,* ed. Jan-Erik Lane (London: Sage, 1987), 58.

13. John A. C. Conybeare, "Bureaucracy, Monopoly, and Competition: A Critical Analysis of the Budget-Maximizing Model of Bureaucracy," *American Journal of Political Science* 28 (1984): 479–502.

14. B. Guy Peters, "The European Bureaucrat: The Applicability of *Bureaucracy and Representative Government* to Non-American Settings," in *The Budget-Maximizing Bureaucrat: Appraisals and Evidence,* ed. André Blais and Stéphane Dion (Pittsburgh: University of Pittsburgh Press, 1991), 303–346; quotation from 318; B. Guy Peters, *The Politics of Bureaucreacy* (White Plains, N.Y.: Longman, 1995).

15. Peters, "European Bureaucrat," 346.

16. Robert E. Goodin, "Possessive Individualism Again," *Political Studies* 24 (1976): 494.

17. Goodin, "Rational Politicians," 26.

18. Patrick Dunleavy, "Bureaucrats, Budgets and the Growth of the State: Reconstructing an Instrumental Model," *British Journal of Political Science* 15 (1985): 299–328; Patrick Dunleavy, *Democracy, Bureaucracy and Public Choice* (London: Harvester Wheatsheaf, 1991), 174–209; Robert A. Young, "Budget Size and Bureaucratic Careers," in *The Budget-Maximizing Bureaucrat: Appraisals and Evidence,* ed. André Blais and Stéphane Dion (Pittsburgh: University of Pittsburgh Press, 1991), 33–58; B. Guy Peters, *Politics of Bureaucracy,* especially 26.

19. P. M. Jackson, *The Political Economy of Bureaucracy* (Oxford: Philip Allen, 1982), 133.

20. Breton and Wintrobe, "Equilibrium Size of a Budget-Maximizing Bureau," 205; Julius Margolis, "Bureaucrats and Politicians: Comment," *Journal of Law and Economics* 29 (1975): 658.

21. Joel D. Aberbach, Robert D. Putnam, and Berta A. Rockman, *Bureaucrats and Politicians in Western Democracies* (Cambridge, Mass.: Harvard University Press, 1981); Mattei Dogan, ed., *The Mandarins of Western Europe* (New York: Wiley, 1975).

22. André Blais and Stéphane Dion, "Are Bureaucrats Budget Maximizers? The Niskanen Model and Its Critics," *Polity* 22 (1990): 673.

23. William A. Niskanen, "A Reflection on *Bureaucracy and Representative Government*," in *The Budget-Maximizing Bureaucrat: Appraisals and Evidence*, ed. André Blais and Stephane Dion (Pittsburgh: University of Pittsburgh Press, 1991), 13–31; quotation from 28.

24. Margaret Thatcher, *The Downing Street Years* (London: HarperCollins, 1993), and *The Path to Power* (London: HarperCollins, 1995); Goodin, "Rational Politicians"; Geoffrey K. Fry, "The Development of the Thatcher Government's 'Grand Strategy' for the Civil Service: A Public Policy Perspective," *Public Administration* 62 (1984); David Heald, "Will the Privatization of Public Enterprises Solve the Problem of Control?" *Public Administration* 63 (1985); Peter Jenkins, *Mrs Thatcher's Revolution* (London: Jonathan Cape, 1987); Gavin Drewry and Tony Butcher, *The Civil Service Today* (Oxford: Basil Blackwell, 1988); Geoffrey K. Fry, "The Thatcher Government, the Financial Management Initiative and the 'New Civil Service,'" *Public Administration* 66 (1988); Kenneth Harris, *Thatcher* (London: Weidenfeld & Nicolson, 1988); Bob Jessop, Kevin Bonnett, Simon Bromley, and Tom Ling, *Thatcherism: A Tale of Two Nations* (Cambridge: Polity Press, 1988); Peter Riddell, *The Thatcher Decade: How Britain Has Changed during the 1980s* (Oxford: Basil Blackwell, 1989); G. W. Jones, "A Revolution in Whitehall? Changes in British Central Government since 1979," *West European Politics* 12 (1989); Brian W. Hogwood, *Trends in British Public Policy: Do Governments Make Any Difference?* (Buckingham, UK: Open University Press, 1992); Jeremy Moon, *Innovative Leadership in Democracy: Policy Change under Thatcher* (Aldershot, UK: Dartmouth, 1993); Donald J. Savoie, *Thatcher, Reagan, Mulroney: In Search of a New Bureaucracy* (Pittsburgh: University of Pittsburgh Press, 1994); André Blais, Donald E. Blake, and Stéphane Dion, *Governments, Parties, and Public Sector Employees: Canada, United States, Britain, and France* (Pittsburgh: University of Pittsburgh Press, 1997); Eric J. Evans, *Thatcher and Thatcherism* (London: Routledge, 1997).

25. Thatcher, *Downing Street*, 122.

26. Savoie, *Thatcher, Reagan, Mulroney*, 99.

27. Jessop et al., *Thatcherism*, 37.

28. Fry, "Development of the Thatcher Government's 'Grand Strategy,'" 323.

29. Goodin, "Rational Politicians," 23.

30. Savoie, *Thatcher, Reagan, Mulroney*, 106.

31. Address by Margaret Thatcher, quoted in Fry, "Development of the Thatcher Government's 'Grand Strategy,'" 322–323.

32. Drewry and Butcher, *Civil Service*, 201.

33. Thatcher, *Path to Power*, 123, 166.

34. Fry, "Development of the Thatcher Government's 'Grand Strategy,'" 330.

35. Thatcher, *Downing Street*, 30–31.

36. Fry, "Thatcher Government."

37. Evans, *Thatcher and Thatcherism*, 53–54.

38. Riddell, *Thatcher Decade*, 204.

39. Thatcher, *Path to Power*, 565.

40. Riddell, *Thatcher Decade*, 3.

41. Savoie, *Thatcher, Reagan, Mulroney.*

42. Max Weber, *From Max Weber: Essays in Sociology,* ed. and trans. H. H. Gerth and C. Wright Mills (New York: Oxford University Press, 1958), 95, 196–197, 214–216.

43. Neil Summerton, "A Mandarin's Duty," *Parliamentary Affairs* 33 (1979): 400–421.

44. Hannah Arendt, *Eichmann in Jerusalem: A Report on the Banality of Evil* (New York: Penguin Group, 1963).

45. F. F. Ridley, "Political Neutrality in the British Civil Service: Sir Thomas More and Mr Clive Ponting v. Sir Robert Armstrong and the Vicar of Bray," in *Politics, Ethics and Public Service,* ed. Bernard Williams, John Stevenson, F. F. Ridley, Sir Kenneth Couzens, Alexander Grey, and Peter Jay (London: Royal Institute of Public Administration, 1985), 31–32, 39.

46. George A. Graham, "Ethical Guidelines for Public Administrators: Observations on Rules of the Game," *Public Administration Review* 34 (1974): 90–92.

47. Glendon A. Schubert Jr., "The Public Interest in Administrative Decision-Making: Theorem, Theosophy, or Theory?" *The American Political Science Review* 51 (1957): 346–368.

48. David K. Hart, "The Virtuous Citizen, the Honorable Bureaucrat, and 'Public' Administration," *Public Administration Review* 44 (1984): 111–120.

49. Dennis F. Thompson, "Moral Responsibility of Public Officials: The Problem of Many Hands," *The American Political Science Review* 74 (1980): 905–916.

50. Terry L. Cooper, *The Responsible Administrator,* 4th ed. (San Francisco: Jossey-Bass, 1998), 254.

51. Carl J. Friedrich, "Public Policy and the Nature of Administrative Responsibility," and Herman Finer, "Administrative Responsibility in Democratic Government," in *Bureaucratic Power in National Politics,* ed. Francis E. Rourke (Boston: Little, Brown, 1965), 165–175 and 176–187. The articles were originally published in 1940 and 1941, respectively.

7. Consequences May Well Be as Intended

1. Robert K. Merton, "The Unanticipated Consequences of Purposive Social Action," *American Sociological Review* 1 (1936): 894–904.

2. For works treating Merton's theory, see, e.g., Lewis A. Coser, ed., *The Idea of Social Structure: Papers in Honor of Robert K. Merton* (New York: Harcourt Brace Jovanovich, 1975); Richard Vernon, "Unintended Consequences," *Political Theory* 7 (1979): 57–73; Michel Crozier and Erhard Friedberg, *Actors and Systems: The Politics of Collective Action* (Chicago: University of Chicago Press, 1980); Susan Barrett and Colin Fudge, eds., *Policy and Action: Essays on the Implementation of Public Policy* (London: Methuen, 1981); Raymond Boudon, *The Unintended Consequences of Social Action* (London: Macmillan, 1982); Angelo Codevilla, *The Cure That May Kill: Unintended Consequences of the INF Treaty* (London: Institute for Eu-

ropean Defence and Strategic Studies, 1988); F. LaMond Tullis, *Unintended Consequences: Illegal Drugs and Drug Policies in Nine Countries* (Boulder, Colo.: Lynne Rienner, 1995); Edward Tenner, *Why Things Bite Back: Technology and the Revenge of Unintended Consequences* (London: Vintage Books, 1996); Ann Dryden Witte, Magaly Queralt Tasneem Chipty, and Harriet Griesinger, "Unintended Consequences? Welfare Reform and the Working Poor" (working paper no. 6798) (Cambridge, Mass.: National Bureau of Economic Research, 1998); Deepak Lal, *Unintended Consequences: The Impact of Factor Endowments, Culture, and Politics on Long-Run Economic Performance* (Cambridge, Mass.: MIT Press, 1998).

3. For a good overview, see Evert Vedung, *Public Policy and Program Evaluation* (New Brunswick, N.J.: Transaction Publishers, 1997).

4. Juan J. Linz and Alfred Stepan, *Problems of Democratic Transition and Consolidation: Southern Europe, South America, and Post-Communist Europe* (Baltimore: Johns Hopkins University Press, 1996), especially 239–254.

5. Y. F. Khong, *Analogies at War* (Princeton, N.J.: Princeton University Press, 1992).

6. A. Baring, *Aussenpolitik in Adenauers Kanzlerdemokratie: Bonns Beitrag zur Europäischen Verteidigungsgemeinschaft* [Foreign politics in Adenauer's chancellor democracy: The contribution of Bonn to the European Defense Community] (Munich: R. Oldenburg Verlag, 1969); D. C. Large, "Grand Illusions: The United States, the Federal Republic of Germany and the European Defense Community, 1950–1954," in *American Foreign Policy and the Reconstruction of West Germany,* ed. J. M. Diefendorf, A. Frohn, and H.-J. Rupieper (Washington, D.C.: Washington German Historical Institute, 1993); Barry Holmström, *Domstolar och demokrati* [Courts of law and democracy] (Uppsala: Acta Universitatis Upsaliensis, 1998), 357–369.

7. Cecilia Garme, *Newcomers to Power* (Uppsala: Acta Universitatis Upsaliensis, 2001).

8. Leif Lewin, *Self-Interest and Public Interest in Western Politics* (Oxford: Oxford University Press, 1991).

9. Formulation from Stephen P. Turner and Regis A. Factor, *Max Weber and the Dispute over Reason and Value: A Study in Philosophy, Ethics, and Politics* (London: Routledge & Kegan Paul, 1984).

10. Charles W. Kegley Jr., "How Did the Cold War Die? Principles for an Autopsy," *Mershon International Studies Review* 38 (1994): 13. Thus does Kegley summarize the theory of which he is the foremost critic.

11. George Melloan, "Military Cutbacks Will Crimp U.S. Foreign Policy," *Wall Street Journal,* 25 January 1993, A17.

12. Beth A. Fischer, *The Reagan Reversal: Foreign Policy and the End of the Cold War* (Columbia: University of Missouri Press, 1997).

13. Ibid., 115–116.

14. Kegley, "Cold War," 14.

15. Alexander L. George and Juliette L. George, *Presidential Personality and Performance* (Boulder, Colo.: Westview Press, 1998), 225–226.

16. Don Oberdorfer, *From the Cold War to a New Era: The United States and the Soviet Union, 1983–1991* (Baltimore: Johns Hopkins University Press, 1998), 23.

17. Kegley, "Cold War," 21, 33.

18. For different interpretations of the motives for and consequences of Reagan's de-

fense policy, see Robert Sheer, *With Enough Shovels: Reagan, Bush, and Nuclear War* (New York: Random House, 1982); Lou Cannon, *President Reagan: The Role of a Lifetime* (New York: Simon & Schuster, 1991); John Prados, *Keepers of the Keys: A History of the National Security Council from Truman to Bush* (New York: William Morrow, 1991); Jay Wink, *On the Brink: The Dramatic, Behind-the-Scenes Saga of the Reagan Era and the Men and Women Who Won the Cold War* (New York: Simon & Schuster, 1996); Fischer, *Reagan Reversal;* Frances Fitzgerald, *Way Out There in the Blue: Reagan, Star Wars, and the End of the Cold War* (New York: Simon & Schuster, 2000). See also the memoirs of three of the central actors: Ronald Reagan, *An American Life* (London: Hutchinson, 1990); Caspar Weinberger, *Fighting for Peace: Seven Critical Years in the Pentagon* (New York: Warner Books, 1990); and George P. Shultz, *Turmoil and Triumph: My Years as Secretary of State* (New York: Scribner's, 1993).

19. Nils Unga, *Socialdemokratin och arbetslöshetsfrågan 1912–34: Framväxten av den "nya" arbetslöshetspolitiken* [The Swedish Social Democratic Party and the issue of unemployment 1912–34: The emergence of the "new" unemployment policy] (Stockholm: Arkiv, 1976).

20. Leif Lewin, *Planhushållningsdebatten* [The debate on the planned economy] (Stockholm: Almqvist & Wiksell, 1967); *Ideology and Strategy: A Century of Swedish Politics* (Cambridge: Cambridge University Press, 1988), 123–158.

21. Gustav Möller, *Arbetslöshetsförsäkringen* [The unemployment insurance] (Stockholm: Tidens Förlag, 1926), especially 16–20.

22. Lewin, *Planhushållningsdebatten,* 45–50, especially 52–53.

23. The account that follows builds on Bo Rothstein's revealing analysis in *Den korporativa staten* [The corporate state] (Stockholm: Norstedts, 1992), 305–331.

24. *Proceedings,* LOs representantskap den 30 november 1930 [Representative body of the Swedish Labour Union, 30 November 1930].

25. Möller, *Arbetslöshetsförsäkringen,* 19–20, 24.

26. Rothstein, *Den korporativa staten,* 315.

27. Ibid., 322.

28. On Weber as the foremost defender of "the classical view," see Chapters 5 and 6.

29. It is said that among mathematicians in Cambridge during the 1920s, the following toast was sometimes proposed: "Pure mathematics. May it never be useful!"

30. For a representative defense of the second view, see Michael Gibbons, Camille Limoges, Helga Nowotng, Simon Schwartzman, Peter Scott, and Martin Trow, *The New Production of Knowledge* (London: Sage, 1994).

31. Alexander L. George, *Bridging the Gap: Theory and Practice in Foreign Policy* (Washington D.C.: United States Institute of Peace Press, 1993), xvii, xviii, 11, 13, 16–17, 21, 31, 140, 143–145.

8. Action Can Be Meaningful Even if Irrational

1. Kaare Strøm, *Minority Government and Majority Rule* (Cambridge: Cambridge University Press, 1990), 23.

2. Kenneth J. Arrow, *Social Choice and Individual Values,* 2nd ed. (New Haven, Conn.: Yale University Press, [1951] 1963); Robert Axelrod, *The Evolution of Co-operation* (New York: Basic Books, 1984); Brian Barry and Russell Hardin, eds., *Rational Man and Irrational Society: An Introduction and Sourcebook* (Beverly Hills, Calif.: Sage, 1982); Garrett Hardin, "The Tragedy of the Commons," *Science* 162 (1968): 1243–1248; James M. Buchanan and Gordon Tullock, *The Calculus of Consent: Logical Foundations of Constitutional Democracy* (Ann Arbor: University of Michigan Press, 1962); Donald Davidson, "Action, Reasons and Causes," *The Journal of Philosophy* 60 (1963); Anthony Downs, *An Economic Theory of Democracy* (New York: Harper & Row, 1957); Jon Elster, *Ulysses and the Sirens: Studies in Rationality and Irrationality* (Cambridge: Cambridge University Press, 1979); Jon Elster, *Sour Grapes: Studies in the Subversion of Rationality* (Cambridge: Cambridge University Press, 1983); Elinor Ostrom, *Governing the Commons: The Evolution of Institutions for Collective Action* (Cambridge: Cambridge University Press, 1990); Anatol Rapoport and Albert M. Chammah, *Prisoner's Dilemma: A Study in Conflict and Cooperation* (Ann Arbor: University of Michigan Press, 1965); William H. Riker, *The Theory of Political Coalitions* (New Haven, Conn.: Yale University Press, 1962); Amartya Sen and Bernard Williams, eds., *Utilitarianism and Beyond* (Cambridge: Cambridge University Press, 1982); Amartya Sen, "Behaviour and the Concept of Preference," in *Choice, Welfare, and Measurement* (Oxford: Basil Blackwell, 1982).

3. John M. Rist, *Epicurus: An Introduction* (London: Cambridge University Press, 1972); Avraam Koen, *Atoms, Pleasure, Virtue: The Philosophy of Epicurus* (New York: Lang, 1995).

4. Robert A. Markus, *Saecuklum: History and Society in the Theology of St Augustine* (Cambridge: Cambridge University Press, 1970); Quentin Skinner, *Machiavelli* (Oxford: Oxford University Press, 1981), 53.

5. Isaiah Berlin, "The Originality of Machiavelli," in *Against the Current: Essays in the History of Ideas,* ed. Henry Hard (Oxford: Clarendon Paperback, [1979] 1989), 25–79; quotations from 75, 40, 69.

6. Jean Hampton, *Hobbes and the Social Contract Tradition* (Cambridge: Cambridge University Press, 1986); Gregory S. Kavka, *Hobbesian Moral and Political Theory* (Princeton, N.J.: Princeton University Press, 1986); David Gauthier, "Taming Leviathan," review of *Hobbes and the Social Contract Tradition,* by Jean Hampton, and *Hobbesian Moral and Political Theory,* by Gregory S. Kavka, *Philosophy and Public Affairs* 16 (1987): 280–298.

7. Duncan Black, *The Theory of Committees and Elections* (Cambridge: Cambridge University Press, 1958).

8. Sen and Williams, *Utilitarianism and Beyond;* Robert Sugden, "Rational Choice: A Survey of Contributions from Economics and Philosophy," *The Economic Journal* 101 (1991): 751–785; Samuel Freeman, "Utilitarianism, Deontology, and the Priority of Right," *Philosophy and Public Affairs* 23 (1994): 313–349; John Rawls, *A Theory of Justice* (Cambridge, Mass.: Harvard University Press, 1971). Rawls can be criticized for insufficient consistency in his rejection of utilitarianism,

inasmuch as the people deliberating under his veil of ignorance consider their self-interest when attempting to form a just society. On Rawls, rights theory, and utilitarianism, see Brian Barry, *Justice as Impartiality* (Oxford: Clarendon Press, 1995), chap. 3.

9. James G. March and Johan P. Olsen, *Rediscovering Institutions: The Organizational Basis of Politics* (New York: Free Press, 1989); James G. March and Johan P. Olsen, *Democratic Governance* (New York: Free Press, 1994).

10. Elster, *Ulysses,* viii.

11. H. R. Trevor-Roper, *The Last Days of Hitler,* 5th ed. (London: Macmillan, [1947] 1978), 123–124.

12. Ibid., 125.

13. Alan Bullock, *Hitler: A Study in Tyranny* (London: Odham Books, 1952); William L. Shirer, *The Rise and Fall of the Third Reich* (New York: Simon & Schuster, 1960); Nicholas Goodrick-Clarke, *The Occult Roots of Nazism* (New York: New York University Press, 1985); Arthur L. Smith Jr., *The War for the German Mind: Re-Educating Hitler's Soldiers* (Providence, R. I.: Berghahn Books, 1996); John Lukacs, *The Hitler of History* (New York: Vintage Books, 1998); Stephen J. Lee, *Hitler and Nazi Germany* (London: Routledge, 1998); Ian Kershaw, *Hitler 1889– 1936: Hubris* (New York: W. W. Norton, 1998); Ian Kershaw, *Hitler 1936–45: Nemesis* (London: Allen Lane, 2000); Martyn Housden, *Hitler: Study of a Revolutionary?* (London: Routledge, 2000); Neil Gregor, ed., *Nazism* (Oxford: Oxford University Press, 2000).

14. Trevor-Roper, *Last Days of Hitler,* 158.

15. Ibid., 195–196.

16. Adolf Hitler, *Mein Kampf,* trans. Ralph Manheim (New York: Mariner Books, [1925] 1999), 654.

17. Trevor-Roper, *Last Days of Hitler,* 5.

18. Eric H. Vieler, *The Ideological Roots of German National Socialism* (New York: Peter Lang, 1999), 87.

19. John Lukacs, *The Last European War* (Garden City, N.Y.: Anchor Press, 1976), 6–7, 519–520.

20. George L. Mosse, *The Crisis of German Ideology: Intellectual Origins of the Third Reich* (New York: Howard Fertig, 1964), 54, 312–317.

21. Martin Broszat, *German National Socialism, 1919–1945* (Santa Barbara, Calif.: Clio Press, 1966), 32, 52, 59.

22. Hermann Rauschning, *Hitler Speaks: A Series of Political Conversations with Adolf Hitler on His Real Aims* (London: Thornton Butterworth, 1939), 14–15.

23. Rudolf Binion, *Hitler among the Germans* (New York: Elsevier, 1976), 109.

24. Binion, *Hitler among the Germans,* 51.

25. John Toland, *Adolf Hitler* (New York: Doubleday, 1976), 849.

26. Ibid., 856–857. The inserted explanation—to the effect that Hitler's reference was to the Soviet Union—is Toland's.

27. Hitler, *Mein Kampf,* 76, 78–81, 91, 450.

28. Vieler, *Ideological Roots,* 121.

29. Rauschning, *Hitler Speaks*, 196–197.
30. Ibid., 199.
31. Kershaw, *Hitler 1889–1936*, 289.
32. Quoted in Fritz Poetzsch-Heffter, "Vom Deutschen Staatsleben" [On German politics], in *Jahrbuch des Öffentlichen Rechts der Gegenwart*, vol. 22 (Tübingen, Germany, 1935), 51.
33. Quoted in Herbert Tingsten, *Nazismens och fascismens idéer* [The ideas of Nazism and Fascism] (Stockholm: Bonniers, [1936] 1965), 90–91.
34. Ibid., 77–85.

9. Conclusion

1. David L. Weimer and Aidan R. Vining, *Policy Analysis: Concepts and Practice*, 3rd ed. (Upper Saddle River, N.J.: Prentice-Hall, [1989] 1999), 280.
2. Henry Kissinger, *The Necessity for Choice: Prospects of American Foreign Policy* (New York: Harper, 1960), 1–6.
3. See Chapter 7, the third section, "Accountability and Expertise."
4. Henry Kissinger, *A World Restored: Metternich, Castlereagh and the Problems of Peace, 1812–22* (London: Weidenfeld & Nicolson, 1957), 324–325.
5. Patricia Day and Rudolf Klein, *Accountabilities: Five Public Services* (London: Tavistock Publications, 1987), 248.
6. Andrew Massey, *Managing the Public Sector: A Comparative Analysis of the United Kingdom and the United States* (Aldershot, UK: Edward Elgar, 1993), 200.
7. Ibid.
8. Ida R. Hoos, *Systems Analysis in Public Policy: A Critique*, rev. ed. (Berkeley: University of California Press, [1972] 1983), 45–46. Cherished children have many names, as the Swedish saying goes. The author points out that the use of such techniques is referred to not just as policy analysis but also as systems analysis, cost/benefit analysis, Planning-Programming-Budgeting-System, risk analysis, and technology assessment.
9. Wayne Parsons, *Public Policy: An Introduction to the Theory and Practice of Policy Analysis* (Cheltenham, UK: Edward Elgar, 1995), 207.
10. William N. Dunn, *Public Policy Analysis: An Introduction*, 2nd ed. (Englewood Cliffs, N.J.: Prentice Hall, [1981] 1994), 19.
11. Ibid.
12. Parsons, *Public Policy*, 433.
13. Fritz W. Scharpf, *Governing in Europe: Effective and Democratic?* (Oxford: Oxford University Press, 1999), 1, 187–204.
14. Giandomenico Majone, *Regulating Europe* (London: Routledge, 1996), especially 284–300.
15. Joseph A. Schumpeter, *Capitalism, Socialism, and Democracy* (New York: Harper, 1942).
16. Isaiah Berlin, *Four Essays on Liberty* (Oxford: Oxford University Press, 1969), 178.

17. Scharpf, *Governing in Europe;* Majone, *Regulating Europe.*

18. Erik Oddvar Eriksen and John Erik Fossum, eds., *Democracy in the European Union: Integration through Deliberation?* (London: Routledge, 2000), xii, 257.

19. Amy Gutmann and Dennis Thompson, *Democracy and Disagreement: Why Moral Conflict Cannot Be Avoided in Politics, and What Should Be Done about It* (Cambridge, Mass.: Belknap, 1996), 28. See also the well-known works by Jürgen Habermas, *The Structural Transformation of the Public Sphere: An Inquiry into the Category of Bourgeois Society,* trans. Thomas Burger and Frederick Lawrence (Cambridge: Polity Press, [1962] 1989); and by John S. Dryzek, *Discursive Democracy* (Cambridge: Cambridge University Press, 1990).

20. Christopher Lord, *Democracy in the European Union* (Sheffield, UK: Sheffield Academic Press, 1998), 129.

21. Juan Linz, "Totalitarian and Authoritarian Regimes," in *Handbook of Political Science,* ed. Fred I. Greenstein and Nelson W. Polsby, vol. 3, *Macropolitical Theory* (Reading, Mass.: Addison-Wesley, 1975), 175–411.

22. Mark N. Franklin, *Voter Turnout and the Dynamics of Electoral Competition in Established Democracies since 1945* (Cambridge: Cambridge University Press, 2004), 121–122.

23. Wolfgang C. Müller and Kaare Strøm, *Coalition Governments in Western Europe* (Oxford: Oxford University Press, 2000); Kaare Strøm, Wolfgang C. Müller, and Torbjörn Bergman, eds., *Delegation and Accountability in Parliamentary Democracies* (Oxford: Oxford University Press, 2002); Hanne Marthe Narud and Henry Valen, "Coalition Membership and Electoral Performance in Western Europe," in *Delegation and Accountability in Parliamentary Democracies,* ed. Kaare Strøm, Wolfgang C. Müller, and Torbjörn Bergman (Oxford: Oxford University Press, 2002); Hanne Marthe Narud, "Har valg noen betydning?" [Do elections matter?], *Tidsskrift for Samfunnsforskning* 43 (2002): 245–258; Olof Petersson, Sören Holmberg, Leif Lewin, and Hanne Marthe Narud, *Demokrati utan ansvar: Demokratirådets rapport 2002* [Democracy without accountability: Report from the Council of Democracy 2002] (Stockholm: SNS, 2002).

24. In Sweden, for example, winning parties stay in power in 57 percent of cases, while losing parties do so in fully 65 percent. Petersson et al., *Demokrati utan ansvar,* 48.

25. Christopher J. Anderson and Christine A. Guillory, "Political Institutions and Satisfaction with Democracy: A Cross-National Analysis of Consensus and Majoritarian Systems," *The American Political Science Review* 91 (1997): 67.

26. Seymour Martin Lipset and William Schneider, *The Confidence Gap: Business, Labor and Government in the Public Mind* (New York: Free Press, 1983); Hans-Dieter Klingemann and Dieter Fuchs, eds., *Citizens and the State* (Oxford: Oxford University Press, 1995); Joseph S. Nye Jr., Philip D. Zelikow, and David C. King, eds., *Why People Don't Trust Government* (Cambridge, Mass.: Harvard University Press, 1997); Leonardo Morlino, *Democracy between Consolidation and Crises: Parties, Groups, and Citizens in Southern Europe* (Oxford: Oxford University Press, 1998); Pippa Norris, ed., *Critical Citizens: Global Support for Democratic Gover-*

nance (Oxford: Oxford University Press, 1999); Susan J. Pharr and Robert D. Putnam, eds., *Disaffected Democracies: What's Troubling the Trilateral Countries?* (Princeton, N.J.: Princeton University Press, 2000).

27. See Robert A. Dahl's comment on some of the studies mentioned, presented at the fifth anniversary of the Johan Skytte Prize in Political Science: Robert A. Dahl, "A Democratic Paradox," in "Special Section: The Future of Democracy," *Scandinavian Political Studies* 23 (2000): 250.

28. Anthony King, "Distrust of Government: Explaining American Exceptionalism," in *Disaffected Democracies: What's Troubling the Trilateral Countries?*, ed. Susan J. Pharr and Robert D. Putnam (Princeton, N.J.: Princeton University Press, 2000), 94–95.

Bibliography

Aberbach, Joel D., Robert D. Putnam, and Berta A. Rockman. *Bureaucrats and Politicians in Western Democracies.* Cambridge, Mass.: Harvard University Press, 1981.

Ahmed, Iftikhar, and Jacobus A. Doeleman, eds. *Beyond Rio: The Environmental Crisis and Sustainable Livelihoods in the Third World.* New York: International Labour Organization, 1995.

Albrow, Martin. *The Global Age: State and Society beyond Modernity.* Oxford: Blackwell, 1996.

Anderson, Christopher J., and Christine A. Guillory. "Political Institutions and Satisfaction with Democracy: A Cross-National Analysis of Consensus and Majoritarian Systems." *The American Political Science Review* 91 (1997): 66–81.

Arendt, Hannah. *Eichmann in Jerusalem: A Report on the Banality of Evil.* New York: Penguin Group, 1963.

Arkes, Hadley. *Bureaucracy, the Marshall Plan, and the National Interest.* Princeton, N.J.: Princeton University Press, 1972.

Arrow, Kenneth J. *Social Choice and Individual Values.* 2nd ed. New Haven, Conn.: Yale University Press, [1951] 1963.

Axelrod, Robert. *The Evolution of Cooperation.* New York: Basic Books, 1984.

Bagehot, Walter. *The English Constitution.* London: Oxford University Press, [1867] 1928.

Bairoch, Paul. "Globalization Myths and Realities." In *States against Markets: The Limits of Globalization,* ed. Robert Boyer and Daniel Drache. London: Routledge, 1996.

Banfield, Edward C. *Political Influence.* Glencoe, Ill.: Free Press, 1961.

Baring, A. *Aussenpolitik in Adenauers Kanzlerdemokratie: Bonns Beitrag zur Europäischen Verteidigunsgemeinschaft* [Foreign politics in Adenauer's chancellor democracy: The contribution of Bonn to the European defense community]. Munich: R. Oldenburg Verlag, 1969.

Barrett, Susan, and Colin Fudge, eds. *Policy and Action: Essays on the Implementation of Public Policy.* London: Methuen, 1981.

Barry, Brian. *Justice as Impartiality.* Oxford: Clarendon Press, 1995.

———. "Political Accommodation and Consociational Democracy." Review of *The*

Politics of Accommodation: Pluralism and Democracy in the Netherlands and "Consociational Democracy," by Arend Lijphart. *British Journal of Political Science* 5 (1975): 477–505.

Barry, Brian, and Russell Hardin, eds. *Rational Man and Irrational Society? An Introduction and Sourcebook.* Beverly Hills, Calif.: Sage, 1982.

Bates, Robert, Avner Greif, Margaret Levi, Jean-Laurent Rosenthal, and Barry R. Weingast. *Analytical Narratives.* Princeton, N.J.: Princeton University Press, 1998.

Bell, Daniel. *The End of Ideology.* New York: Free Press, 1960.

Bennett, Andrew, and Alexander L. George. *Case Study and Theory Development.* Cambridge, Mass.: MIT Press, 1998.

Benson, Bruce L. "Why Are Congressional Committees Dominated by 'High-Demand' Legislators? A Comment on Niskanen's View of Bureaucrats and Politicians." *Southern Economic Journal* 48 (1981): 68–77.

Berlin, Isaiah. *Four Essays on Liberty.* Oxford: Oxford University Press, 1969.

———. "The Originality of Machiavelli." In *Against the Current: Essays in the History of Ideas,* ed. Henry Hardy. Oxford: Clarendon Paperback, [1979] 1989.

Binion, Rudolf. *Hitler among the Germans.* New York: Elsevier, 1976.

Black, Duncan. *The Theory of Committees and Elections.* Cambridge: Cambridge University Press, 1958.

Blais, André, Donald E. Blake, and Stéphane Dion. *Governments, Parties, and Public Sector Employees: Canada, United States, Britain, and France.* Pittsburgh: University of Pittsburgh Press, 1997.

Blais, André, and Stéphane Dion. "Are Bureaucrats Budget Maximizers? The Niskanen Model and Its Critics." *Polity* 22 (1990): 655–674.

Bogdanor, Vernon. *What Is Proportional Representation?* Oxford: Martin Robertson, 1984.

Boudon, Raymond. *The Unintended Consequences of Social Action.* London: Macmillan, 1982.

Boutros-Ghali, Boutros. "Global Leadership after the Cold War." *Foreign Affairs* 75 (March/April 1996): 86–98.

Boyer, Robert, and Daniel Drache, eds. *States Against Markets: The Limits of Globalization.* London: Routledge, 1996.

Breisach, Ernst. *Historiography: Ancient, Medieval, and Modern.* Chicago: University of Chicago Press, 1983.

Breton, Albert. *The Economic Theory of Representative Government.* London: Macmillan, 1974.

Breton, Albert, and Ronald Wintrobe. "The Equilibrium Size of a Budget-Maximizing Bureau: A Note on Niskanen's Theory of Bureaucracy." *Journal of Political Economy* 83 (1975): 195–208.

Brinkley, Douglas, and Clifford Hackett, eds. *Jean Monnet: The Path to European Unity.* London: Macmillan, 1991.

Broszat, Martin. *German National Socialism, 1919–1945.* Santa Barbara, Calif.: Clio Press, 1966.

Bruin, Gert T. de. "Economic Theory of Bureaucracy and Public Good Allocation." In *Bureaucracy and Public Choice,* ed. Jan-Erik Lane. London: Sage, 1987.

Bruun, H. H. *Science, Values and Politics in Max Weber's Methodology.* Copenhagen: Munksgaard, 1972.

Buchanan, James M., and Gordon Tollock. *The Calculus of Consent: Logical Foundations of Constitutional Democracy.* Ann Arbor: University of Michigan Press, 1962.

Bufacchi, Vittorio, and Simon Burgess. *Italy since 1989: Events and Interpretations.* London: Macmillan, 1998.

Bull, Martin, and Martin Rhodes, eds. *Crisis and Transition in Italian Politics.* London: Frank Cass, 1997.

Bullock, Alan. *Hitler: A Study in Tyranny.* London: Odham Books, 1952.

Burnett, Stanton H., and Luca Mantovani. *The Italian Guillotine: Operation Clean Hands and the Overthrow of Italy's First Republic.* Lanham, Md.: Rowman & Littlefield, 1998.

Burns, Timothy, ed. *After History? Francis Fukuyama and His Critics.* London: Littlefield Adams, 1994.

Cannon, Lou. *President Reagan: The Role of a Lifetime.* New York: Simon & Schuster, 1991.

Castles, Francis, and Robert D. McKinley. "Does Politics Matter? An Analysis of the Public Welfare Commitment in Advanced Democratic States." *European Journal of Political Research* 7 (1979): 169–186.

Cerny, Philip. *The Politics of Grandeur.* Cambridge: Cambridge University Press, 1980.

Chiarante, Giuseppe. *Italia 1995: La Democrazia Difficile* [Italy 1995: The difficult democracy]. Rome: Edizioni Sisifo, 1995.

Clark, Ian. *Globalization and Fragmentation: International Relations in the Twentieth Century.* Oxford: Oxford University Press, 1997.

———. *Globalization and International Relations Theory.* Oxford: Oxford University Press, 1999.

Clark, Martin. *Modern Italy, 1871–1982.* London: Longman, 1984.

Clarke, Michael, ed. *Corruption, Causes, Consequences and Control.* London: Frances Pinter, 1983.

Codevilla, Angelo. *The Cure That May Kill: Unintended Consequences of the INF Treaty.* London: Institute for European Defence and Strategic Studies, 1988.

Collier, David, and James Mahoney. "Insights and Pitfalls: Selection Bias in Qualitative Research." *World Politics* 49 (1996): 56–91.

Conybeare, John A. C. "Bureaucracy, Monopoly, and Competition: A Critical Analysis of the Budget-Maximizing Model of Bureaucracy." *American Journal of Political Science* 28 (1984): 479–502.

Cooper, Terry L. *The Responsible Administrator.* 4th ed. San Francisco: Jossey-Bass, 1998.

Cornforth, Maurice. *The Open Philosophy and the Open Society: A Reply to Sir Karl Popper's Refutations of Marxism.* London: Lawrence & Wishart, 1968.

Coser, Lewis A., ed. *The Idea of Social Structure: Papers in Honor of Robert K. Merton.* New York: Harcourt Brace Jovanovich, 1975.

Crepaz, Markus M. L., Thomas A. Koelble, and David Wilsford, eds. *Democracy and Institutions: The Life Work of Arend Lijphart.* Ann Arbor: University of Michigan Press, 2000.

Crozier, Michel, and Erhard Friedberg. *Actors and Systems: The Politics of Collective Action.* Chicago: University of Chicago Press, 1980.

Cumings, Bruce. "The End of History or the Return of Liberal Crisis?" *Current History* 98 (1999): 9–16.

Daalder, Hans. "The Consociational Democracy Theme." Review of *The Politics of Accommodation: Pluralism and Democracy in the Netherlands,* by Arend Lijphart. *World Politics* 26 (1974): 604–621.

Dahl, Robert A. *Democracy and Its Critics.* New Haven, Conn.: Yale University Press, 1989.

———. "A Democratic Paradox." In "Special Section: The Future of Democracy." *Scandinavian Political Studies* 23 (2000): 246–251.

———. *A Preface to Democratic Theory.* Chicago: Phoenix Books, 1956.

Davidson, Donald. "Action, Reasons and Causes." *The Journal of Philosophy* 60 (1963): 685–700.

Day, Patricia, and Rudolf Klein. *Accountabilities: Five Public Services.* London: Tavistock Publications, 1987.

della Porta, Donatella. "The System of Corrupt Exchange in Local Government." In *The New Italian Republic: From the Fall of the Berlin Wall to Berlusconi,* ed. Stephen Gundle and Simon Parker. London: Routledge, 1996.

Deutscher, Isaac. *Stalin: A Political Biography.* London: Oxford University Press, 1967.

Dictionary of the History of Ideas. New York: Scribner's, 1973.

Diebold, William, Jr. *The Schuman Plan: A Study in Economic Cooperation 1950–1959.* New York: Praeger, 1959.

Di Natale, Francesco. *Appunti di storia della Prima Republica* [Note on the history of the First Republic]. Perugia, Italy: Guerra Edizioni, 1994.

Di Palma, Giuseppe. *Surviving without Governing: The Italian Parties in Parliament.* Berkeley: University of California Press, 1977.

Dodds, Felix, ed. *The Way Forward: Beyond Agenda 21.* London: Earthscan, 1997.

Dogan, Mattei, ed. *The Mandarins of Western Europe.* New York: Wiley, 1975.

Downs, Anthony. *An Economic Theory of Democracy.* New York: Harper & Row, 1957.

Drewry, Gavin, and Tony Butcher. *The Civil Service Today.* Oxford: Basil Blackwell, 1988.

Dryzek, John S. *Discursive Democracy.* Cambridge: Cambridge University Press, 1990.

Duchêne, Francois. *Jean Monnet: The First Statesman of Interdependence.* New York: Norton, 1994.

Dulles, Allen W. *The Marshall Plan.* Providence, R.I.: Berg, 1993.

Dunleavy, Patrick. "Bureaucrats, Budgets and the Growth of the State: Reconstructing an Instrumental Model." *British Journal of Political Science* 15 (1985): 299–328.

Dunleavy, Patrick. *Democracy, Bureaucracy and Public Choice.* London: Harvester Wheatsheaf, 1991.

Dunn, William N. *Public Policy Analysis: An Introduction.* 2nd ed. Englewood Cliffs, N.J.: Prentice Hall, [1981] 1994.

Eckstein, Harry. "Case Study and Theory in Political Science." In *Handbook of Political Science,* ed. Fred I. Greenstein and Nelson W. Polsby. Vol. 7, *Strategies of Inquiry.* Reading, Mass.: Addison-Wesley, 1975.

Elster, Jon. *Sour Grapes: Studies in the Subversion of Rationality.* Cambridge: Cambridge University Press, 1983.

———. *Ulysses and the Sirens: Studies in Rationality and Irrationality.* Cambridge: Cambridge University Press, 1979.

Encyclopaedia of Philosophy. Repr. ed. New York: Macmillan, 1972.

Eriksen, Erik Oddvar, and John Erik Fossum, eds. *Democracy in the European Union: Integration through Deliberation?* London: Routledge, 2000.

Evans, Eric J. *Thatcher and Thatcherism.* London: Routledge, 1997.

Ferguson, Niall, ed. *Virtual History: Alternatives and Counterfactuals.* London: Papermac, [1997] 1998.

Ferrell, Robert H. *The American Secretaries of State and Their Diplomacy.* New York: Cooper Square, 1966.

Finer, Herman. "Administrative Responsibility in Democratic Government." In *Bureaucratic Power in National Politics,* ed. Francis E. Rourke. Boston: Little, Brown, 1965.

Fischer, Beth A. *The Reagan Reversal: Foreign Policy and the End of the Cold War.* Columbia: University of Missouri Press, 1997.

Fisher, David Hackett. *Historians' Fallacies: Toward a Logic of Historical Thought.* New York: Harper & Row, 1970.

Fitzgerald, Frances. *Way Out There in the Blue: Reagan, Star Wars, and the End of the Cold War.* New York: Simon & Schuster, 2000.

Fogel, Robert W. "The New Economic History: Its Findings and Methods." *The Economic History Review* 19 (1966): 642–656.

———. *Railroads and American Economic Growth.* Baltimore: Johns Hopkins University Press, 1964.

Franklin, Mark N. *Voter Turnout and the Dynamics of Electoral Competition in Established Democracies since 1945.* Cambridge: Cambridge University Press, 2004.

Freeman, Samuel. "Utilitarianism, Deontology, and the Priority of Right." *Philosophy and Public Affairs* 23 (1994): 313–349.

Friedrich, Carl J. *The Pathology of Politics: Violence, Betrayal, Corruption, Secrecy, and Propaganda.* New York: Harper & Row, 1972.

———. "Public Policy and the Nature of Administrative Responsibility." In *Bureaucratic Power in National Politics,* ed. Francis E. Rourke. Boston: Little, Brown, 1965.

———, ed. *Responsibility.* New York: Liberal Arts Press, 1960.

Fry, Geoffrey K. "The Development of the Thatcher Government's 'Grand Strategy' for the Civil Service: A Public Policy Perspective." *Public Administration* 62 (1984): 322–335.

———. "The Thatcher Government, the Financial Management Initiative and the 'New Civil Service'." *Public Administration* 66 (1988): 1–20.

Fukuyama, Francis. "The End of History." *The National Interest,* no. 16 (1989): 3–18.

———. *The End of History and the Last Man.* New York: Free Press, 1992.

Fuller, Timothy. "More Responses to Fukuyama." *The National Interest,* no. 17 (1989): 93–95.

Furlong, Paul. *Modern Italy: Representation and Reform.* London: Routledge, 1994.

Gane, Nicholas. "Max Weber on the Ethical Irrationality of Political Leadership." *Sociology: The Journal of the British Sociological Association* 31 (1997): 549–564.

Garme, Cecilia. *Newcomers to Power.* Uppsala: Acta Universitatis Upsaliensis, 2001.

Gauthier, David. "Taming Leviathan." Review of *Hobbes and the Social Contract Tradition,* by Jean Hampton, and *Hobbesian Moral and Political Theory,* by Gregory S. Kavka. *Philosophy and Public Affairs* 16 (1987): 280–298.

George, Alexander L. *Bridging the Gap: Theory and Practice in Foreign Policy.* Washington D.C.: United States Institute of Peace Press, 1993.

———. "Case Studies and Theory Development: The Method of Structured, Focused Comparison." In *Diplomacy: New Approaches in History, Theory, and Policy,* ed. Paul Gordon Lauren. New York: Free Press, 1979.

George, Alexander L., and Juliette L. George. *Presidential Personality and Performance.* Boulder, Colo.: Westview Press, 1998.

Gibbons, Michael, Camille Limoges, Helga Nowotny, Simon Schwartzman, Peter Scott, and Martin Trow. *The New Production of Knowledge.* London: Sage, 1994.

Gilbert, Mark. *The Italian Revolution: The End of Politics, Italian Style?* Boulder, Colo.: Westview Press, 1995.

Gillingham, John. *Coal, Steel, and the Rebirth of Europe, 1945–1955: The Germans and French from Ruhr Conflict to Economic Community.* Cambridge: Cambridge University Press, 1991.

Gimbel, John. *The Origins of the Marshall Plan.* Stanford, Calif.: Stanford University Press, 1976.

Goodin, Robert E. "Possessive Individualism Again." *Political Studies* 24 (1976): 488–501.

———. "Rational Politicians and Rational Bureaucrats in Washington and Whitehall." *Public Administration* 60 (1982): 23–41.

Goodrick-Clarke, Nicholas. *The Occult Roots of Nazism.* New York: New York University Press, 1985.

Graham, George A. "Ethical Guidelines for Public Administrators: Observations on Rules of the Game." *Public Administration Review* 34 (1974): 90–92.

Gray, J. *Liberalisms.* London: Routledge & Kegan Paul, 1989.

Greentsone, J. David. "Corruption and Self-Interest in Kampala and Nairobi." In *Political Corruption: Readings in Comparative Analysis,* ed. Arnold Heidenheimer. New York: Holt, Rinehart & Winston, 1970.

Gregor, Neil, ed. *Nazism.* Oxford: Oxford University Press, 2000.

Grumley, John. "Fukuyama's Hegelianism—Historical Exhaustion or Philosophical Closure." *History of European Ideas* 21 (1995): 379–392.

Guiner, Lani. *The Tyranny of the Majority: Fundamental Fairness in Representative Democracy.* New York: Free Press, 1994.

Guistino, David de, ed. *A Reader in European Integration.* London: Longman, 1996.

Gundle, Stephen, and Simon Parker, eds. *The New Italian Republic: From the Fall of the Berlin Wall to Berlusconi.* London: Routledge, 1996.

Gustavsson, Sverker. "Varför överstat utan demokrati?" [Why suprastate without democracy?]. In *Europaperspektiv 1998: Årsbok för Europaforskning inom ekonomi, juridik och statskunskap.* [European perspectives 1998. The annual review of European research within the fields of economics, law and political science], ed. Ulf Bernitz, Sverker Gustavsson, and Lars Oxelheim. Stockholm: Nerenius & Santérus Förlag, 1998.

Gutmann, Amy, and Dennis Thompson. *Democracy and Disagreement: Why Moral Conflict Cannot Be Avoided in Politics, and What Should Be Done about It.* Cambridge, Mass.: Belknap, 1996.

Habermas, Jürgen. *The Structural Transformation of the Public Sphere: An Inquiry into the Category of Bourgeois Society.* Trans. Thomas Burger and Frederick Lawrence. Cambridge: Polity Press, [1962] 1989.

Hadenius, Axel. *Institutions and Democratic Citizenship.* Oxford: Oxford University Press, 2001.

Halliday, Fred. "An Encounter with Fukuyama." *New Left Review* (May–June 1992).

Hampton, Jean. *Hobbes and the Social Contract Tradition.* Cambridge: Cambridge University Press, 1986.

Hardin, Garrett. "The Tragedy of the Commons." *Science* 162 (1968): 1243–1248.

Hare, Thomas. *The Machinery of Representation.* London: W. Maxwell, 1857.

———. *A Treatise on the Election of Representatives, Parliamentary and Municipal.* London: Longman, Brown, Green, Longmans & Roberts, 1859.

Harris, Kenneth. *Thatcher.* London: Weidenfeld & Nicolson, 1988.

Hart, David K. "The Virtuous Citizen, the Honorable Bureaucrat, and 'Public' Administration." *Public Administration Review* 44 (1984): 111–120.

Hart, Jenifer. *Proportional Representation: Critics of the British Electoral System 1820–1945.* Oxford: Clarendon Press, 1992.

Hayek, Friedrich A. *The Constitution of Liberty.* London: Routledge & Kegan Paul, 1976.

———. *The Road to Serfdom.* London: Routledge & Kegan Paul, 1944.

Heald, David. "Will the Privatization of Public Enterprises Solve the Problem of Control?" *Public Administration* 63 (1985): 7–22.

Heidenheimer, Arnold, ed. *Political Corruption: Readings in Comparative Analysis.* New York: Holt, Rinehart & Winston, 1970.

Held, David, Anthony McCrew, David Goldblatt, and Jonathan Perraton. *Global Transformations: Politics, Economics and Culture.* Cambridge: Polity Press, 1999.

Hine, David. *Governing Italy: The Politics of Bargained Pluralism.* Oxford: Clarendon Press, 1993.

Hirst, Paul, and Grahame Thompson. *Globalization in Question.* 2nd ed. Cambridge: Polity Press, [1996] 1999.

Hitler, Adolf. *Mein Kampf.* Trans. Ralph Manheim. New York: Mariner Books, [1925] 1999.

Hobbes, Thomas. *Leviathan.* Harmondsworth, UK: Penguin, [1651] 1968.

Hogan, Michael J. *The Marshall Plan: America, Britain, and the Reconstruction of Western Europe, 1947–1952.* Cambridge: Cambridge University Press, 1987.

Hogwood, Brian W. *Trends in British Public Policy: Do Governments Make Any Difference?* Buckingham, UK: Open University Press, 1992.

Holmes, Stephen. "The Scowl of Minerva." *The New Republic* 23 (March 1992).

Holmström, Barry. *Domstolar och demokrati* [Courts of law and democracy]. Uppsala: Acta Universitatis Upsaliensis, 1998.

Hoos, Ida R. *Systems Analysis in Public Policy: A Critique.* Rev. ed. Berkeley: University of California Press, [1972] 1983.

Hoskyns, Catherine, and Michael Newman, eds. *Democratising the European Union: Issues for the 21st Century.* Manchester, UK: Manchester University Press, 2000.

Housden, Martyn. *Hitler: Study of a Revolutionary?* London: Routledge, 2000.

Huntington, Samuel P. "No Exit: The Errors of Endism." *The National Interest,* no. 17 (1989): 3–11.

Iggers, Georg G. *The German Conception of History: The National Tradition of Historical Thought from Herder to the Present.* Middletown, Conn.: Wesleyan University Press, 1983.

International Encyclopedia of the Social Sciences. New York: Macmillan, 1968.

Jackson, P. M. *The Political Economy of Bureaucracy.* Oxford: Philip Allen, 1982.

Jamieson, Alison. *Political Corruption in Western Europe.* London: Research Institute for the Study of Conflict and Terrorism, 1996.

Jenkins, Peter. *Mrs Thatcher's Revolution.* London: Jonathan Cape, 1987.

Jessop, Bob, Kevin Bonnett, Simon Bromley, and Tom Ling. *Thatcherism: A Tale of Two Nations.* Cambridge: Polity Press, 1988.

Johnson, Paul. "The End of History and the Last Man." *Commentary* 93 (March 1992): 51–53.

Jones, G. W. "A Revolution in Whitehall? Changes in British Central Government since 1979." *West European Politics* 12 (1989): 238–261.

Karlsson, Christer. *Democracy, Legitimacy and the European Union.* Uppsala: Acta Universitatis Upsaliensis, 2001.

Katz, Richard S., and Piero Ignazi, eds. *Italian Politics: The Year of the Tycoon.* Boulder, Colo.: Westview Press, 1996.

Kavka, Gregory S. *Hobbesian Moral and Political Theory.* Princeton; N.J.: Princeton University Press, 1986.

Kegley, Charles W., Jr. "How Did the Cold War Die? Principles for an Autopsy." *Mershon International Studies Review* 38 (1994): 11–41.

Kennan, George F. *American Diplomacy, 1900–1950.* Chicago: University of Chicago Press, 1951.

———. *Memoirs, 1925–1950.* London: Hutchinson, 1968.

X [Kennan, George F.]. "The Sources of Soviet Conduct." *Foreign Affairs* 25 (July 1947): 566–582.

Kershaw, Ian. *Hitler 1889–1936: Hubris.* New York: W. W. Norton, 1998.

———. *Hitler 1936–45: Nemesis.* London: Allen Lane, 2000.

Khong, Y. F. *Analogies at War.* Princeton, N.J.: Princeton University Press, 1992.

King, Anthony. "Distrust of Government: Explaining American Exceptionalism." In *Disaffected Democracies: What's Troubling the Trilateral Countries?* ed. Susan J. Pharr and Robert D. Putnam. Princeton; N.J.: Princeton University Press, 2000.

King, Gary, Robert O. Keohane, and Sidney Verba. *Designing Social Inquiry: Scientific Inference in Qualitative Research.* Princeton, N.J.: Princeton University Press, 1994.

Kiser, Edgar. "The Revival of Narrative in Historical Sociology: What Rational Choice Theory Can Contribute." *Politics and Society* 24 (1996): 249–271.

Kissinger, Henry. *The Necessity for Choice: Prospects of American Foreign Policy.* New York: Harper, 1960.

———. *A World Restored: Metternich, Castlereagh and the Problems of Peace, 1812–22.* London: Weidenfeld & Nicolson, 1957.

Klingemann, Hans-Dieter, and Dieter Fuchs, eds. *Citizens and the State.* Oxford: Oxford University Press, 1995.

Koen, Avraam. *Atoms, Pleasure, Virtue: The Philosophy of Epicurus.* New York: Lang, 1995.

Koff, Sondra Z., and Stephen P. Koff. *Italy: From the First to the Second Republic.* London: Routledge, 2000.

Krugman, Paul. *Pop Internationalism.* Cambridge; Mass.: MIT Press, 1996.

Kumar, Kristan. "The Revolution of 1989: Socialism, Capitalism, and Democracy." *Theory and Society* 21 (1992): 309–356.

Lacouture, Jean. *De Gaulle: The Ruler, 1945–1970.* London: Harvill, [1985, 1986] 1991.

Lafferty, William M., ed. *Implementing LA21 in Europe: New Initiatives for Sustainable Communities.* Oslo: ProSus, 1999.

Lafferty, William M., and Katarina Eckerberg, eds. *From the Earth Summit to Local Agenda 21: Working towards Sustainable Development.* London: Earthscan, 1998.

Lafferty, William, and James Meadowcroft, eds. *Implementing Agenda 21: Strategies and Initiatives in High Consumption Societies.* Oxford: Oxford University Press, 2000.

Lal, Deepak. *Unintended Consequences: The Impact of Factor Endowments, Culture, and Politics on Long-Run Economic Performance.* Cambridge, Mass.: MIT Press, 1998.

Lane, Jan-Erik, ed. *Bureaucracy and Public Choice.* London: Sage, 1987.

LaPalombara, Joseph. *Democracy, Italian Style.* New Haven, Conn.: Yale University Press, 1987.

Large, D. C. "Grand Illusions: The United States, the Federal Republic of Germany and the European Defense Community, 1950–1954." In *American Foreign Policy and the Reconstruction of West Germany,* ed. J. M. Diefendorf, A. Frohn, and H.-J. Rupieper. Washington; D.C.: Washington German Historical Institute, 1993.

Lee, Stephen J. *Hitler and Nazi Germany.* London: Routledge, 1998.

Le Monde, 9 May 1970 (Monnet's memorandum on the European Coal and Steel Community).

Lenin, Vladimir Iljitj. *Imperialism, the Highest Stage of Capitalism: A Popular Outline.* Beijing: Foreign Language Press, [1917] 1969.

Levi, Margaret. "A Model, a Method, and a Map: Rational Choice in Comparative and Historical Analysis." In *Comparative Politics: Rationality, Culture, and Structure,* ed. Mark Irving Lichbach and Alan S. Zuckerman. Cambridge: Cambridge University Press, 1997.

Levinson, Roland B. *In Defense of Plato.* Cambridge, Mass.: Harvard University Press, 1953.

Lewin, Leif. *"Bråka inte!" Om vår tids demokratisyn* ["Don't be a trouble-maker!" The democratic theory of our time]. Stockholm: SNS, 2002.

———. *Ideology and Strategy: A Century of Swedish Politics.* Cambridge: Cambridge University Press, 1988.

———. *Planhushållningsdebatten* [The debate on the planned economy]. Stockholm: Almqvist & Wiksell, 1967.

———. *Self-Interest and Public Interest in Western Politics.* Oxford: Oxford University Press, 1991.

Lewin, Leif, and Evert Vedung, eds. *Politics as Rational Action: Essays in Public Choice and Policy Analysis.* Dordrecht: D. Reidel, 1980.

Lewis, David W. P. *The Road to Europe: History, Institutions, and Prospects of European Integration, 1945–1993.* New York: Peter Lang, 1993.

Lieberson, Stanley. "Small *N*s and Big Conclusions: An Examination of the Reasoning in Comparative Studies Based on a Small Number of Cases." In *What Is a Case? Exploring the Foundations of Social Inquiry,* ed. Charles C. Ragin and Howard S. Becker. Cambridge: Cambridge University Press, 1992.

Lijphart, Arend. "Consensus and Consensus Democracy: Cultural, Structural, Functional, and Rational-Choice Explanations." *Scandinavian Political Studies* 21 (1998): 99–108.

———. "Democracies: Forms, Performance, and Constitutional Engineering." *European Journal of Political Research* 25 (1994): 1–17.

———. *Democracies: Patterns of Majoritarian and Consensus Government in Twenty-One Countries.* New Haven, Conn.: Yale University Press, 1984.

———. *Democracy in Plural Societies: A Comparative Exploration.* New Haven, Conn.: Yale University Press, 1977.

———. *Patterns of Democracy: Government Forms and Performance in Thirty-Six Countries.* New Haven, Conn.: Yale University Press, 1999.

———. *The Politics of Accommodation: Pluralism and Democracy in the Netherlands.* Berkeley: University of California Press, 1968.

Linz, Juan J. "Totalitarian and Authoritarian Regimes." In *Handbook of Political Science,* ed. Fred I. Greenstein and Nelson W. Polsby. Vol 3, *Macropolitical Theory.* Reading, Mass.: Addison-Wesley, 1975.

Linz, Juan J., and Alfred Stepan. *Problems of Democratic Transition and Consolidation: Southern Europe, South America, and Post-Communist Europe.* Baltimore: Johns Hopkins University Press, 1996.

Lipgens, Walter, and Wilfried Loth, eds. *Documents on the History of European Integration.* 4 vols. Berlin: Walter de Gruyter, 1985–1991.

Lipset, Seymour Martin. *Political Man.* London: Mercury Books, 1963.

Lipset, Seymour Martin, and William Schneider. *The Confidence Gap: Business, Labor and Government in the Public Mind.* New York: Free Press, 1983.

Lipset, Seymour Martin, Martin A. Trow, and James S. Coleman. *Union Democracy: The Internal Politics of the International Typographical Union.* Glencoe, Ill.: Free Press, 1956.

Longman Dictionary of Contemporary English. 2nd ed. Essex, UK: Longman House, 1987.

Lord, Christopher. *Democracy in the European Union.* Sheffield, UK: Sheffield Academic Press, 1998.

Lukacs, John. *The Hitler of History.* New York: Vintage Books, 1998.

———. *The Last European War.* Garden City, N.Y.: Anchor Press, 1976.

Lundström, Mats. "Is Anti-Rationalism Rational? The Case of F. A. Hayek." *Scandinavian Political Studies* 15 (1992): 235–248.

———. *Politikens moraliska rum: En studie i F. A. Hayeks politiska filosofi* [The moral space of politics: An analysis of the political philosophy of F. A. Hayek]. Uppsala: Almqvist & Wiksell, 1993.

MacDonald, Mary. *Agendas for Sustainability: Environment and Development into the Twenty-First Century.* London: Routledge, 1998.

Machiavelli, Niccolò. *The Prince and the Discourses.* New York: Random House, [1513] 1950.

Mack Smith, Denis. *Modern Italy: A Political History.* New Haven, Conn.: Yale University Press, 1997.

Majone, Giandomenico. *Regulating Europe.* London: Routledge, 1996.

March, James G., and Johan P. Olsen. *Democratic Governance.* New York: Free Press, 1994.

———. *Rediscovering Institutions: The Organizational Basis of Politics.* New York: Free Press, 1989.

Margolis, Julius. "Bureaucrats and Politicians: Comment." *Journal of Law and Economics* 29 (1975): 645–659.

Markus, Robert A. *Saecuklum: History and Society in the Theology of St Augustine.* Cambridge: Cambridge University Press, 1970.

Martin, Hans-Peter, and Harald Schumann. *The Global Trap: Globalization and the Assault on Democracy and Prosperity.* London: Zed Books, [1996] 1997.

Marwick, Arthur. Review of *The End of History and the Last Man,* by Francis Fukuyama. *History: The Journal of the Historical Association,* n.s., 79 (1994): 83–84.

Massey, Andrew. *Managing the Public Sector: A Comparative Analysis of the United Kingdom and the United States.* Aldershot, UK: Edward Elgar, 1993.

Matthews, Richard K., ed. *Virtue, Corruption and Self-Interest: Values in the Eighteenth Century.* London: Associated University Press, 1994.

McCagg, William O., Jr. *Stalin Embattled, 1943–1948.* Detroit, Mich.: Wayne State University Press, 1978.

McCarthy, Patrick. *The Crisis of the Italian State: From the Origins of the Cold War to the Fall of Berlusconi and Beyond.* London: Macmillan, 1995.

McKay, David. *Federalism and European Union: A Political Economy Perspective.* Oxford: Oxford University Press, 1999.

Mee, Charles L., Jr. *The Marshall Plan: The Launching of the Pax Americana.* New York: Simon & Schuster, 1984.

Melloan, George. "Military Cutbacks Will Crimp U.S. Foreign Policy." *Wall Street Journal,* 25 January 1993, A17.

Mershon, Carol, and Gianfranco Pasquino, eds. *Italian Politics: Ending the First Republic.* Boulder, Colo.: Westview Press, 1995.

Merton, Robert K. "The Unanticipated Consequences of Purposive Social Action." *American Sociological Review* 1 (1936): 894–904.

Mignone, Mario B. *Italy Today: A Country in Transition.* New York: Peter Lang, 1995.

Mill, John Stuart. "Considerations of Representative Government" [1861]. In *Collected Works of John Stuart Mill,* ed. John Mercel Robson. Vol. 19, *Essays on Politics and Society.* London: Routledge, 1977.

———. "Recent Writers on Reform" [1859]. In *Collected Works of John Stuart Mill,* ed. John Mercel Robson. Vol. 19, *Essays on Politics and Society.* Toronto: University of Toronto Press, 1977.

———. *A System of Logic: Ratiocinative and Inductive.* Toronto: University of Toronto Press, [1843] 1967.

Miller, Gary J., and Terry M. Moe. "Bureaucrats, Legislators, and the Size of Government." *The American Political Science Review* 77 (1983): 297–322.

Milward, Alan S. *The European Rescue of the Nation-State.* London: Routledge, 1993.

———. *The Reconstruction of Western Europe, 1945–51.* London: Methuen, 1984.

Mishra, Ramesch. *Globalization and the Welfare State.* Cheltenham, UK: Edward Elgar, 1999.

Möller, Gustav. *Arbetslöshetsförsäkringen* [The unemployment insurance]. Stockholm: Tidens Förlag, 1926.

Mommsen, T. E. "St. Augustine and the Christian Idea of Progress." In *Medevial and Renaissance Studies,* ed. Eugene F. Rice Jr. Ithaca, N.Y.: Cornell University Press, 1959.

Monnet, Jean. *Memoirs.* London: Collins, [1976] 1978.

Montanelli, Indro, and Mario Cervi. *L'Italia di Berlusconi, 1993–1995* [Berlusconi's Italy, 1993–1995]. Milan: Rizzoli, 1995.

Moon, Jeremy. *Innovative Leadership in Democracy: Policy Change under Thatcher.* Aldershot, UK: Dartmouth, 1993.

Moravcsik, Andrew. *The Choice for Europe: Social Purpose and State Power from Messina to Maastricht.* Ithaca, N.Y.: Cornell University Press, 1998.

———. "Europe without Illusions: A Category Error." *Prospect* (July 2005).

Morgan, Roger. *West European Politics since 1945: The Shaping of the European Community.* London: Batsford, 1972.

Morgenthau, Hans J. *Politics among Nations: The Struggle for Power and Peace.* New York: Knopf, 1948.

Morlino, Leonardo. *Democracy between Consolidation and Crises: Parties, Groups, and Citizens in Southern Europe.* Oxford: Oxford University Press, 1998.

Mosley, Leonard. *Marshall: Hero for Our Times.* New York: Hearst Books, 1982.

Mosse, George L. *The Crisis of German Ideology: Intellectual Origins of the Third Reich.* New York: Howard Fertig, 1964.

Müller, Wolfgang C., and Kaare Strøm. *Coalition Governments in Western Europe.* Oxford: Oxford University Press, 2000.

Mussolini, Benito. *The Doctrine of Fascism.* Florence: Vallechi editore, 1938.

Narud, Hanne Marthe. "Har valg noen betydning?" [Do elections matter?]. *Tidsskrift for Samfunnsforskning* 43 (2002): 245–258.

Narud, Hanne Marthe, and Henry Valen. "Coalition Membership and Electoral Performance in Western Europe." In *Delegation and Accountability in Parliamentary Democracies,* ed. Kaare Strøm, Wolfgang C. Müller, and Torbjörn Bergman. Oxford: Oxford University Press, 2002.

Newman, Michael. *Democracy, Sovereignty and the European Union.* London: Hurst, 1997.

Niskanen, William A. *Bureaucracy and Representative Government.* Chicago: Aldine-Atherton, 1971.

———. "Bureaucrats and Politicians." *Journal of Law and Economics* 18 (1975): 617–643.

———. "A Reflection on *Bureaucracy and Representative Government.*" In *The Budget-Maximizing Bureaucrat: Appraisals and Evidence,* ed. André Blais and Stéphane Dion. Pittsburgh: University of Pittsburgh Press, 1991.

Norris, Pippa. "Choosing Electoral Systems: Proportional, Majoritarian and Mixed Systems." *International Political Science Review* 18 (1997): 297–312.

———, ed. *Critical Citizens: Global Support for Democratic Governance.* Oxford: Oxford University Press, 1999.

Nozick, Robert. *The Examined Life.* New York: Simon & Schuster, 1989.

Nye, Joseph S., Jr., Philip D. Zelikow, and David C. King, eds. *Why People Don't Trust Government.* Cambridge, Mass.: Harvard University Press, 1997.

Oberdorfer, Don. *From the Cold War to a New Era: The United States and the Soviet Union, 1983–1991.* Baltimore: Johns Hopkins University Press, 1998.

Ohmae, Kenichi. *The End of the Nation State.* London: HarperCollins, 1996.

———. *Triad Power: The Coming Shape of Global Competition.* New York: Free Press, 1985.

O'Riordan, Tim, and Heather Voisey, eds. *The Transition to Sustainability: The Politics of Agenda 21 in Europe.* London: Earthscan, 1998.

Osborn, Derek, and Tom Bigg. *Earth Summit II: Outcomes and Analysis.* London: Earthscan, 1998.

Ostrom, Elinor. *Governing the Commons: The Evolution of Institutions for Collective Action.* Cambridge: Cambridge University Press, 1990.

Parri, Ferrico. "Panorama of 1950." In *Documents on the History of European Integration,* ed. Walter Lipgens and Wilfried Loth. Vol. 3, *The Struggle for European Union by Political Parties and Pressure Groups in Western European Countries, 1945–1950.* Berlin: Walter de Gruyter, 1991.

Parsons, Wayne. *Public Policy: An Introduction to the Theory and Practice of Policy Analysis.* Cheltenham, UK: Edward Elgar, 1995.

Partridge, Hilary. *Italian Politics Today.* Manchester, UK: Manchester University Press, 1998.

Pasquino, Gianfranco, and Patrick McCarthy, eds. *The End of Post-War Politics in Italy: The Landmark 1992 Elections.* Boulder, Colo.: Westview Press, 1993.

Peet, Richard. "I. Reading Fukuyama: Politics at the End of History." *Political Geography* 12 (1993): 64–78.

Peters, B. Guy. "The European Bureaucrat: The Applicability of *Bureaucracy and Representative Government* to Non-American Settings." In *The Budget-Maximizing Bureaucrat: Appraisals and Evidence,* ed. André Blais and Stéphane Dion. Pittsburgh: University of Pittsburgh Press, 1991.

———. *The Politics of Bureaucracy.* White Plains, N.Y.: Longman, 1995.

Petersson, Olof, Sören Holmberg, Leif Lewin, and Hanne Marthe Narud. *Demokrati utan ansvar: Demokratirådets rapport 2002* [Democracy without accountability: Report from the Council of Democracy 2002]. Stockholm: SNS, 2002.

Pharr, Susan J., and Robert D. Putnam, eds. *Disaffected Democracies: What's Troubling the Trilateral Countries?* Princeton, N.J.: Princeton University Press, 2000.

Plamenatz, John. *Ideology.* London: Macmillan, 1970.

Poetzsch-Heffter, Fritz. "Vom Deutschen Staatsleben" [On German politics]. In *Jahrbuch des Öffentlichen Rechts der Gegenwart.* Vol. 22. Tübingen, Germany, 1935.

Popper, Karl R. *Conjectures and Refutations: The Growth of Scientific Knowledge.* London: Routledge & Kegan Paul, 1963.

———. *The Open Society and Its Enemies I–II.* London: Routledge & Kegan Paul, 1945.

———. "Popper on Democracy: The Open Society and Its Enemies Revisited." *Economist,* 23 April 1988.

———. *The Poverty of Historicism.* London: Routledge & Kegan Paul, 1957.

Powell, G. Bingham. *Elections as Instruments of Democracy: Majoritarian and Proportional Visions.* New Haven, Conn.: Yale University Press, 2000.

———. "Political Responsiveness and Constitutional Design." In *Democracy and Institutions: The Life Work of Arend Lijphart,* ed. Markus M. L. Crepaz, Thomas A. Koelble, and David Wilsford. Ann Arbor: University of Michigan Press, 2000.

———. Review of *Democracy in Plural Societies,* by Arend Lijphart. *The American Political Science Review* 73 (1979): 295–297.

Prados, John. *Keepers of the Keys: A History of the National Security Council from Truman to Bush.* New York: William Morrow, 1991.

Price, Harry Bayard. *The Marshall Plan and Its Meaning.* Ithaca, N.Y.: Cornell University Press, 1955.

Proceedings. LOs representantskap den 30 November 1930 [Representative body of the Swedish Labour Union, 30 November 1930].

Przeworski, Adam, and Henry Teune. *The Logic of Comparative Social Inquiry.* New York: Wiley, 1970.

Ragin, Charles C., and Howard S. Becker, eds. *What Is a Case? Exploring the Foundations of Social Inquiry.* Cambridge: Cambridge University Press, 1992.

Ranke, Leopold von. *Sämtliche Werke.* Vols. 33–34, *Geschichten der romanischen und germanischen Völker von 1494 bis 1514* [History of the Romanic and Germanic peoples from 1494 to 1514]. Leipzig, [1824] 1874.

Rapoport, Anatol, and Albert M. Chammah. *Prisoner's Dilemma: A Study in Conflict and Cooperation.* Ann Arbor: University of Michigan Press, 1965.

Rauschning, Hermann. *Hitler Speaks: A Series of Political Conversations with Adolf Hitler on His Real Aims.* London: Thornton Butterworth, 1939.

Rawls, John. *A Theory of Justice.* Cambridge, Mass.: Harvard University Press, 1971.

Reagan, Ronald. *An American Life.* London: Hutchinson, 1990.

Reich, Robert B. *The Work of Nations: Preparing Ourselves for 21st Century Capitalism.* New York: Knopf, 1991.

Riddell, Peter. *The Thatcher Decade: How Britain Has Changed during the 1980s.* Oxford: Basil Blackwell, 1989.

Ridley, F. F. "Political Neutrality in the British Civil Service: Sir Thomas More and Mr. Clive Ponting v. Sir Robert Armstrong and the Vicar of Bray." In *Politics, Ethics and Public Service,* ed. Bernard Williams, John Stevenson, F. F. Ridley, Sir Kenneth Couzens, Alexander Grey, and Peter Jay. London: Royal Institute of Public Administration, 1985.

Riker, William. *Liberalism against Populism: A Confrontation between the Theory of Democracy and the Theory of Social Choice.* San Francisco: W. H. Freeman, 1982.

———. *The Theory of Political Coalitions.* New Haven, Conn.: Yale University Press, 1962.

Riker, William H., and Peter C. Ordeshook. *An Introduction to Positive Political Theory.* Englewood Cliffs, N.J.: Prentice-Hall, 1973.

Rist, John M. *Epicurus: An Introduction.* London: Cambridge University Press, 1972.

Roberts, Adam, and Benedict Kingsbury, eds. *United Nations, Divided World: The UN's Roles in International Relations.* Oxford: Clarendon Press, 1993.

Román, Mikael. *The Implementation of International Regimes: The Case of the Amazon Cooperation Treaty.* Uppsala: Uppsala University, Department of Government, 1998.

Rose, Richard. *Understanding Big Government: The Programme Approach.* London: Sage, 1984.

Rosenau, James N. *Along the Domestic-Foreign Frontier: Exploring Governance in a Turbulent World.* Cambridge: Cambridge University Press, 1997.

Ross, George. *Jacques Delors and European Integration.* Cambridge: Polity Press, 1995.

Roth, Guenther, and Wolfgang Schluchter. *Max Weber's Vision of History: Ethics and Methods.* Berkeley: University of California Press, 1979.

Rothstein, Bo. *Den korporativa staten* [The corporate state]. Stockholm: Norstedts, 1992.

Rousseau, Jean-Jacques. *The Social Contract.* Trans. Maurice Cranston. Harmondsworth, UK: Penguin Books, [1762] 1968.

Ruigrok, Winfried, and Rob van Tulder. *The Logic of International Restructuring.* London: Routledge, 1995.

Russett, Bruce. *Grasping the Democratic Peace: Principles for a Post–Cold War World.* Princeton, N.J.: Princeton University Press, 1993.

Sassen, Saskia. *Losing Control? Sovereignty in an Age of Globalization.* New York: Columbia University Press, 1996.

Sassoon, Donald. *Contemporary Italy: Economy, Society and Politics since 1945.* 2nd ed. London: Longman, [1986] 1997.

Savoie, Donald J. *Thatcher, Reagan, Mulroney: In Search of a New Bureaucracy.* Pittsburgh: University of Pittsburgh Press, 1994.

Scharpf, Fritz W. *Governing in Europe: Effective and Democratic?* Oxford: Oxford University Press, 1999.

Scharpf, Fritz W., and Vivien A. Schmidt, eds. *Welfare and Work in the Open Economy.* Vols. 1–2. Oxford: Oxford University Press, 2000.

Schmitt, Carl. *Politische Theologie* [Political theology]. Berlin: Duncker & Humblot, [1922] 1993.

Schmitter, Philippe C. "If the Nation-State Were to Wither Away in Europe, What Might Replace It?" In *The Future of the Nation-State: Essays on Cultural Pluralism and Political Integration,* ed. Sverker Gustavsson and Leif Lewin. Stockholm: Nerenius and Santérus, 1996.

Schubert, Glendon A., Jr. "The Public Interest in Administrative Decision-Making: Theorem, Theosophy, or Theory?" *The American Political Science Review* 51 (1957): 345–368.

Schumpeter, Joseph A. *Capitalism, Socialism, and Democracy.* New York: Harper, 1942.

Scott, James C. *Comparative Political Corruption.* Englewood Cliffs, N.J.: Prentice-Hall, 1972.

Seindal, René. *Mafia, Money and Politics in Sicily, 1950–1997.* Copenhagen: Museum Tusculanum Press, 1998.

Self, Peter. *Political Theories of Modern Government.* London: George Allen & Unwin, 1985.

Selznick, Philip. "Reflections on Responsibility: More Than Just Following Rules." *The Responsive Community* 10 (Spring 2000): 57–61.

Sen, Amartya. "Behaviour and the Concept of Preference." In *Choice, Welfare, and Measurement.* Oxford: Basil Blackwell, 1982.

Sen, Amartya, and Bernard Williams, eds. *Utalitarianism and Beyond.* Cambridge: Cambridge University Press, 1982.

Sheer, Robert. *With Enough Shovels: Reagan, Bush, and Nuclear War.* New York: Random House, 1982.

Shirer, William L. *The Rise and Fall of the Third Reich.* New York: Simon & Schuster, 1960.

Shultz, George P. *Turmoil and Triumph: My Years as Secretary of State.* New York: Scribner's, 1993.

Skinner, Quentin. *Machiavelli.* Oxford: Oxford University Press, 1981.

Smith, Arthur L., Jr. *The War for the German Mind: Re-Educating Hitler's Soldiers.* Providence, R.I.: Berghahn Books, 1996.

Spinelli, Altiero. "Report on the Proposal for a European Assembly to Draft a Pact of Federal Union." In *Documents on the History of European Integration,* ed. Walter Lipgens and Wilfried Loth. Vol. 4, *Transnational Organizations of Political Parties and Pressure Groups in the Struggle for European Union, 1945–1950.* Berlin: Walter de Gruyter, 1991.

Spotts, Frederic, and Theodor Wieser. *Italy: A Difficult Democracy.* Cambridge: Cambridge University Press, 1986.

Stove, David. "More Responses to Fukuyama." *The National Interest,* no. 17 (1989): 97–98.

Strange, Susan. "Finance, Information and Power." *Review of International Studies* 16 (1990): 259–274.

———. *The Retreat of the State: The Diffusion of Power in the World Economy.* Cambridge: Cambridge University Press, 1996.

Strøm, Kaare. *Minority Government and Majority Rule.* Cambridge: Cambridge University Press, 1990.

Strøm, Kaare, Wolfgang C. Müller, and Torbjörn Bergman, eds. *Delegation and Accountability in Parliamentary Democracies.* Oxford: Oxford University Press, 2002.

Sugden, Robert. "Rational Choice: A Survey of Contributions from Economics and Philosophy." *The Economic Journal* 101 (1991): 751–785.

Summerton, Neil. "A Mandarin's Duty." *Parliamentary Affairs* 33 (1979): 400–421.

Tangen Page, Michael von. *Prisons, Peace and Terrorism.* London: Macmillan, 1998.

Tenner, Edward. *Why Things Bite Back: Technology and the Revenge of Unintended Consequences.* London: Vintage Books, 1996.

Tetlock, Philip E., and Aaron Belkin, eds. *Counterfactual Thought Experiments in World Politics.* Princeton, N.J.: Princeton University Press, 1996.

Thatcher, Margaret. *The Downing Street Years.* London: HarperCollins, 1993.

———. *The Path to Power.* London: HarperCollins, 1995.

Thody, Philip. *An Historical Introduction to the European Union.* London: Routledge, 1997.

Thomas, Caroline. *The Environment in International Relations.* London: Royal Institute of International Affairs, 1992.

Thompson, Dennis F. "Moral Responsibility of Public Officials: The Problem of Many Hands." *The American Political Science Review* 74 (1980): 905–916.

Tilly, Charles. *Coercion, Capital, and European States, AD 990–1990.* Cambridge: Basil Blackwell, 1990.

Tingsten, Herbert: *Nazismens och fascismens idéer* [The ideas of Nazism and Fascism]. Stockholm: Bonniers, [1936] 1965.

Toland, John. *Adolf Hitler.* New York: Doubleday, 1976.

Trevor-Roper, H. R. *The Last Days of Hitler.* 5th ed. London: Macmillan, [1947] 1978.

Tullis, F. LaMond. *Unintended Consequences: Illegal Drugs and Drug Policies in Nine Countries.* Boulder, Colo.: Lynne Rienner, 1995.

Turner, Stephen P., and Regis A. Factor. *Max Weber and the Dispute over Reason and Value: A Study in Philosophy, Ethics, and Politics.* London: Routledge & Kegan Paul, 1984.

Unga, Nils. *Socialdemokratin och arbetslöshetsfrågan 1912–34: Framväxten av den "nya" arbetslöshetspolitiken* [The Swedish Social Democratic Party and the issue of unemployment 1912–34: The emergence of the "new" unemployment policy]. Stockholm: Arkiv, 1976.

United Nations Conference on Environment and Development. *Agenda 21: Earth Summit—The United Nations Programme of Action from Rio.* New York: United Nations Department of Public Information, 1993.

United Nations, Economic and Social Council, Commission on Sustainable Development. *Agriculture, Land and Desertification: Report of the Secretary-General.* 2001. E/CN.17/2001/PC/13.

———. *Changing Consumption Patterns: Report of the Secretary-General.* 2001. E/CN.17/2001/PC/8.

————. *Energy and Transport: Report of the Secretary-General.* 2001. E/CN.17/2001/ PC/20.

————. *Finance and Trade: Report of the Secretary-General.* 2001. E/CN.17/2001/PC/10.

————. *Global Status of Biological Diversity: Report of the Secretary-General.* 2001. E/CN.17/2001/PC/18.

————. *Implementing Agenda 21: Report of the Secretary-General.* 2001. E/CN.17/2002/ PC.2/7.

————. *Oceans and Seas: Report of the Secretary-General.* 2001. E/CN.17/2001/PC/16.

————. *Protection of the Atmosphere: Report of the Secretary-General.* 2001. E/CN.17/ 2001/PC/12.

————. *Review of Progress in Forests since the United Nations Conference on Environmental Development: Report of the Secretary-General.* 2001. E/CN.17/2001/PC/15.

————. *Water: A Key Resource for Sustainable Development: Report of the Secretary-General.* 2001. E/CN.17/2001/PC/17.

United Nations Environment Programme. *Global Environment Outlook (GEO-1).* Nairobi: United Nations Environment Programme, 1997.

United Nations General Assembly. 19th Special Session. *Programme for the Further Implementation of Agenda 21: Resolution Adopted by the General Assembly,* A/RES/S-19/2. 1997. New York: United Nations Department of Public Information, 1998.

Vedung, Evert. *Public Policy and Program Evaluation.* New Brunswick, N.J.: Transaction Publishers, 1997.

Vernon, Richard. "Unintended Consequences." *Political Theory* 7 (1979): 57–73.

Vieler, Eric H. *The Ideological Roots of German National Socialism.* New York: Peter Lang, 1999.

Weaver, R. Kent. "The Politics of Blame Avoidance." *Journal of Public Policy* 6 (1986): 371–398.

Weber, Max. *From Max Weber: Essays in Sociology,* ed. and trans. H. H. Gerth and C. Wright Mills. New York: Oxford University Press, 1958.

————. "Politics as a Vocation." In *From Max Weber: Essays in Sociology,* ed. and trans. H. H. Gerth and C. Wright Mills. London: Routledge & Kegan Paul, [1919] 1948.

————. "Science as Vocation." In *From Max Weber: Essays in Sociology,* ed. and trans. H. H. Gerth and C. Wright Mills. London: Routledge & Kegan Paul, [1919] 1948.

Weimer, David L., and Aidan R. Vining. *Policy Analysis: Concepts and Practice.* 3rd ed. Upper Saddle River, N.J: Prentice-Hall, [1989] 1999.

Weinberger, Caspar. *Fighting for Peace: Seven Critical Years in the Pentagon.* New York: Warner Books, 1990.

Williams, Robert. *Political Corruption in Africa.* Aldershot, UK: Gower, 1987.

Wink, Jay. *On the Brink: The Dramatic, Behind-the-Scenes Saga of the Reagan Era and the Men and Women Who Won the Cold War.* New York: Simon & Schuster, 1996.

Witte, Ann Dryden, Magaly Queralt, Tasneem Chipty, and Harriet Griesinger. "Unintended Consequences? Welfare Reform and the Working Poor." Working paper no. 6798. Cambridge, Mass.: National Bureau of Economic Research, 1998.

World Commission on Environment and Development. *Our Common Future: The*

World Commission on Environment and Development. Oxford: Oxford University Press, 1987.

Young, Robert A. "Budget Size and Bureaucratic Careers." In *The Budget-Maximizing Bureaucrat: Appraisals and Evidence,* ed. André Blais and Stéphane Dion. Pittsburgh: University of Pittsburgh Press, 1991.

Zevin, Robert B. "Are World Financial Markets More Open? If So, Why and with What Effects?" In *Financial Openness and National Autonomy: Opportunities and Constraints,* ed. Tariq Banuri and Juliet B. Schor. Oxford: Clarendon Press, 1992.

Acknowledgments

This study has been generously sponsored by The Bank of Sweden Tercentenary Fund.

The following research assistants provided valuable help with this project: Anna Danielsson, Charlotta Eriksson, Liv Hammargren, Karolina Larfors, and Lina Westin.

From the beginning, this book has been planned for an English-speaking audience. Peter Mayers has transformed my text into idiomatic English.

As usual, I have benefited from the constructive criticism of my colleagues at the Department of Government Skytteanum, Uppsala University: Karl-Göran Algotsson, Sverker Gustavsson, Axel Hadenius, Jörgen Hermansson, and Barry Holmström. In addition, I am grateful for the recommendations of two anonymous reviewers at Harvard University Press.

Index